Appeals to Interest

Appeals to Interest

Language, Contestation, and the Shaping of Political Agency

DEAN MATHIOWETZ

The Pennsylvania State University Press
University Park, Pennsylvania

LIBRARY OF CONGRESS CATALOGING-IN-PUBLICATION DATA

Mathiowetz, Dean, 1972–

   Appeals to interest : language, contestation, and the shaping of political agency / Dean Mathiowetz.

      p. cm.

Includes bibliographical references and index.

Summary: "Explores the theoretical and political implications of self-interest within the context of neoliberal political, theoretical, and methodological imperatives"—Provided by publisher.

ISBN 978-0-271-04850-5 (cloth : alk. paper)

ISBN 978-0-271-04851-2 (pbk. : alk. paper)

1. Self-interest—Political aspects.

2. Political psychology.

I. Title.

JA74.5.M38   2011

320.01'9—dc22

2010039084

Copyright © 2011 The Pennsylvania State University
All rights reserved
Printed in the United States of America
Published by The Pennsylvania State University Press,
University Park, PA 16802-1003

The Pennsylvania State University Press is a member of the Association of American University Presses.

It is the policy of The Pennsylvania State University Press to use acid-free paper. Publications on uncoated stock satisfy the minimum requirements of American National Standard for Information Sciences—Permanence of Paper for Printed Library Material, ANSI Z39.48–1992.

In memory of MICHAEL ROGIN

Contents

Acknowledgments ix

1 Introduction: The Politics of Interest 1

2 Property, Usury, and the Juridical Subject of Interest 31

3 Appeals to Interest in Seventeenth-Century England 58

4 Contesting Sovereignty: Interest in Thomas Hobbes 106

5 A Historiography of Liberal Interest and the Neoliberal Self 140

6 Interest in Political Studies: Action, Grouping, and Government 169

Epilogue: The Language of Interest as a Critical Theory of Politics 205

Selected Bibliography 209

Index 221

Acknowledgments

A book writes its author, most of all through the relationships that it creates, sustains, and even tests at times. The debt of my gratitude to friends and interlocutors for working through this book and its process is humbling to reckon. Foremost I thank my advisers and teachers for the challenges and inspiration: Wendy Brown, Mary Dietz, Lisa Disch, James Farr, Hanna Pitkin, Michael Rogin, and Paul Thomas. Many others commented on various parts of this work throughout its several stages of development and maturation. Stephen Engelmann in particular labored generously over the entire manuscript more than once to provide many helpful suggestions and criticisms, large and small, for its improvement. I am also thankful for the work of a congeries of friends, colleagues, mentors, reviewers, and interlocutors: Mark Anderson, Douglas Dow, Elisabeth Ellis, John Gunnell, Jimmy Klausen, Bronwyn Leebaw, Patchen Markell, Robert Meister, Benjamin Read, Melvin Richter, Ronald Schmidt Jr., Vanita Seth, Anna Marie Smith, Sandy Thatcher, Megan Thomas, Toon van Houdt, and Darren Walhof. For assistance with research, I thank Paul Held and Alex Hirsch. Sarah Johnson prepared the index. Andrew Lewis's work on the details and prose of the text was helpful beyond measure. It goes without saying that the remaining shortcomings of this work are mine alone.

For many years of intellectual camaraderie and friendship, I am grateful to Ivan Asher, Mary Bellhouse, Cristina Beltrán, John Cioffi, Julie Cooper, Kennan Ferguson, Michaele Ferguson, Jason Frank, Jill Frank, Jennet Kirkpatrick, Nancy Luxon, Robyn Marasco, James Martel, Keally McBride, Susan McCarthy, Kirstie McClure, Davide Panagia, Elliot Posner, Torrey Shanks, Sharon Stanley, Simon Stow, Brian Weiner, and Gillian Weiss. And thanks to friends and colleagues at UC Santa Cruz, whose encouragement was indispensable: Cindy Bale, Eva Bertram, Michael Brown, Annette Clear, Glenda Dixon, Kent Eaton, Debbie Gould, Phil Hammack, Kimberly Lau, Ronnie Lipschutz, Eleonora

Pasotti, Dana Rohlf, Pat Sanders, Marianna Santana, Roger Schoenman, Anne Tuttle, Michael Urban, and Dan Wirls.

The love, support, and diversions of family and friends outside the academy have underwritten my effort every step of the way. Thanks of course to my family: Mom, Dad, Jeff, and Allison. I am particularly grateful to Peter Maleitzke for his partnership in this and so many endeavors. Many thanks as well to John Cronin, Jennifer DeToy, Matthew Ferguson, Niels Hooper, James Loduca, Stephen Massey, Kimberly Milbrath, Yingwei Qi, Ruth Woodruff, and last but never least, Bella the Dog.

I benefited from opportunities to present parts of this work to the Political Science Department at Williams College, to the Center for Cultural Studies at UC Santa Cruz, to the Political Theory Colloquium at the University of Wisconsin, Madison, and at the University of Minnesota. A version of Chapter 2 appeared as "The Juridical Subject of 'Interest,'" in *Political Theory* 35, no. 4 (August 2007). Parts of Chapter 6 appeared as "'Interest' Is a Verb: Arthur Bentley and the Language of Interest," in *Political Research Quarterly* 61, no. 4 (December 2008). I am grateful for permission to publish new versions of these works.

1 INTRODUCTION

The Politics of Interest

When a thing ceases to be a subject of controversy, it ceases to be a subject of interest.
—WILLIAM HAZLITT, "THE SPIRIT OF CONTROVERSY"

What's the Matter with Interest?

Thomas Frank's 2004 best seller, *What's the Matter with Kansas?* spoke to the puzzlement of many Democratic voters regarding the ability of the Republicans to win the votes of people who were harmed financially by GOP policies.[1] Frank claims that white and rural working- and middle-class Kansans—and their counterparts in states whose electoral votes are up for grabs—act "against their interests" when they support Republican candidates at the polls. The power of Republicans to induce these folks to vote "against their interests" seemed, to many observers, a formidable barrier to the pursuit of better economic and social policies for all Americans.[2] Frank points to the "culture war" that began with Nixon, and then to the galvanization of abortion opponents in Wichita in the early 1990s, to explain this subversion of interest. This political development was fatefully turned to the advantage of the Right when the Democratic Leadership Council began to drop planks of economic benefit to the middle class from the party platform. All of these developments, he says, "turned the politics of this country upside down."[3] Turning politics right side up again, as Frank sees it, means restoring rationality by convincing voters to attend to their bottom line when calculating how to spend their votes—getting them to act, once again, in their interests.

---

1. Thomas Frank, *What's the Matter with Kansas? How Conservatives Won the Heart of America* (New York: Metropolitan Books, 2004).
2. See also Thomas Frank, "The Culture Crusade of Kansas," *New York Times*, August 8, 2006.
3. Ibid.

While the cultural turn played out in American politics and academic disciplines over several decades, the financial crisis of fall 2008 also brought the centrality of interest to economy and government into sharp relief, and again interest became a puzzle. In the wake of cascading bank failures, the demise of Wall Street giant Bear Stearns, and an unprecedented government bailout of financial institutions like the American Insurance Group, Alan Greenspan testified before the House Committee of Oversight and Government Reform on October 23, 2008. Greenspan's thousand-word statement addressed several areas of concern, but just twenty-five of those words became the sound bite that was played and replayed across the news media. "Those of us who have looked to the self-interest of lending institutions to protect shareholder's equity—myself especially," he said, "are in a state of shocked disbelief." With these words, Greenspan registered the degree to which the primacy of self-interest had been an article of faith among policymakers, as well as a linchpin of finance capitalism, while at the same time attesting to its fallibility—an admission all the more notable coming from a self-professed disciple of Ayn Rand. This potent morsel was mostly ignored by the Right, but was greeted by a chorus of self-satisfaction by a few left commentators in the media and academia. To these latter critics, Greenspan's confession exposed the fundamental bankruptcy at the heart of neoclassical economics and the neoliberal free-market policy prescriptions that had defined American policymaking since Ronald Reagan.

This hand-wringing over the culture war and the failure of financial regulation by self-interest alone says much, not only about the drift of American politics at the turn of the twenty-first century, but also about the very terms that structure our understanding of political life. Our astonishment that interest fails us, tendered at moments of crisis, speaks to the absolute and self-evident salience of interest as a fundamental concept for narrating our lives. It is a fundamental part of our language of explanation and justification. But while interest seems to forsake that narrative time and again, a rigidly narrow view of what interests are, of what their role in politics and government is, nonetheless typically carries the day. Interest, the story goes, is a rational motivation, universal among modern persons (if not among persons everywhere and at all times). Interest, according to observers of politics from the armchair to the academy, is a psychology of calculating self-regard for which economic benefit is paradigmatic, if not the whole story. Interest, we are assured, is inside of each of us; it is the spring of individual action. It is the reliable, true, and right foundation of modern political and economic practices and institutions. Viewed in a historical register, interest is the great seventeenth-century discovery finally assimilated by eighteenth-century philosophy. Madison, Hamilton, and Jay's parsing of constitutional power in the *Federalist Papers* and Adam Smith's defense of laissez-faire economics in *Inquiry into the Nature and Causes of the Wealth of Nations* stand at the gateway to our modern life of checked-and-balanced powers and the free flow of commodities in a global market—regulated by none other than the spontaneously rational machinations of interest. Yet such a conception of interest provides the puzzle that lies at the heart of Frank's account, and the anxiety of Democratic partisans and left-leaning observers for the last quarter-century.

By now it should be clear that there are deep fissures in this bedrock of interest. But what to make of the cracks, and how deeply they run, is a muddled affair. Consider again Greenspan's brief remark, which bore both the man's and the concept's characteristic ambiguity: did self-interest induce financial catastrophe—in which case, greed is the problem—or did financial markets prevent the bankers, traders, and investors from following (or even knowing) their interests? Each of these possibilities in Greenspan's statement hews to interest as calculating self-regard. And each has engendered a predictable response. Business schools begin to urge their graduates to sign oaths of ethical conduct. Bernard Madoff is sentenced to 125 years in prison for orchestrating a $65 billion Ponzi scheme. Congress is called upon to regulate complex financial derivatives that are blamed for catastrophically masking the risks posed by "toxic assets." The link between self-interest and the financial collapse, drawn most prominently by Greenspan but claimed by many, poses a problem not only for neoliberal regulatory regimes, but also for the ethical underpinnings of liberal government and theories more generally. *What if* greed is not good? And *what if* the ability to know one's own interests, indeed to know *oneself*, is dramatically limited?

Scholarly response to Frank's *New York Times* article "The Culture Crusade of Kansas" opened similar lines of questioning—and similarly left untouched a conception of interest as essentially about calculating self-regard. Finding that the Kansan political climate examined at length by Frank does not represent trends in the American electorate as a whole, Larry Bartels promptly shored up the self-interestedness of the electorate by parsing electoral surveys.[4] In the course of a subsequent exchange, Frank and Bartels redrew the markers of class, from differences in income to differences in educational attainment. This

---

4. Larry M. Bartels, "What's the Matter with *What's the Matter with Kansas?*" *Quarterly Journal of Political Science* 2006, no. 1 (2006).

redrawing suggested that perhaps the problem of interest could be settled by settling a question of identity: what is the working class? The implication was that Kansans voted against their interests out of ignorance.[5] While even this revised claim did not, in the end, satisfy Bartels as a good account of American politics as a whole, it does highlight questions that have provoked political theorists for generations. These questions concern who has an interest, who or what determines that interest, and how we know either—points at which questions of interests become questions of politics.

To speak only in the broadest terms for now, Marx distilled one tradition of handling these questions by applying the philosophical language of "subjective" and "objective" to interests, and by invoking ideology as an explanation for the difference between the two.[6] In the twentieth century, the prevailing response of liberals—whether approached by way of Rawls or Dworkin, or via the tradition of critical theory that ends with Habermas—has been to articulate systems of normatively objective principles against which to gauge perceptions and articulations of interests. So aside from interest in its subjective guise, as a motivation, we encounter objective interests in justice, in autonomy, or in communicative competence.[7] In other words, we limn the extent to which interests conform to proper selves, properly understood. The impulse of political philosophy, in short, has been to remove the question of interest from politics and quarantine it instead in the realm of theory. Of course, skeptics abound, as critics continue to raise the questions of who knows what these interests are, by what means they are known, who decides, and by what modes of power these interests are made effective.

Fifty years into the linguistic turn, we know by now that if interest lies at the foundation of political and social order, then it is also a point at which this foundation encounters language. And in language we confront the persistence, indeed the indispensability of the language of interest in political argument and its intransigence in political philosophy. The very word "interest," we find, is a contradiction: it opposes itself as soon as it is voiced. When viewed as individual preference, "interest" implies an impenetrable interiority, a hidden origin of desire, but this very invocation of interest is always an

---

5. Ibid., 204.

6. Karl Marx, *The German Ideology* (New York: Prometheus Books, 1998). I explore the "objective/subjective" distinction in political studies and critical theory in Chapter 6.

7. John Rawls, *A Theory of Justice* (Cambridge: Harvard University Press, 1971); Ronald Dworkin, *Sovereign Virtue: The Theory and Practice of Equality* (Cambridge: Harvard University Press, 2000); Jürgen Habermas, *The Theory of Communicative Action*, vol. 1, *Reason and the Rationalization of Society* (New York: Beacon Press, 1985). Regarding Rawls, see also note 21.

opening into the idea of an external standard. So, for example, we see a poor Kansan woman voting Republican as revealing her interest as a purely individual preference. Yet in the face of Republican economic policies, we aver, voting Republican cannot truly be in this woman's interest. The same problem can be writ on a collective scale, where perhaps it reveals itself more readily: to end an argument by invoking, say, "the national interest" easily raises in many the incongruence of this interest with a competing view and the space to disagree. Is the American national interest a robust national defense, or a robust defense of civil liberties? We are apt to suppose that such a question can be answered, or indeed its dilemma dissolved, by a clear picture of who this Kansan woman is, or what America truly is. Identity will lead to us to interest. And yet, despite all the powers of social science, these questions go unresolved.

Though the linguistic turn has matured, we have not come to grips with the insights it holds for these questions. This instability of "interest," the inevitable sliding of its senses and jostling of its referents, is enormously important to politics. It reveals, at the level of everyday language, how the claims that we stake in the face of the pervasive uncertainty of political life are ever provisional, but no less powerful for that. Appeals to interest are action-oriented; in appealing to interest, we say, "*Here*, and not there, is where we should be going," understanding only partly or not at all that the "we" that appears as prior to the claim is, in truth, the called-for effect. It is one complex America that can be said both to have an interest in a powerful national defense apparatus and in robust civil liberties, but a different America is likely to emerge tomorrow, depending upon which of these appeals to interest carries the day. Tracing the source of this power in appeals to interest to provoke identity, exploring its effects in political life, and tallying the cost of its denial are my objectives in this book. My fundamental argument is that appeals to interest are sites of identity formation, rather than simply products of calculating self-regard. In other words, the usual priority that we accord to identities in the pairing of identities and interests must be turned around. The ambiguities and slippages in the language of interest (as well as the pretense of interest claims to stand above dispute) are all necessary conditions if appeals to interest are to have any power in political argument.

The best way to understand the instability of this language of interest and its importance to politics is to consider the concept of interest at the junctures of its history—and the junctures at which the instability of this language have been obscured and denied, perhaps out of hope that the contingency and uncertainty of politics can be held at bay. And so while the conceptual history of interest is a terrain that appears to have been well mapped, the recurrent theme of these explorations has been to reassure us that interest, by virtue of its amalgamation of individualism and rationality, provides a clear and even path from the interiority of the modern self to the institutions and events of politics. The source of this individualism, we may be told, is private property: Karl Marx's analysis of the bourgeois language of interest in *The German Ideology* is perhaps the most prominent example. The source of interest's rationalism, Albert O. Hirschman tells us, derives from the origin of the term "interest" as a euphemism for "usury." In other words, the financial roots of interest ground its fundamental rationality. Its individualism intrudes from an altogether different vector: the early modern reason-of-state literature, with its focus on rightly directing the action of a prince. Hirschman describes the confluence of these uses of the term in a moral vocabulary as securing interest's fundamental political character as an individual, rational motivation.[8] As such, interest is a prime marker of individual rationality and autonomy.

Hirschman's conceptual history of interest is a linchpin of his broader and widely admired thesis regarding the emergence of moral justifications for commercial society. Hirschman finds this justification in the regularity, rationality, and inevitability of self-interested behavior that are typically characteristic of markets and trade, and he shows the deep roots of this justification in earlier discourses of morality and reason-of-state. However entangled its history, the conception of interest at the center of his tale is dazzling in its simplicity and self-evidence. "Interest has stood for the fundamental forces," he writes, "based on the drive for self-preservation and self-aggrandizement, that motivate or should motivate actions of the prince or the state, [and] of the individual."[9] With this notion of interest as a backdrop, he cites as a "simple fact" that "each person is best informed about his or her own [interests]," because he or she is "best informed about his or her *own* desires, satisfactions, disappointments, and sufferings."[10] Part of the burden of my argument is to show that this "simple fact" is a prejudice of a recent, broadly liberal discourse. It is, moreover, a prejudice that induces a late modern blindness to what the language of interest does in and for political discourse. In the shadow of this prejudice, both the rich histories of the concept of interest, and the richness of the patterns of the term's usage in present-day political talk, have become inaudible to us.

8. Albert O. Hirschman, *The Passions and the Interests: Political Arguments for Capitalism Before Its Triumph* (Princeton: Princeton University Press, 1977); Albert O. Hirschman, "The Concept of Interest: From Euphemism to Tautology," in *Rival Views of Market Society and Other Recent Essays* (Cambridge: Harvard University Press, 1992).
9. Hirschman, "Concept of Interest," 35.
10. Ibid., 36.

Theorizing an Alternative: Interest as Juridical and Plural

Faced with the prominent and widely known histories offered in support of interest as calculating self-regard, we must begin from new historical and analytical points of departure if we are to revisit interests. While one aspect of my argument is to chart how the idea of interest as calculating self-regard has been "constructed"—in that it is widely taken for granted, historically contingent, and yet insufficient for grappling with political life[11]—the main thrust of my argument is itself a positive one that explores an alternative. While a better account of interests is needed, however, we must also hesitate to overdraw the unity of this alternative. We need a better "way of hearing" the language of interests, with all its variety, not simply a more sharply focused image of the concept itself. The imperatives of this shift may be best navigated by borrowing a metaphor from Ludwig Wittgenstein and theorizing a "family resemblance" among appeals to interest in political life.[12] In the account of interest that I am about to give, the legal inflections of the term "interest" will provide both the alternative point of departure for theorizing interest we will need if we are to begin again, and a touchstone for seeking out the family resemblances among appeals to interest that we will need if we are to embrace their complexity.

Searching for this family resemblance in the seventeenth-century vogue of interest and its medieval prehistory, and finding its resonance in the contemporary language of interest (even, and especially, when invoked outside a legal context), I find that the legal aspects of interest have gone almost unnoticed in existing scholarship. The legal past of interest, with its roots in scholasticism, is distinct from the economic and humanist roots of interest that Marx, Hirschman, and many others have explored. This legal side, with its suggestion of authoritative ties between persons and their properties, gave rise to and sustains the contested and identity-provoking power of appeals to interest in present-day political language. Like others, I will call this forgotten side of interest "juridical."[13]

---

11. I adopt this outline of "social construction" arguments from Ian Hacking, *The Social Construction of What?* (Cambridge: Harvard University Press, 1999).
12. Ludwig Wittgenstein, *Philosophical Investigations* (New York: Macmillan, 1958), §67. Most of Wittgenstein's examples of traits that make up family resemblances are visual, but not all: he also cites "temperament."
13. Among contributors to the study of interests in political thought, Stephen Engelmann alone has noted the older juridical meaning of interest; see Stephen G. Engelmann, *Imagining Interest in Political Thought: Origins of Economic Rationality* (Durham: Duke University Press, 2003), 5. I am informed in many ways by his account, which traces the consolidation of monistic and economic interest in the eighteenth century, as I explore the significance of juridical interest prior to that development and its erasure from the intellectual life of the twentieth century.

But in so doing I intend to push beyond the typical equation of the juridical with the rule of law and the system of punishments and rewards.[14] As I will use the term, juridical interest draws our attention to broader relations among three elements: (1) a norm, (2) a conflict or contest over application of the norm, and (3) a decision (including a "who decides").[15] Incorporating contestation and decision into a picture of the juridical expands and enriches this notion, which is generally seen as restricted to matters of legal right.[16] Such an expanded notion of the juridical also tempers views of decision as sovereign, because to render a decision is at the same time to acknowledge, however tacitly, the norm and the contestation in question.[17]

In order to emphasize that, when it comes to politics, contestation rather than decision is the more conspicuous aspect of the language of interest, I will often refer to this side of interest as "juridical and plural." This combination speaks to the life of juridical interests in political contexts. Simple observations of political discourse suggest the improbability, if not the impossibility, of arriving at an uncontested statement of anyone's interest. I take the unlikelihood of an uncontested appeal to interest as a starting point for grappling with the language of interest, rather than an impasse that can and must be resolved by a better theory of objective interest. This is not to argue simply for viewing interest as an "essentially contested" or even "contingently contested" concept. To do so would be simply to note that the term has uses that are irreducibly at odds with one another; practically all terms are liable to disagreements about their applicability.[18] Instead, it is a means of attending to how contests that pertain especially to "interest" are critical to the politics of interest. Contests are

14. James Tully, "Governing Conduct," in *Conscience and Casuistry in Early Modern Europe*, ed. E. Leites (Cambridge: Cambridge University Press, 1988), 40.
15. For a conception of the juridical drawn along these lines, see Carl Schmitt, *Political Theology* (Chicago: University of Chicago Press, 2005), 30–31, 59, and T. M. Knox, ed., *Hegel's Philosophy of Right* (New York: Oxford University Press, 1967), §§219–22.
16. See, for example, James Tully, "Wittgenstein and Political Philosophy: Understanding Practices of Critical Reflection," *Political Theory* 17, no. 2 (1989): 188–89.
17. Ernesto Laclau, "Identity and Hegemony: The Role of Universality in the Constitution of Political Logics," in *Contingency, Hegemony, Universality: Contemporary Dialogues on the Left*, by Judith Butler, Ernesto Laclau, and Slavoj Žižek (New York: Verso, 2000), 83. My view of the juridical and its relation to decisionism is also informed by Andreas Kalyvas's reading of Arendt; see Andreas Kalyvas, "From the Act to the Decision: Hannah Arendt and the Question of Decisionism," *Political Theory* 32, no. 3 (2004).
18. For an elaboration of "essentially contested concepts" in politics, see William Connolly, *The Terms of Political Discourse* (Princeton: Princeton University Press, 1993). I discuss Connolly's treatment of "interest" as a conceptually contested concept in Chapter 6. For a corrective caution regarding how to deploy the notion of "essentially contested concepts" in political studies, see John G. Gunnell, "Time and Interpretation: Understanding Concepts and Conceptual Change," *History of Political Thought* 19, no. 4 (1998): 648.

fertile openings to examine the point of appeals to interest, to elucidate what's at stake in these appeals, and to limn the power of the language of interest in politics more generally. A conceptual history of interest that incorporates the juridical and the plural offers a theory of interest that replaces a view of interest as essentially about calculating self-regard with a view of interest as a medium of contestation, self-understanding, and action, and therefore of contested self-constitution. It exposes and theorizes a family of resemblances among appeals to interest—characterized by contestation, plurality, identity, collective action, bodies, and agency—which no handy, univocal conception (or "definition") of interest could encompass.

The legal backdrop to the term "interest" also draws our attention to something deeply paradoxical about interest. And in attending to this paradox, my argument takes a decisive step in the positive direction of offering a better view of interests, because it encompasses the one that I work to displace. Appeals to interest are statements of "what matters," "what is of importance," or "what makes a difference" at sites of conflict and contestation. But while contest is the context in which an interest claim is animated in the first place, the structure (or one might say, the conceit) of a such a claim, like that of legal claims in general, is to deny the plausibility of an alternative statement of affairs regarding what matters, or is of importance, or makes a difference to the matter at hand. Each claim, though born of contest, masquerades as a statement for which no further contest is warranted.[19] Both contestability and its denial must be seen as integral parts of the language of interest, even in the case of self-interest; for too long, the denial has been taken as the whole story. Finding plurality and contest as the basis of an appeal to interest, and recognizing the openness of this appeal to further contestation, is the work for which a critical theory of interest—one attuned to language, rather than to historical materialism or recent liberal prejudices—is urgently needed.

With the juridical as my point of departure, I argue that the language of interest is a means of shaping and reshaping agents, and is therefore fundamental to the constitution of political identity and agency. Arguments from interest, I show, are claims about "who" somebody is, and provocations to act in such a way that this "who" is realized. If such claims were not already contested, they would be pointless: the actions would be preordained. Identity is not a backdrop to interest; rather, an appeal to the interest of an agent is

---

19. This paradox is an instance of what Richard Rorty has called the "performative contradiction" inherent in language. See Richard Rorty, *Contingency, Irony, and Solidarity* (New York: Cambridge University Press, 1989), 7–10.

an ascription to that agent of *an* identity against a field of possibilities. While appeals to interest depend on agency, they also shape it in the give-and-take of interest claims and action. Therefore, the autonomy of political agency and the independence of political identity, so often presumed to be reflected by a politics of interest, are called into question by how the language of interest works in political discourse more broadly.

Losing Interest in Political Studies

Political studies must grapple with this side of the language of interest in their engagements with political life. Students of politics continue to marshal the conception of interest common to Frank, Greenspan, Hirschman, and others, but in the context of a broad intellectual *disengagement* from the concept of interest in the last twenty years across political science and, with few exceptions, in political theory as well.[20] Yet the withdrawal of political studies from the language of interest must be understood as a symptom of, rather than a solution to, the ways that appeals to interest trouble our impulse to locate a stable ontology of political life.

20. The concept of interest was subject to much conceptual-analytic attention in political theorizing and philosophy of social science upon the arrival of the linguistic turn in political science in the 1960s and 1970s. See, for examples, S. I. Benn, "'Interests' in Politics," *Proceedings of the Aristotelian Society* 60 (1960); Frank J. Sorauf, "The Conceptual Muddle," in *Nomos V: The Public Interest*, ed. Carl J. Friedrich (New York: Atherton Press, 1962); Virginia Held, *The Public Interest and Individual Interests* (New York: Basic Books, 1970); Isaac D. Balbus, "The Concept of Interest in Pluralist and Marxian Analysis," *Politics and Society* 1, no. 2 (1971); Clarke E. Cochran, "The Politics of Interest: Philosophy and the Limitations of the Science of Politics," *American Journal of Political Science* 17, no. 4 (1973); Connolly, *Terms of Political Discourse*; Theodore M. Benditt, "The Concept of Interest in Political Theory," *Political Theory* 3, no. 3 (1975); Terence Ball, "Interest-Explanations," *Polity* 12, no. 2 (1979); and Robert Q. Parks, "Interests and the Politics of Choice," *Political Theory* 10, no. 4 (1982). The concepts "public interest" and "interest groups" were given similar scrutiny during this period. See Glendon Schubert, *The Public Interest: A Critique of the Theory of a Political Concept* (Glencoe, Ill.: The Free Press, 1961); Anthony Downs, "The Public Interest: Its Meaning in a Democracy," *Social Research* 29 (1962); Carl J. Friedrich, ed., *Nomos V: The Public Interest* (New York: Atherton Press, 1962), vol. 5; Richard E. Flathman, *The Public Interest: An Essay Concerning the Normative Discourse of Politics* (New York: John Wiley & Sons, 1966); and Graham Wootton, *Interest-Groups*, ed. Robert A. Dahl, Foundations of Modern Political Science (Englewood Cliffs, N.J.: Prentice Hall, 1970). Subsequent to this avalanche of criticism, which was directed at Marxist and behaviorist social science and theory alike, the impossibility of knowing or operationalizing interests must have seemed obvious to any researcher who wanted to grapple with fundamental concepts. Rawlsian liberalism and rational choice theory stepped in to fill the gaps and hesitations that these analyses abetted in behavioralist research programs and critical theorizing. For their part, rational choice elaborated models of political interaction on the basis of a choosing agent bearing preferences, not "interests." See, for example, Bruce Bueno de Mesquita, *Predicting Politics* (Columbus: Ohio State University Press, 2002), 51.

Among political theorists, this disengagement appears as contemporary liberal theory renders interest (as self-interest) a presumption and precursor to theorizing the problems of political life, problems that take shape in questions of rights and cultural difference. For example, individual interest is axiomatic to John Rawls's theory of justice and political liberalism.[21] Disengagement from interest also appears where the mainstream of democratic theory figures interests as akin to non-negotiable, prepolitical prejudices. Seyla Benhabib, for example, sharply contrasts these interests with the continuing and integrative dialogue of deliberation.[22] When political theorists have engaged directly with interests, their tendency has been to draw on the power of this language to invoke individuals endowed with calculating powers of rational self-regard as subjects of their study, while ignoring everything in the language of interest that complicates and troubles such a picture. While theorists as diversely inclined as Stephen Holmes, David Gauthier, and Stephen White offer recent examples of such an approach, this picture of interest as coextensive with self-regard and individualism, and these as coextensive with modernity itself, is a pervasive one among political theorists for whom the works of Max Weber, Leo Strauss, and Sheldon Wolin serve as reference texts. While some theorists express dissatisfaction with this individual and prepolitical picture of interests from time to time, an alternative has never been systematically explored. And last, abandoning the language of interest to the rationalist and individualist presuppositions of its most liberal defenders, much of contemporary critical political theory and cultural studies has decisively turned away from examining interests in political life and language. These studies are prone to discounting the prevalence of interest talk in politics or dismissing it as ideological window dressing and false consciousness. Many have instead turned to desires, affect, or the body (to name only three examples), as nonrational or intersubjective sites for the formation of identity and the play of power.

While mainstream political theory ignores interest because it seems obvious, and while cultural theorists ignore interest because it seems too neat, social scientists concede, in their way, that an inherent messiness of interest

---

21. In *A Theory of Justice*, Rawls cursorily and neatly packages interest (as self-interest) as an axiom of the theory; as such, it has not been subject to the many revisions that Rawls and his readers have elaborated over the years. Interests, says Rawls, are shared to the extent that individuals "live better" with one another than they would in isolation. They conflict to the extent that each person wants a greater rather than a lesser share of the goods to be distributed in society. See Rawls, *Theory of Justice*, 4 and 11.

22. Seyla Benhabib, *The Claims of Culture: Equality and Diversity in the Global Era* (Princeton: Princeton University Press, 2002).

impedes their attempts to put unitary agency at the foundations of social science analysis. Sensing the contestability, incompleteness, and even illiberality of interests, recently ascendant programs of research in the social sciences have abandoned the term as well. In turning to formal methods adopted from mathematics and theoretical physics by way of economics, rational-choice theorists and other postpositivist political scientists are increasingly apt to speak of preferences and utility instead of interests.[23] They can thereby focus all the more easily on this pregiven agent, an individual defined in terms of the calculating form of its rationality, namely, the ordering of preferences. An analogous shift away from interests and toward preferences can be seen in recent international relations theorizing.[24]

If this turn away from interests is consolidated, what will have been lost? Given the ubiquity of this language in political argument, one effect would be to sever political studies from political life, wherein the language of interest is everywhere. It would abet the substitution of simple or complex abstractions for sustained engagement in the complexities of that life. And it would render political inquiry prone to miss how the language of interest, precisely because of its complexity and contestation, is itself a democratic resource—albeit more agonistic or participatory than representative—for modern polities.

To restore the language of interest to its full potential for the student of politics, then, let us start again. Engaging the language of interest as a resource for a democratic politics rooted in contestation, difference, and collective action, we may recover a critical theory of interest, one that departs from the mainstays of contemporary liberal theorizing, formal modeling, and empirical social science. In so doing, we may even discover a resource for critical engagement with long-standing problems, like the nature and sources of collective identity, and for approaching new ones, like the ways that neoliberalism stages forms of government that evade and erode citizen's democratic impulses.[25]

---

23. For an account of the ascendancy of "self-interest" in the earlier years of formal modeling, and the crisis within formal modeling that prompted the abandonment of "interest" as a rubric of positive political theory, see Jane Mansbridge, "Self-Interest in Political Life," *Political Theory* 18, no. 1 (1990): 137–44.

24. See, for example, John J. Mearsheimer, *The Tragedy of Great Power Politics* (New York: W. W. Norton, 2001).

25. Wendy Brown, "American Nightmare: Neoliberalism, Neoconservatism, and De-Democratization," *Political Theory* 34, no. 6 (2006). By "government" here I mean the broad sense described by James Tully: "the multiple, complex, and overlapping ways of governing individuals and groups." James Tully, "Political Philosophy as a Critical Activity," *Political Theory* 30, no. 4 (2002): 538. Stephen Engelmann argues, in *Imagining Interest*, that the language of interest plays a powerful supportive role in economic rationality and neoliberal government.

In the Beginning Was the Word

I have asserted that it is important not to overdraw the unity of an alternative conception of interest, and I have offered Wittgenstein's notion of "family resemblances" as a model for how to proceed otherwise. I would now like to examine this notion more closely and explain how attending to the juridical uses of "interest"—which may at first seem to be merely another "sense" or "meaning" of interest, alongside interest as a psychological faculty of calculating self-regard—can yield a more comprehensive and general theory of interest. The search for family resemblances signals a bit of a departure from many approaches to conceptual history or analysis, which more commonly begin by breaking down a term into "senses" and "meanings"—cutting language at the joints, as it were—as a prophylactic against unaccountable slippages from one sense of a term to another. This approach seems wise in light of Wittgenstein's view that each use of a term should be considered a particular case. A craving for *generality*, he writes, underwrites a great deal of philosophical puzzlement about concepts.[26]

Even so, it would be a mistake to suppose that the uses of words can be divided and categorized into parts—for example, "self-regarding calculation is a kind of interest"—and to leave it at that, for Wittgenstein notes how we use words "in an enormous number of different and *differently related* ways."[27] Therefore, a conception of interest that Hirschman historicizes, for example, must be seen as inseparable from the relations among ways that the word "interest" was used in early modern discourse. Even though calculating self-regard may have emerged in political discourse toward the end of the seventeenth century, when calculating self-regard gets expressed by the term "interest," the articulation of this motivation becomes intimately connected to the other applications of "interest" in its contemporary lexicon. While the conceptual analyst declares various senses distinct, the political rhetorician happily deploys their points of intersection. With this in mind, I pursue a linguistic argument throughout this book to support recovering juridical interest for political studies. I argue that a focus on the word "interest" is the best way to study the concept interest, because the historical and analytical study of language must emphasize heterogeneity and account for, or at least be open to, the variegated and even contradictory uses of words in political discourses. To

---

26. Ludwig Wittgenstein, *The Brown and Blue Books* (New York: Harper & Row, 1958), 17–18.
27. Wittgenstein, *Philosophical Investigations*, §47; emphasis added.

the extent that a conceptual approach reduces this heterogeneity in the name of parsimony or precision—for example, seeing interest as essentially about calculating self-regard—it misses the importance of conflict, slippage, and contestation in the language of interest.

An emphasis on how a term's various uses are "differently related" displaces the search for a conceptual center around which a concept such as "interest" can be historicized, on the one hand, or formalized, on the other. Wittgenstein explores this idea by way of the term "language." "Instead of producing something common to all that we call language," he writes, "I am saying that these phenomena have no one thing in common which makes us use the same word for all—but that they are *related* to one another in many different ways. And it is because of this relationship, or these relationships, that we call them all 'language.'"[28] Wittgenstein famously characterizes these relationships as "family resemblances"—a notion that I have already said informs the alternative view of interest that I offer in this book.[29] If we leave Wittgenstein's view at this, however, a history of interest as calculating self-regard still seems possible—after all, if there is no *thing* in common, partial histories are all we have. Yet Wittgenstein does not leave it at that. Though the relationships are multiple, concepts are not liable to pure dispersion; although Wittgenstein never explicitly notes that the word itself is what these relations have in common, in practice he offers the appearance of words ("game," "description") as occasions for exploring the multiplicity of relationships among each word's heterogeneous uses. So, for example, if one wants to know what "game" means, one needs to get a broad view of its many uses; none can be excluded *ex ante* in a full account of the concept. In other words, while games may be heterogeneous, all are called games despite their myriad differences. Just as the word "interest" has a variety of uses in the language, none of which captures all the others, so, too, the word is what calls up and renders family resemblances visible in the first place and signals possibilities among their relations.

Therefore, not only does mindfulness of a word's many uses work against setting any one use as primary or central to all the others, this mindfulness suggests how any one use of a word does not exclude other uses. Interest is not a thing independent of the use of the word "interest," but rather is known through it. No one use of the word is independent of the open multiplicity of relationships that comprise the way we use it. To this end, Wittgenstein

---

28. Ibid., §65.
29. Ibid., §67.

emphasizes how concepts are compounds; these compounds are made up of, and indeed partly owe their usefulness to, the heterogeneity of their uses—just as a rope gets its strength from the continuous twisting and overlapping of many fibers, rather than from any one fiber running its entire length.[30] James Tully explores a similar idea with a notion of "equivocity," which he explains as "a linguistic signal that two items are related in some way; a relation which might go unnoticed if two different terms were used. In this respect," he writes, "equivocity is different from ambiguity, where two items bear the same name but do not stand in any relation one to another. 'Bank,' referring to the sides of rivers and to institutions which safeguard and lend money, is ambiguous. 'Politics,' referring to a range of activity and to the body of knowledge of that range of activity, is equivocal."[31] When we aim to give historical or semantic accounts of our concepts, we ignore the heterogeneity of their uses—their equivocity—at our peril. By the same token, use of a word other than "interest" that is a near synonym (e.g., "self-love") cannot simply be said to be "really" about interest, because this use leaves the complexity of "interest" behind and imports the complexity and equivocity of the near synonym instead.[32]

Despite the ready root-and-branch arboreal metaphor commonly used to discuss word histories, which misleads us with the notion of a conceptual

30. Ibid.
31. James Tully, *A Discourse on Property: John Locke and His Adversaries* (Cambridge: Cambridge University Press, 1980), 61.
32. How best to figure the relationship between words and concepts for writing conceptual history has been clouded by an example, first offered by Quentin Skinner but often repeated among writers of critical conceptual history, namely the relation of the concept of originality and the word "originality." Terence Ball extends Skinner's argument about words and concepts on the basis of "originality." Skinner argues that John Milton's expressed desire to write about "things unattempted yet in prose or rhyme" shows originality to be "clearly central to [Milton's] thought, [even though] the word ["originality"] did not enter the language until a century or more after his death." The usefulness of Skinner's distinction between words and concepts, elaborated with reference to "originality," is compromised by his argument from a concept expressed by a neologism. If a word is available in the author's time, the claim that she had it in mind when she used other words encounters trouble. Equating the author's distinct term (e.g., self-love) to the scholar's object of inquiry (e.g., interest) amounts to the implausible claim that these terms are perfect synonyms. It also discounts the possibility that her choice of other terms signals a difference and a decision. See Quentin Skinner, "Language and Political Change," in *Political Innovation and Conceptual Change*, ed. Terence Ball, James Farr, and Russell L. Hanson (New York: Cambridge University Press, 1989), 8, and Terence Ball, *Transforming Political Discourse: Political Theory and Critical Conceptual History* (New York: Blackwell, 1988), 15. Working to clarify this discussion, John Gunnell has taken the distinction between words and concepts in a somewhat different direction, arguing that words may change their meanings over time to refer to different concepts. See Gunnell, "Time and Interpretation," 649–51. Gunnell leaves room in this discussion for a perspective that ties a concept closely to words in the way I have done here, particularly when it comes to what he calls "theoretical concepts" of natural kinds, including "in the sense of the conventions of a natural language" (649).

"trunk" holding the senses of a word together, language is instead rhizomic: conceptual relationships cut across a word's many uses.[33] Conceptualizations, then, draw from the rhizomic relations among uses of the term; relations of possibility that are reflected in the term's versatility, recognizing with Wittgenstein how terms are multiply and differently related, and often possibly equivocal. While this point is widely understood in principle, and often accepted by conceptual historians, it is seldom practiced by political theorists when they give accounts of their concepts. And it has never been adequately pursued in discussions of interest. I contend throughout the book that it is generally insufficient and often misleading to equate "interest" with other words or phrases (such as "self-love," "usury," and "rational desire"). Instead we have much to learn from how the word "interest" uniquely brings together these disparate associations, and we therefore stand to gain much by making the uniqueness of this word's equivocity the point around which our studies turn.

Once we stop thinking of self-interest as a center or origin of interest, and allow these other uses to have their say, we can begin to see what the various threads in the concept of interest *bring to* notions of selfhood that "interest" is called upon to characterize.[34] This is true when it comes to the word's history and its present-day uses; these also bear a complexity far exceeding the notion of calculating self-regard. Adding a juridical history to this story is not to say simply that one particular sense of interest has been ignored, but rather to examine how the legally inflected uses of the term contribute to all the others, by way of their common and indeed intrinsic connections to the word "interest." These inflections have remained effective throughout a series of conceptual changes. As we shall see, when the legal side of interest comes into contact with financial language, this interest becomes a matter of contingent futurity; when it comes into contact with statecraft and politics, it becomes a matter of shaping specific identities of states, citizens, and polities out of plural possibilities. In this light, psychological interest too, in the sense of attention or regard, can be seen as a consciousness of a stake or a share, leading to action on behalf of realizing that stake or share. Even the most trivial side of interest—captured by Heidegger's complaint that "today's interest . . . is the sort of thing that can freely be regarded as indifferent in the next moment, and be displaced by something else, which then concerns us just as little as what went

---

33. Gilles Deleuze and Felix Guattari, *A Thousand Plateaus* (Minneapolis: University of Minnesota Press, 1987), chap. 1; see also Hanna Fenichel Pitkin, *Wittgenstein and Justice* (Berkeley and Los Angeles: University of California Press, 1993), 70, 85.

34. For a discussion of ways selfhood is conceived and lived in modernity, see Charles Taylor, *Sources of the Self: The Making of Modern Identity* (Cambridge: Harvard University Press, 1989).

before"—reflects the utmost sense of a person's presumed privilege to arbitrate what's at stake in his or her action or inaction, and the drifting and listing of that privilege when it is loosed from purpose or obligation.[35] Rather than these uses of the term being distinct or even quarantined from one another because they express different "concepts" of interest, these uses represent a diversity of applications, which nonetheless buttress and inform one another.[36]

In order to foreground how uses of the term "interest" constitute what is supposed to be known and explained by way of interest, I focus on uses of the word (as a noun and a verb, and their close cognates, "interesting," "interested," and so on). Verbs in particular highlight the actively constituting, as opposed to representing, aspect of appeals to interest—yet they have been all but ignored in conceptual histories and analyses of interest. My emphasis on uses of the term, rather than its ostensive referents, shapes my account in another way. Throughout, I will focus on how using the word "interest" is a means by which a particular political argument or inquiry proceeds; I am less concerned about what the actors and authors in question say about interest than what they *do* by appealing to interest.

Language, Bodies, Agency

My word-focused linguistic approach to studying interest, and the juridical picture of interest I will draw out of this approach, raises a few broader philosophical questions regarding ontology and agency.

The ways that language shapes the self have been extensively examined in terms of how the self is reflexively mediated by diverse historical languages and practices of politics.[37] And the language of interest supports these findings. But to examine how the language of interest shapes agency is to cast a

---

35. Martin Heidegger, *What Is Called Thinking?* trans. Fred D. Wieck and J. Glenn Gray (New York: Harper & Row, 1968), 5.

36. While words do change their meanings, my approach is to emphasize that the change in the uses of "interest" from the late medieval into the modern period are not so radical as has been supposed. Instead, I emphasize how the range of the term's application, and therefore the points at which its juridical and plural inflections are brought to bear, expanded into various political discourses since the late medieval period. Interest as calculating self-regard is, from this point of view, not a distinct or separate concept of interest, but a particular case masquerading as the general one. To summon Gunnell's framework, we might see it as an analytical concept, drawn from behavioralist social science and neoliberal discourses, masquerading as a theoretical one drawn from natural language. See Gunnell, "Time and Interpretation," 648–51.

37. Taylor, *Sources of the Self*; Jerrold E. Seigel, *The Idea of the Self* (New York: Cambridge University Press, 2005), 12–14.

wider net, because it attends to how the constitution of the self is, in some critical respects, like the constitution of (other?) collective identities. The point here is to suspend the distinction between individual and collective interest—as though these are two different "kinds" of interest—and to interrogate the priority that is usually ascribed to the former, as though individual interests are real and group interests merely metaphorical or aggregative. To that end, I will use the term "interested bodies" to speak of the entities that are said to have an interest, or to be interested, in light of the fact that not only individuals but also collectivities are said to have or be bodies (e.g., "the body politic"). In keeping with my larger argument about interest, it's worth noting here that the word "body" is sometimes used to ascribe identity by fiat to an abstract or amorphous collectivity, including those to which one generally does not ascribe agency (e.g., "a body of water"). This ascription of identity may involve including certain elements of a heterogeneous and complex set, specifying the relations among them, and excluding other relations and elements.

Turning to bodies as nonindividual and unstable sites for identification has an analogue in juridical language, where "the person" is a legally recognized complex of relationships and properties. Bearing in mind that "property" means "a characteristic" as well as "a positive right to something"—in other words, that "property" is itself equivocal—we can see how legal determinations of the properties that shape and animate persons mirror the ascriptions of identity to bodies. Therefore, in replacing interest as a calculating and self-regarding faculty of individuals with a view of "interest" as limning the property of bodies, we shift our focus to something that is not given prior to interpretation, and whose unity is only provisionally achieved.[38]

My intention to suspend the priority of individuals or groups when it comes to appeals to interest brings my argument into the vicinity of the large and complex question of social ontology. When we study the phenomena that interest us as students of politics, should we assign ontological priority to individuals or to systems (in this case, groups)? This question arises as a matter of course when we strive to explain social phenomena. Yet as we examine a part of the language of political life—appeals to interest—and theorize the entailments of that language, we find ourselves somewhat off to the side of explanation, and of the question of social ontology proper. In other words, the argument of this book turns not on "what interests are, really"—the question

---

38. On the Nietzschean positioning of "the body" as a foundation for analysis against the Cartesian "consciousness" as a site and ontology for critical reflection, see David Couzens Hoy, *Critical Resistance* (Cambridge: MIT Press, 2004), 13–14, 20–21.

for which ontology would be an appropriate exercise—but rather "what appeals to interest *do*."

As I have said, the notion that interest is intrinsically individual is one that I aim to criticize. In that regard, I do take aim at a tenet of methodological individualism that has broad appeal to students of politics.[39] And the aspect of appeals to interest that has been given short shrift in political studies, namely, the plural side that emerges from its juridical history, has strong affinities with the tradition of social holism that stretches at least from Georg Friedrich Hegel and through Émile Durkheim. This tradition found its American expression in philosophers such as Arthur Bentley and John Dewey, and it continues to animate debate in philosophy today.[40] These affinities account in part for why I begin my story of juridical interest with Hegel and draw my discussion of its plural dimensions to a close with a reading of Bentley. At the very least, these affinities are evidence that, much to the contrary of the standard view that both empirically and formally minded social scientists are apt to take today, interests are not in themselves individual phenomena, nor does the importance of interests to politics in itself lend credence to methodological individualism in the study of politics and society. But the affinity of my approach and argument to aspects of social holism ends there. The insights I draw from the historical and present-day uses of "interest" do not respect distinctions between individual and collective phenomena, let alone prioritize one over the other. Rather, I treat an appeal to interest as an ascription of identity to the body said to be interested, which awaits further action for its realization. This, I argue, is itself a potent heuristic for understanding modern political agency.

---

39. For the classic, influential, and most strident defense of methodological individualism when it comes to interests, see Mancur Olson, *The Logic of Collective Action: Public Goods and the Theory of Groups* (Cambridge: Harvard University Press, 1965).

40. Holism is a complex theory with several dimensions and variations; for a catalog of these, see Dennis Charles Phillips, *Holistic Thought in Social Science* (Stanford: Stanford University Press, 1976). For a very recent and comprehensive statement of social ontology, see David Weissman, *A Social Ontology* (New Haven: Yale University Press, 2000). John Searle advances a somewhat different thesis regarding social reality under the heading of social ontology. This theory of social reality is interested in systems rather than in institutions, and it presumes the priority of individual cognition. See John R. Searle, "Social Ontology: Some Basic Principles," *Anthropological Theory* 80 (2006). While a thorough engagement with Searle's argument is beyond the scope of my own, the importance of action, of contestation, and of becoming to appeals to interest in politics may speak to a lacuna in Searle's analysis of social ontology. As I shall argue in Chapter 2, appeals to interest are useful precisely at the limits of our epistemically objective knowledge about agents and at points where observers disagree regarding their independence and relativity.

Such a picture of agency has two immediate implications: first, its location of agency in address or voice, and second, its situating of agency as irreducibly plural.

Seeing appeals to interest as provocations to realize political identity means seeing agency as mediated in language and as a matter of voice, rather than as secured in conscience or consciousness, or as privileged and protected by communicative conditions and competencies.[41] And while agency is often exercised in the voice of the so-called natural person, even here we are reminded (by Hobbes and by others) that the Latin term from which "person" derives, *persona*, is a mask, namely, that through which (*per*) one speaks (*sona*), and whose authority stems from myriad possible sources. In its most literal sense, therefore, *persona* is the animation of a mask by the voice.[42] Seen from this angle, agency may reside as easily in the voice of the artificial person or institution: a county clerk issues a marriage license; a person says "I do." In neither instance does the person speak only in her own voice, or words entirely of her choosing. In the latter instance, we see clearly how the speaker's very agency is shaped by her utterance itself.

Any account of agency that begins with its mediation in language must attend to the presence of others who act and speak in response; the need for such a response highlights the fact that agency is a matter of beginning, rather than a matter of achieving ends. An appeal to interest is such a beginning. Its effect awaits another action (one's own or another's) toward the achievement of that identity. Here the language of interest brings some important peculiarities to the general ways that the constitution of selves is caught up in and mediated by language. In the space of waiting for the next action comes the possibility that what will come will instead be an opposing appeal to interest, with a different action to be taken and a different identity to be realized. When the president claims the national interest is served by preemptive war, among strategies for derailing action toward this end is a competing articulation of the national interest. The identities invoked by such appeals are likely to be articulated in terms of contemporaneous differences with others—what we might call identity's "spatial" dimension, as in the United States versus an adversary. And each of these appeals to interest bears the conceit of being the final say. But the appeal to interest and the agency it provokes is a temporal one. To continue our example, they speak to what the United States becomes, which of its many

---

41. Adriana Cavarero, *For More than One Voice: Toward a Philosophy of Vocal Expression* (Stanford: Stanford University Press, 2005), 10–16.

42. Seigel, *Idea of the Self*, 16.

aspects is promoted and which are attenuated by a particular action. Therefore, appeals to interest offer a rich and complex picture of agency not captured by classical liberal notions of autonomy or neoliberal notions of maximization, where the only plurality involved is the pair or bundle of "choices" facing a subject whose interests are presumed to precede, but be realized in, choosing.

Seeing plurality as intrinsic to the agency supported by "interest," rather than as embodied merely in a plurality of choices that interest reduces to one choice at the moment of decision, reveals that the ultimate realization of interest is always deferred. For if an appeal to interest is a call to action, this appeal therefore depends on the open horizon of future possibility that underwrites all action. Temporal identity is never fully consolidated, an insight that works against the static quality of emphasis on the spatial aspects of identity that prevail in political-theoretical discussions. Identity politics, where group affiliations (and persons at the intersection of these affiliations) are perceived primarily in terms of contemporaneous difference with others, provides a particularly apt example. With such a view of agency in mind, provocation and incompletion become conditions of possibility for agency, rather than impediments to it. Just as the perspective on interest developed in the chapters that follow notes the power of appeals to interest to forge self-identity and collective identity by prompting action that promotes that identity, it also emphasizes the incompleteness, and contestability, of these appeals.

Recovering the Plurality of the Present

Up until now, I have been unpacking my argument in a largely philosophical register, but I have remarked time and again that I am engaging in conceptual history as a means toward offering a more encompassing theorization of interest. A few words are in order, then, about the kind of history that I aim to write, and what historical study has to offer the kind of political theorizing that I undertake in this work. As I have noted, many of the texts and historical moments that I will examine in this book have been treated by historians of political thought before. Most of these historians represent the "Cambridge school" of scholarship, whose approach is to emphasize historical context as a means of elucidating authors' intentions, and more specifically their intention to act politically, in writing certain texts.[43] This line of scholarship has

---

43. For a discussion of the methods of the Cambridge school, see Quentin Skinner, *Visions of Politics*, vol. 1, *Regarding Method* (Cambridge: Cambridge University Press, 2002).

provided me with invaluable schooling in early modern political thought. The work of Quentin Skinner, who is regarded as the developer and guardian of Cambridge school methods, in particular offers many touchstones, and a few points of dispute, for my argument along the way. But while I am engaged in a process of historical study and interpretation, the historical attitude that informs my study takes its cues more from a hermeneutic approach, one that resonates broadly with the work of Charles Taylor, Hans-Georg Gadamer, or even Michel Foucault, than from Skinner and other Cambridge-style historians, or Leo Strauss, or Sheldon Wolin, or others whose work has inspired this rich field.[44] In other words, my primary concern is not elucidating the intentions of historical actors. Instead, I focus on the significance of their verbal actions for an evolving language of interest, one that implicates us today. And I am equally concerned with the effects of this language upon these verbal actions and actors, including the ways that these effects may exceed or trouble speakers' intentions. And where other scholars have emphasized innovation and change, I attend equally to what persists over time, tracing the effects of persistent entailments in novel contexts.[45]

My exploration of the conceptual history of interest begins, therefore, by directing our attention to what appears marginal, strange, or unfamiliar about it. In the account that I offer, catching moments of prolepsis serves not to correct the fine points of a historical record, but instead to diagnose the present-day preoccupations that have led us to overemphasize novelty or conceptual homogeneity. In other words, we can employ word histories, as

---

44. Charles Taylor, "Theories of Meaning," in *Human Agency and Language: Philosophical Papers I* (New York: Cambridge University Press, 1985); Charles Taylor, "The Hermeneutics of Conflict," in *Meaning and Context: Quentin Skinner and His Critics*, ed. James Tully (Princeton: Princeton University Press, 1988); Hans-Georg Gadamer, *Truth and Method*, trans. Joel Weinsheimer and Donald G. Marshall (New York: Continuum, 1975); Leo Strauss, *Persecution and the Art of Writing* (Chicago: University of Chicago Press, 1988); Sheldon Wolin, *Politics and Vision* (Boston: Little, Brown, 1960).

45. Regarding techniques of writing conceptual history, as my discussion in note 32 suggests, Cambridge school methods serve as a key point of departure for my argument. In addition to the works cited in that note, see J. G. A. Pocock, "Introduction: The State of the Art," in *Virtue, Commerce, and History* (Cambridge: Cambridge University Press, 1985), and J. G. A. Pocock, "The Concept of a Language and the *métier d'historien*: Some Considerations on Practice," in *The Languages of Political Theory in Early-Modern Europe*, ed. Anthony Pagden (Cambridge: Cambridge University Press, 1987). Consistent with the word-focused approach I advocate, I have found it useful in practice to follow the cues of *Begriffsgeschichte* when patterning my own engagement with the history of interest. Gadamer has also reflected on the contribution of hermeneutics to conceptual history; see Hans-Georg Gadamer, "Vom Wort zum Begriff. Die Aufgabe der Hermeneutik als Philosophie," in *Menschliche Endlichkeit und Kompensation*, ed. Odo Marquand et al. (Bamberg: Fränkischer Tag Verlag, 1995).

Hanna Pitkin suggests, "as didactic devices, for stressing aspects of our own concept which we have neglected or forgotten," taking special care to open, rather than close or displace, our appreciation for historical and present-day uses, and for present-day uses *as* historical.[46] For his part, Taylor urges us to connect conceptual peculiarities with their counterparts in past practices and philosophical formations in order to better articulate "important parts of the reality implicit in our practices" that are "blocked out or denied" by dominant, generally accepted prejudices.[47] Following Taylor, we may read the dominance of perspectives on interest as individual and calculating as "a typical case of a distorted or partial formulation acting as a screen." "In order to understand what is going on in a case like this," he says, "we have to go back. We have to recover the last full-blooded formulation of the side that is being thus suppressed. . . . Because this last full formulation will give us the theory with which our society is out of tune, it is an indispensable part of the story."[48] Recovering an indispensable part of our story, a history of the juridical and plural side of interest offers a context in which to theorize the politics of contested, collective, and active senses already available in the language of interest. And examining how political theorists have invoked conceptual history in ways that shut down or foreclose aspects of interest points to those theoretical concerns to which the reopening of interest most urgently speaks.[49] In sum, what I offer is not a corrected compendium of the intellectual history of interest, noting every concept to which the word has been related and documenting each of its internal changes at various points. Instead, I offer a study of crucial changes and transformations whose selection and juxtapositions serve to reinvigorate our appreciation for the language of interest in political life and political study today.

46. Pitkin, *Wittgenstein and Justice*, 213.
47. Charles Taylor, "Philosophy and Its History," in *Philosophy in History*, ed. Richard Rorty, J. B. Schneewind, and Quentin Skinner (Cambridge: Cambridge University Press, 1984), 26.
48. Ibid., 27.
49. Here and throughout, I follow David Couzens Hoy's way of negotiating differences between Gadamer's and Derrida's distinct appropriations of Heidegger's view of understanding as the basic form of knowledge, and interpretation as the inescapable practice of understanding. Hoy reads Heidegger's account of meaning as pluralistic, that is to say, as "recogniz[ing] both [Gadamerian] reconstruction and [Derridean] deconstruction as necessary moments of interpretation." See David Couzens Hoy, "Heidegger and the Hermeneutic Turn," in *The Cambridge Companion to Heidegger*, ed. Charles B. Guignon (New York: Cambridge University Press, 1993), 189–90, 92. Modern hermeneutical interpretation, as Hoy describes it, must tack between a Gadamerian "attempt to construct a comprehensive totality" and a Derridean "healthy skepticism about the possibility of a complete success in doing so." Hoy continues: "Reading would thus be the interplay between a construction (or rational reconstruction) and deconstruction. The latter moments would be necessary to guard against reading familiar expectations into the text, and would have the benefit of allowing the strangeness of the text to appear." Hoy, *Critical Resistance*, 44.

While the remainder of this book is devoted primarily to unpacking "the last full-blooded formulation" of interest "that is being . . . suppressed," I should take a moment now to acknowledge that the prevailing, if "partial formulation" of interest—as calculating self-regard—has a history of its own. What are *its* origins? One of the pillars of my historical argument is that the twentieth century is one such origin. Throughout the chapters that follow, I argue that a conception of interests prejudicial to present-day liberalism, empirical social sciences, and formal modeling in political science underwrites and saturates political theorists' "discovering" the *seventeenth*-century origins of interest defined primarily as self-regarding calculation. Only since the middle of the twentieth century, I argue, has calculating and monistic self-regard come to be considered the essence of interest. In other words, the relevance of plural, individual, and nonrational interest was edged out of political studies from the 1950s to the 1970s. It is perhaps not coincidental that this blindness is coeval with the ascendance of positivism and the dominance of behavioralism, with their emphasis on the observation and measurement of individual behaviors and attitudes. It seems to me, therefore, that positivism and behavioralism, not early modernity, swept juridical and plural perspectives on interest from political studies. Despite the various ways that students of politics have moved beyond behavioralism, we have not discarded monistic, utilitarian, and behaviorist views of interest as calculating self-regard. The modern view of interests has survived the declining fortunes of behavioralism because it underwrites a more pervasive current of present-day political studies and politics more generally, namely, neoliberalism.

The distinctively individual and rationalist view of interests that animates twentieth-century political theory and social science, and which has from there colonized the dominant tradition of writing interest's conceptual history, has its own history in two developments. These developments have been ably examined by other scholars, whose accounts buttress my effort to focus on the persistent resonance and power of an older conception and to see how it supports the emergence of a newer one. The first, as James Tully has explored, was a roughly eighteenth-century change in how theorists conceptualized the juridical. They displaced its older sense, of apportioning stakes and shares, with a newer picture of the law as a system of reward and punishment.[50] Although John Locke was an early and prominent advocate for the newer conception of the law, the work of later theorists, including the third Earl of Shaftesbury,

---

50. Tully, "Governing Conduct," 71.

Jeremy Bentham, and Cesare, the Marquis of Beccaria, exemplified efforts to assimilate the language of interest from the older association to such a system of punishment and reward.[51] Perhaps more important is how they put this new language of interest to work. As Stephen Engelmann has more recently explained, these and other theorists deployed the language of interest in their efforts to displace moral pluralism—the view that persons have many, perhaps conflicting, motives and desires—with a master, monistic desire. Bentham and Shaftesbury in particular marshaled the term "interest" to this end.[52] This conception of interests, as promoted by Bentham, Claude Helvétius, and others, has had a broad influence. Seen as the single unifying and rational principle behind human conduct, and as a reflection of human agency, this picture of interest is a fundamental premise of behavioralism, political psychology, rational choice, and formal modeling. This monistic interest furthermore animates a form of economic rationality that informs neoliberal impulses in political discourse today. In other words, it supports a picture of rationality limited to an individual's (or nation's) arrangement of qualitatively incommensurable goals into ordered preferences, and a picture of agency as limited to that of choosing among them.[53]

But monistic interest must not be viewed as having reduced the language of interest once and for all. Present-day uses of the term to describe nonindividual bodies, and the intimacy of appeals to interest and contestation do suggest the extent to which the older juridical and even plural side of interest still circulates in our language. And it is for this reason that examining juridical interest, prior to and into the seventeenth century, presents an opportunity to disclose what the eighteenth-century monistic theorizations of interest and their twentieth-century progeny deny, namely, how the language of interest resists neoliberal assumption of monism and sovereign agency. Rewriting the conceptual history of interest with this purpose in mind supports opening political studies to the question of identity that Locke, Bentham, and many others sought to foreclose.

In restoring a juridical and plural side of interest to its proper place in conceptual history and analysis, I aim to reestablish continuities where others have

---

51. For the sake of brevity and convenience, from this point onward, "the juridical" and "juridical interest" will refer to the older conception.

52. Engelmann, *Imagining Interest,* chap. 4. Engelmann's thesis is of special importance to my account, both in that it offers points of contrast with my own, but also in that our accounts are in many ways complementary. While his focus is monistic rather than juridical interest, he stands as a notable exception to the rule that interest's juridical and plural aspect has been ignored in histories of interest.

53. Ibid., 1–6.

posited breaks. I do this not in order to deny change, but to restore heterogeneity to the present, so that heterogeneity may be recognized as an important, and indeed integral, resource of political languages. In sum, my conceptual history of interest aims to disrupt the self-evidence of the present by reopening the artifacts of interest's conceptual history to a more wide-ranging perspective, and asks what this ersatz self-evidence does to us when it foreshortens our appreciation of the power of the language of interest in politics.

The Plan of the Book

Each chapter of the book attends to an episode that has figured prominently in standard histories of interest and explores how standard accounts have tended to obscure, rather than to reveal, the crucial importance of juridical and plural aspects of interest to that history. In each chapter, I examine how political actors and political theorists grappled with and responded to interest's juridical and plural side while they dealt with matters like property, sovereignty, agency, and democracy. I examine these episodes in roughly chronological order, one that follows the transformation of juridical interest as it passed into political discourse, then into political philosophy, and ultimately into political science. But this chronology is "rough" in that each of these chapters also gestures to a more recent history, regarding the point at which juridical and plural interest was all but occluded in political studies. And each chapter draws on the present as I turn to showing how traces of the juridical language that animated actors' and writers' responses to political problems long ago live on in political language today. Given that present-day political theory is deeply informed by the perspectives on sovereignty, autonomy, democracy, and agency that come out of these histories, and given the way juridical interest still animates the language of interest, restoring the juridical has much to offer to contemporary theoretical engagement with these ideas.

In Chapter 2, I begin with the putative financial origins of interest, but examine the neglected and all-important legal aspects of this origin. Looking at the uses of "interest" as a Roman legal term, and the relations of this term to property and usury, I tell a story that departs from the presumption of interest's calculability and self-determination. Invoking Hegel's discussion of property and personality in relation to this area of law, I interpret interest-related subjectivity—the "who" that is said to have interests and be interested—in light of the term's legal extension from property damage to money loans. Locating the conceptual changes that made interest relevant to money in historical context, I find that the monetary inflation of the sixteenth century is critical for interpreting the expansion of the term beyond strictly legal uses, and for conceiving the new contested and future-oriented forms of interest-related subjectivity it precipitates. The importance of contested futurity to the concept of interest—that is, this strengthening of its plural side—is a key backdrop, I argue, to the role played by the language of interest in seventeenth-century debates regarding state sovereignty and democratic participation.

These debates are the subject of Chapter 3. Turning to seventeenth-century England with the juridical history of interest as an alternative point of departure, I examine reason-of-state and civil war–era pamphlets, especially the English reception of *The Interest of the Princes and States of Christendom* by Henri, duc de Rohan, and the circulation of Marchamont Nedham's *Interest Will Not Lie*. These pamphlets made "interest" a catchword of political argument, and have therefore drawn the attention of conceptual historians. But the effects of interest's juridical—and now, plural—side have escaped these scholars' scrutiny, and so the full significance of these pamphlets on political discourse has not been drawn out. I set the old juridical connection of interest to status, regarding estates and other property, at the fore in my rereading of these texts. Thus exposing the role of interest's identity-provoking power in these and other works, and the effects of this power in the term's early political vogue, I bring to light the transformative power of appeals to interest in the making and remaking of the political personality of citizens and the state. Turning to the Putney Debates and then to patterns in the present-day language of interest that echo the patterns that animated those debates, I argue that the pluralistic side of the language of interest that derives from its juridical past promotes a distinctly agonistic and participatory form of democratic contestation.

While Rohan, Nedham, and their contemporaries placed the language of interest at the center of political debate, Thomas Hobbes is often said to have theorized the centrality of interests in *Leviathan*. This would seem to be an uncontroversial point among political philosophers, given how frequently they have characterized his work as founding sovereignty in universal self-interest. Recent historians of political thought, by contrast, have noted that Hobbes opposed the intrusion of interests in political life, but they have traced neither the sources, nor the philosophical significance, of this opposition. In Chapter 4, I transcend this familiar split between analytical and critical political theory on the one hand, and history of political thought on the other, by historicizing the former readings of Hobbes and theorizing the latter. I argue that Hobbes's political philosophy—and his articulation of proper personality in particular—is addressed to the same contested and, more important, legalistic notions of interest that I have shown were vitally at play in seventeenth-century political debates. My close examination of how Hobbes himself uses the term "interest" in *Leviathan* and other works reveals the distinctive power of juridical interests and their pluralization to disrupt sovereignty. In the face of these forces, I argue, Hobbes works to construct a theory of propriety, of "one's own" in relation to sovereignty, that excludes interests from representation and proper personality. I use this analysis to examine the shared preoccupation that drives readings of Hobbes as diverse as Sheldon Wolin's and David Gauthier's. I also offer it as a critical amendment to Quentin Skinner's speculative suggestion that Hobbes's objection to interest arises from his exposure to the writings of Rohan during his Continental exile.

Hobbes famously made the relation of sovereignty to political knowledge a central problem for political science: geometry provided a model of knowledge, and sovereignty secured its verbal building blocks. Present-day liberalism and social science, by contrast, ostensibly get around Hobbes's absolutist answer to the problem by positing the regularity and sovereignty of the blocks—that is, in individuals (or states) having, and being motivated by, interests. The last two chapters of the book examine liberalism and social science in turn, to elaborate the insights—regarding liberalism, and for social science—to be had when juridical interest is allowed to complicate this picture of interest as the regular and sovereign motivation of political agents.

The persistence of juridical interest, and its importance in classical liberalism, animates my critique of Stephen Holmes's widely read article "The Secret History of Self-Interest" in Chapter 5.[54] Holmes locates the emergence of liberalism in the acceptance of individual, rational self-interest. But the historical sources that Holmes sees as containing the kernels of this "liberal" idea—from Richard Hooker to J. S. Mill—illustrate instead these early modern and classical liberal thinkers' acknowledgment of, and reckoning with, the juridical side of interests. Examining Mill's elaboration of the Harm Principle in particular illustrates how the juridical moment of interest promotes subjectivities proper to a liberal conception of autonomy. I argue that Holmes's erasure of this juridical moment is characteristic of neoliberal government—a very recent

---

54. Stephen Holmes, "The Secret History of Self-Interest," in *Beyond Self-Interest*, ed. Jane J. Mansbridge (Chicago: University of Chicago Press, 1990). A revised version of this article makes up chapter 2 of Stephen Holmes, *Passions and Constraint* (Chicago: University of Chicago Press, 1995).

intellectual and policy development that not only depends upon the "self-evidence" of interest as calculating self-regard, but also upon the suppression of its juridical other. Recovering the classical liberal response to interests that Holmes's conceptual history suppresses also provides an opportunity to reflect upon the political and theoretical consequences of prolepsis in conceptual history. Positing a conceptual center of interest to the exclusion of heterogeneity in a word's uses, I argue, is neoliberal in its foreclosure of alternatives to interest as calculating self-regard, making this self seem natural and indeed intrinsic to interest. Resuscitating what is suppressed in Holmes's account reveals how appeals to interest, rather than buttressing neoliberal movements tout-court, may be seen as disrupting neoliberalism in political thought and discourses.

Holmes's obliviousness to classical liberalism's engagement with interest stems from a way of conceptualizing interest that underwrites nearly all of the histories of this concept that I examine in this book.[55] In Chapter 6, I explore the sources and effects of this neoliberal conceptualization in political science. In so doing, I return to the problems that the concept of interest—as invoked, to recall the examples with which I began this introduction, by Thomas Frank and by Alan Greenspan—poses for empirical political science and for traditional critical theory.

In this chapter, I use the ascendancy and dominance of behavioralism in political science to frame the erasure of political and juridical notions of interest in political studies. Arthur Bentley's *The Process of Government,* which brought the term "interest group" into the English language in 1908, provides an intriguing benchmark from which to gauge behavioralism's effects. Bentley's account, as I read it, sets the juridical and plural side of interest at the center of political analysis. David Truman's midcentury and insistently liberal appropriation of the "interest group" promoted instead an individual conception of interest that ostensibly reflects and respects the sovereign agency of subjective interests while rendering the emanations of that interest into objects available for empirical study. This conception establishes the congruence of empirical research with the pervasive motif of parsing interest into subjective and objective senses—a practice that, as I mentioned earlier in this introduction, has provided the template for most of modern political philosophy's engagement with interests. William Connolly's *Terms of Political Discourse* provides a highly regarded example of how this modern pattern, and its liberal prejudice

---

55. As I mentioned earlier, Engelmann would be the clearest and only consistent exception to this rule; see Engelmann, *Imagining Interest.*

regarding agency, has persisted in critiques of behavioralism, just as it has in the many prominent conceptual histories of interest examined in my previous chapters. Indeed, I suggest that these studies reflect the stubborn legacy of behavioralist conceptions of interest in scholarly efforts far removed from behavioralist research programs. The contingency and fluidity that Bentley ascribes to group phenomena, and his way of drawing on the language of interest to support this contingency, model steps that students of politics may take to move beyond preoccupations with sovereign agency and the presumption of empirical research that interest is a thing. Interest, we see, is activity; appeals to interest are provocations to action. Political studies that attend to interests must attend to this activity.

In light of these explorations, in the epilogue I offer the language of interest as itself a template for a genuinely critical theory of political life, one that illustrates the moments of constitution and dissolution of political identity and sheds light on agents' contingent participation in these moments.[56] Such a theory points beyond how recently dominant traditions in political studies have handled agency, by making room for a picture of agency shaped in fundamental ways by contingency, contestation, and collective action.

Reclaiming the legal side of interest—as seen in its various juridical and pluralistic inflections—calls upon students of politics to recognize that invocations of interest are, in practice, claims of various kinds. This entails recognizing the contested aspect of these claims, the claims' orientation toward the provocation of action, and the uncertainty about which of these claims would be effective in the future. It is a call to suspend the presumption of interest as individual self-regard, which has hitherto led students of politics to disregard these ready features of the language of interest as nothing more than rhetoric and nothing less than conceptual confusion, and to attend to the peculiar power of the language of interest in political discourse. A conception of interest that is usually associated with liberal theories of democratic representation gives way to a way of seeing how a family of uses of interest, related to each other by means of shared connection to a legal history and its entailments, support agonistic conceptions of democratic argument and action.

---

56. Laclau, "Identity and Hegemony," 48–49.

2 PROPERTY, USURY, AND THE JURIDICAL SUBJECT OF INTEREST

Displacing Humanistic "Interest"

In *Keywords,* Raymond Williams notes that "interest" exemplifies how "our most general words for attraction and involvement . . . have developed from a formal objective term in property and finance."[1] Williams elaborates no further on this point, but his remark gestures toward the centrality of interests for comprehending modern subjectivity and politics. Among political theorists and conceptual historians, however, emphasis on a financial origin of the term "interest" has obscured its other origin suggested in Williams's brief remark, namely, in legal matters pertaining to real property.[2] In so doing, these scholars deflect attention from juridical traces in the uses of the term "interest" in early modern and present-day political discourses—to the detriment of political theory's appreciation for interest-related subjectivity. Without a study of these traces, and how they speak to the present-day conviction that interest is critical to politics and political inquiry, we cannot fully appreciate the power of appeals to interest in politics today.

Albert O. Hirschman's classic essay *The Passions and the Interests* and Stephen Holmes's defense of liberalism in *Passions and Constraint* both argue that the origin of "interest" as a euphemism for usury binds the concept of interest

---

1. Raymond Williams, *Keywords: A Vocabulary of Culture and Society* (New York: Oxford University Press, 1983), 173.
2. Williams indicates that "interest" entered early modern English through the French term *intérêt,* meaning "damage or loss." He does not note that this is a legal term.

to the rational preoccupations of commercial culture.[3] Hirschman in particular argues that the emergence of interest as a category of moral, social, and political discourses is a key element in the change from feudal to bourgeois society.[4] A new, essentially humanist language of interest, he tells us, brought a new science of motivation into political study, schooling and legitimating a new style of reasoning in political life. This new style of reasoning had its origins in statecraft, where it applied to the actions of princes, who were said to be motivated by interests. But the applicability of this motivation to all persons was secured when the same term found a home in early modern moral speculation about the passions. With moralists' exhortations to virtue losing their hold on the imagination, early modern writers turned to the strategy of harnessing passions, or setting them against each other, as a means of controlling humanity's most destructive behaviors.[5]

This strategy, according to Hirschman, turned on the ability of reason as a species of prudence—always a virtue of the head—to choose among passions in way that harnessed or "countervailed" their destructive power. But "interest" played a unique role in such schemes, Hirschman argues, because of its early euphemistic link to usury. Owing to its affinity with avarice, it contended directly with the other motions within human beings. But thanks to its affinity with finance, Hirschman says, it remained rational. Hence humanistic interest was, like passion, an internal motion albeit a rational one.[6] While Hirschman remains ambivalent about the loss of a richer moral language for examining economic and political life, Holmes builds on elements of his story, but takes a more sanguine view of the developments it describes, arguing that the egalitarian (if somewhat cynical) implications of the ascent of interest set the stage for a greater moral good, namely, liberal democracy.[7] Harvey Mansfield, exploring the same historical and literary terrain as Hirschman and Holmes, concludes that early modern discussions of interest signal the distinctively modern view of a commercial rationality that "leads men more surely than unaided reason."[8]

For all of these authors, the confluence of this financial origin of the term with its uses in humanist reason-of-state discourse of motivations secures the

---

3. Hirschman, *The Passions and the Interests*; Holmes, *Passions and Constraint*. See also Hirschman, "Concept of Interest."
4. Hirschman, *The Passions and the Interests*, 4–5.
5. Ibid., 12–31.
6. Ibid., 31–36.
7. Holmes, *Passions and Constraint*, 4, 26–66.
8. Harvey C. Mansfield, "Self-Interest Rightly Understood," *Political Theory* 21, no. 1 (1995): 49.

fundamentally individual and rational character of interest for politics.⁹ The kind of reason thus imputed to the individual accords with a picture of interest as calculable in ways amenable to exchange: a person acting in her interest is said to choose among options after weighing their perceived benefits.¹⁰ On this basis, Hirschman in particular identifies "two essential elements" that he says "characterize interest-propelled action: *self-centeredness,* that is, predominant attention of the actor to the consequences of any contemplated action for himself; and *rational calculation,* that is, a systematic attempt at evaluating prospective costs, benefits, satisfaction, and the like."¹¹ Owing to this conceptual peculiarity of "interest," Hirschman cites as a "simple fact" that "each person is best informed about his or her own [interests]," because he or she is "best informed about his or her *own* desires, satisfactions, disappointments, and sufferings"—interest being little more than a rational amalgamation of these and similar emotions.¹²

In this chapter and the subsequent ones, I follow Hirschman's, Holmes's, and Williams's program of interpreting the history of interest as a window into elements of modern subjectivity. But in order to enrich and deepen this story of interest, I take the roots of "interest" in the Roman-legal formula *id quod interest* for the adjudication of real property and indemnity as an alternative point of departure.¹³ It is by way of this formula that the word "interest" was first disseminated across Europe in the practice of Roman law.¹⁴ *Id quod interest,* which means "that which matters," "that which is of importance," or "that which makes a difference," was the name for the area of Roman law addressed

---

9. Hirschman, *The Passions and the Interests,* 32–33.
10. See Connolly, *Terms of Political Discourse,* esp. 64.
11. Hirschman, *The Passions and the Interests,* 36.
12. Hirschman, "Concept of Interest," 36. For an account of how interest came to be such an amalgam, see Engelmann, *Imagining Interest.*
13. In so structuring my account, I distinguish first-order and second-order interpretations. In the accounts of Hirschman and Holmes, the first-order interpretation situates "interest" as a feature of modern subjectivity; the second-order interpretation interprets this subjectivity in terms of calculating rationality and humanism. I accept the first-order interpretation, noting that it *is* an interpretation of subjectivity, while enriching it with a more encompassing second-order interpretation. See Hoy, *Critical Resistance,* 39.
14. The *Oxford English Dictionary* and the *Middle English Dictionary* indicate that another form related to *intérêt,* the middle-French *interesse* (and its spelling variants, *enteresse, entrest,* and *intrest*), came directly into Middle English legal usage from French much earlier, arriving with the Normans as a term of art in Law French; this idiom survived and influenced English into the early modern period. See J. G. A. Pocock, *The Ancient Constitution and the Feudal Law* (Cambridge: Cambridge University Press, 1957), 34. From Law French "interest" entered Middle English vernaculars, as illustrated by Chaucer's use of *interesse* in his poem, *Fortune,* to mean a right or a share that extends well beyond the pecuniary.

to matters of indemnity and reparation regarding contracts on loans of objects that were fixed (like land), or were unique or varied significantly in their qualities (like houses or oxen). When such an object was damaged while it was under contract, jurists had to sort out the extent of these damages by determining what difference the damage had made to the value of the lent object in question. By considering how this process connected to Roman-legal adjudication of personality more generally, my aim is to recover the juridical side of "interest," as it appeared before and changed throughout its shifting status vis-à-vis financial practices, as a means of enriching our picture of subjectivity, both early modern and present-day.[15]

Whereas the typical conceptual history of interest emphasizes that the word "interest" is extended *to* a financial practice, my story takes into account the *from where* it is extended, namely, legal matters involving real property and personality associated with *id quod interest*. I track the legal side of interest's relation to financial practices, and trace how this side is still at work in present-day patterns of interest talk. On this basis, I argue that as changing economic conditions and practices interact with the law, appeals to interest are revealed as a medium for justifying action, on the part of selves and others, as a means of realizing an identity from among a field of possibilities. In other words, appeals to interest enjoin the active realization of *who* somebody is. Connecting interest to its legal past further suggests how these articulations of identity are contested and incomplete, as indicated by the difficulty of arriving at a final, unproblematic, or uncontested claim about interests in political discourse and political studies alike.[16] The alternative story I lay out in this chapter suggests ways that interpretations of the period, such as those offered by Hirschman, Holmes, and others, as well as interpretations of its most prominent political thinker, Thomas Hobbes, may be revisited—matters I will take up in the chapters that follow.

I begin this chapter by bringing the word-focused approach that I justified in the introduction to bear on Hirschman's thesis. In so doing, I open a path for reconsidering his emphasis on the financial origins of interest, replacing them with a broader legal perspective. In light of Hirschman's turn to interest to elucidate the development of commercial society, I then turn to Hegel's *Philosophy of Right* to explore his precedent for theorizing commercial life in terms of its relation to the law. In this work, Hegel turns to the adjudication of

---

15. On recovering historical practices and ideas for philosophy, see Taylor, "Philosophy and Its History."
16. See Connolly, *Terms of Political Discourse*, chap. 1.

property claims covered by *id quod interest* as he develops a theory of legal subjectivity, or personality.¹⁷ The persistence of the term "interest" as a watchword of political argument links Roman law to the present in a historical register; briefly drawing on *Philosophy of Right* establishes a philosophical link between Roman legal categories and modern practices that helps to shed light on the meaning of the historical linkage.

With these points in mind, I then turn to literatures pertaining to interest and usury offered by historians of economic thought, economic historians, and the *Geschichtliche Grundbegriffe*, a detailed conceptual history reference.¹⁸ These materials draw our attention to the erosion of Roman-legal categorical thinking at the end of the medieval period, especially as it pertains to the ownership and productive capacities of money. I find that the incursion of money into legal matters associated with real property, a domain from which money was earlier excluded, reflects changing legal views of money and changing economic practices during the age of exploration and the early colonial period. The sixteenth-century price revolution, during which price increases were unprecedented in their degree, temporal persistence, and geographical extent, is of special interpretive importance for my argument. Then turning to my interpretive account, I argue that the mixture of juridical interest with financial practice adds inflationary considerations to the adjudication of real-property concerns. In so doing, it adds futurity and uncertainty to the picture of interest-related subjectivity, making the contestation at the root of juridical interest into a basis for a plurality intrinsic to the language of interest. In the final part of this chapter, I reflect by way of conclusion on how this history of interest can help us to reflect on the relation of the juridical and agency in political theory.

History, Heterogeneity, and the Word

Despite their nods to word history, Hirschman's and Holmes's studies pay little attention to the variety of applications of the word "interest." Instead, they search for precursors of a concept of interest that focuses from the outset on a propensity

---

17. Knox, *Hegel's Philosophy of Right*; Istvan Hont, "Commercial Society and Political Theory in the Eighteenth Century: The Problem of Authority in David Hume and Adam Smith," in *Main Trends in Cultural History*, ed. Willem Melching and Wyger Velema (Atlanta: Rodopi, 1994), 61.

18. For a discussion of *Begriffsgeschichte* scholarship and the *Geschichtliche Grundbegriffe*, including its relation to Anglophone conceptual history, see Melvin Richter, *The History of Political and Social Concepts: A Critical Introduction* (New York: Oxford University Press, 1995).

for self-regarding calculation commensurate with the individual's orientation to money. Their treatment of interest is therefore incomplete, and in ways that matter greatly to how we think about the role of interests in political life.

Hirschman briefly acknowledges that the term "interest" has forebears (e.g., *intérêt* and *interesse*), but says that the "idea" or "concept" of interest "has stood for the fundamental forces, based on the drive for self-preservation and self-aggrandizement, that motivate or should motivate actions of the prince or the state, [and] of the individual."[19] As I noted above, Hirschman identifies self-centeredness and rational calculation as two "essential elements" that "characterize interest-propelled action."[20] So Hirschman, like others, treats self-interest as central to, and even an origin of, the concept of interest.[21] As for squaring this conceptual definition with evidence, Hirschman sometimes points out the appearance of the word "interest" in a text, but often he identifies "*the* notion of interest" or "*the* idea of interest" as being "used" in various contexts independent of the appearance of the word.[22] He does not say how the forebears and cognates of "interest" supported this concept or what they might have indicated prior to Renaissance and early modern discourses on statecraft and individualism, or the term's eventual ("euphemistic") employment in financial matters. These earlier (pre-euphemistic) uses do not accord with the propensity for rational calculation, since prior to the sixteenth century, the adjudication of interest excluded rational calculation, a point to which I will return.[23]

An approach to conceptual history that is closely attuned to the uses of words offers the possibility of seeing more clearly the means by which Hirschman's "two essential elements" of interest came to be *a* sense of "interest" and a form of subjectivity. A word-focused approach can help us to decouple this sense and this form, and suggest other possibilities within the language of interest. It turns out that earlier (pre-euphemistic) uses of the term do not accord with the propensity for rational calculation that Hirschman sees at the heart of the

---

19. Hirschman, "Concept of Interest," 35.
20. Hirschman, *The Passions and the Interests*, 36.
21. Stephen Holmes goes so far as to make the plainly anachronistic assertion that various uses of "interest" have self-interest at their origin. See Holmes, *Passions and Constraint*, 64; see also Jane Mansbridge, "Self Interest in Political Life," *Political Theory* 18, no. 1 (1990): 132–53. For a history of calculating self-regard before "self-interest," see Pierre Force, *Self-Interest Before Adam Smith: A Genealogy of Economic Science* (Cambridge: Cambridge University Press, 2003).
22. Hirschman, *The Passions and the Interests*, 33, 38; emphasis added.
23. Hirschman also errs in neglecting the extent of humanist or economic discourses' appropriation of "interest" from late-medieval scholastic, Roman-legal, and religious-mystical language—possibilities I examine briefly in Chapter 3.

concept of interest, since prior to the sixteenth century the adjudication of interest excluded rational calculation. The way that the earlier legal uses of the term resist rational calculation, and the way that the financial changes paradoxically preclude the certainty that rational calculation is meant to offer, have much to tell us about the kind of subjectivity appeals to interest provoke. If we may follow Hirschman and others in bringing the history of economic thought and economic history to bear on matters related to agency, the legal aspect of the term "interest" aside from its relation to usury must be given its due.

But restoring the legal side of interest to its proper place involves suspending a second critical assumption about interests that has obscured the juridical side of interests—namely, that "interest" was originally a euphemistic financial term. The financial practice to which the terms "interest" or "usury" have been applied masquerades as a conceptual origin, and the reason for calling the practice "interest" falls from view. Historians of economic thought generally presume from the outset that interest is essentially a permanent net income owed to the individual owner of a capital sum in the form of a fee charged on a money loan.[24] From that starting point they treat the medieval wrangling over interest mainly as the struggle of scholastics, jurists, moneylenders, and others to square the law with a timeless economic fact in a way that minimizes coercion and extortion—an approach that makes it all the easier for Hirschman and others to view interests as intrinsically rational. Very few mention *id quod interest* or other uses of "interest" aside from the pecuniary at all, and none give them sustained attention. If we begin instead with an ear to how multiple uses of a term interact over time, we become attuned to how the earlier application of "interest" to property and personality changed when the term became associated with the practices of charging a fee on a money loan. We can hear *how* "interest" came to refer to calculating self-regard, and

24. The definitions here are Böhm-Bawerk's. See Eugen von Böhm-Bawerk, *Capital and Interest*, trans. George D. Huncke and Hans F. Sennholz, vol. 1, *History and Critique of Interest Theories* (South Holland, Ill.: Libertarian Press, 1959), 1, 9, 12–13. Although subsequent studies have greatly refined and extended scholarly appreciation of the routes by which charging a fee on a money loan has been legitimated, these definitions are practically unchanged. See Joseph Schumpeter, *History of Economic Analysis* (New York: Routledge, 1992); John Thomas Noonan, *The Scholastic Analysis of Usury* (Cambridge: Harvard University Press, 1957); Raymond de Roover, "Economic Thought, Ancient and Medieval Thought," in *International Encyclopedia of the Social Sciences* (1968 edition); Odd Inge Langholm, *The Aristotelian Analysis of Usury* (New York: Columbia University Press, 1984); and Toon van Houdt, "'Lack of Money': A Reappraisal of Lessius' Contribution to the Scholastic Analysis of Money-Lending and Interest-Taking," *European Journal of the History of Economic Thought* 5, no. 1 (1998). Across this literature, interest (like the time value of money, which it is said to express) is an ahistorical phenomenon, even if it is only fully realized, and realizable, in developed capitalist economies.

more important, we become sensitive to aspects of interest-related subjectivity that are presupposed by—and can even exceed—rational, self-regarding calculation.

Other thinkers have looked into the more distant past of interest to explore its implications for subjectivity—but here too, the legal uses of the term that were the practical vector of its reach into modern idioms have gone unnoticed. Perhaps the best known of these premodern explorations, among political theorists at least, is Hannah Arendt's. Her remark in *The Human Condition* on the Romans' language of interest has become a touchstone for attempts by political theorists to rethink the place of interests in politics against the social-scientific trend of the modern age.[25] "Action and speech go on between men," she writes, "even if their content is exclusively 'objective,' concerned with the matters of the world of things in which men move, which physically lies between them and out of which arise their specific, objective, worldly interests. These interests constitute," she continues, "in the word's most literal significance, something which *inter-est*, which lies between people and therefore can relate and bind them together" (182). Behind Arendt's observation is the insight that the Latin helping-verb "esse" combined with the preposition "inter," spawning a verb whose uses included the spatial sense of "to be situated between" or "to be among." The potential of this between- or amongness animates Arendt's often cited argument for recovering the intrinsic plurality of interest.

Describing the idea that "the only thing people have in common is their private interests" as "the obvious contradiction" in modern government, Arendt diagnoses the modern preoccupation with interests—as material, individual, calculating self-regard—to be a symptom of the simultaneously atomizing and aggregating political tendencies she attributes to the rise of "the social" in politics.[26] Among her many theoretical antidotes to this tendency, Arendt argues for a political recovery of the plural side of *interesse* as seen in "to be between" or "among"—such a recovery would disclose the "overgrowing" of the political by the social.[27] Her call to view interest by means of a literal, if forgotten, meaning is a helpful step. Prying the concept away from

---

25. Hannah Arendt, *The Human Condition* (Chicago: University of Chicago Press, 1958), 182; recent discussions of Arendt's etymology include Adam Sitze, "Flight in Dark Times," *Theory & Event* 6, no. 2 (2002).

26. Arendt, *Human Condition*, 69.

27. Sitze, "Flight in Dark Times," 6–7.

its uses at the hands of liberal theorists or behaviorists, for example, allows her to invoke the objectivity (or, in her idiom, worldliness) of interests as known by means of plurality—that is, by acknowledging how they are rooted in a irreducible variety of perspectives—rather than by way of philosophy or science.

However imaginative and evocative ("more truth than fact") Arendt's story about interest may be, it nonetheless promotes the etymological fallacy of locating a word's "true" significance in a distant past from which modern political language has been severed.[28] Arendt, like Hirschman, overplays the significance of financial uses to the "whole story" of interests in modern politics when she presents interest as a most difficult case for exploring the essential plurality of the world, owing to the overwhelming individualism and materialism of interests related to money.[29] And in the end, Arendt, like Hirschman, obscures how juridical notions of interest open and sustain plurality in the language of interest in present-day politics. She calls upon us to resurrect a sense of interest from a distant past, namely, as "something which . . . lies between people and therefore can relate and bind them together" (*Human Condition*, 182), as though this *were* alien to us today. Yet present-day speakers do appeal to interests in the sense she endorses, that is, as shared, and these uses are sustained in the practices of our political life. To make good on Arendt's insight, therefore, we had better examine how this sense of interest as shared has been—and is—used in coherent ways, albeit in ways that may be unfamiliar or even anathema to present-day theoretical perspectives.

In drawing out the continuity between the language of the ancient Romans and today's language of interest, we find that the actual if circuitous connection between interest and plurality is worth careful examination. *Interesse* also meant, among other things, "it makes a difference" or "it is of importance," "it affects" or "it matters."[30] It is from this final grouping of senses—what makes a difference, or what matters—that *interesse* begins its journey into modern European languages, by route of a specialized usage of *interesse* in Roman law as a noun. This noun, meaning "the hand one has in play" and "what makes a difference," was subsequently codified in the medieval Roman-legal term *id*

---

28. Regarding storytelling in Arendt, see Lisa Disch, "More Truth Than Fact: Storytelling as Critical Understanding in the Writings of Hannah Arendt," *Political Theory* 21, no. 4 (1993).

29. Sitze, "Flight in Dark Times."

30. Ernst Wolfgang Orth, "Interesse," in *Geschichtliche Grundbegriffe*, ed. Otto Brunner, Werner Conze, and Reinhart Koselleck (Stuttgart: Ernst Klett Verlag, 1982), 306.

quod interest, and from there made its way into European vernaculars.[31] The original use of *id quod interest* characterized legal duties in general, as the matter—or the object of legal contestation—which brought one to the court of law. And so if we wish to locate plurality in interests, the notions of "having a hand in play" and "differences that matter" rather than the sense of "between or among" deserve our close attention.

As disseminated across Europe in the practice of Roman law, the title *id quod interest* came to be concerned primarily with matters of identifying and diagnosing damages or changes in an object of property under contract and properly apportioning those differences to the parties of the contract. Arendt and others would read these as moments of interest's privatization and atomization, but looked at through another lens, they reflect and buttress the most basic forms of political participation and the roots of collective life. Hegel in particular was concerned to theorize property in this light, and so his philosophy offers touchstones for tracing the importance of juridical interest to political life more generally.

Id Quod Interest and Hegel's Theory of Personality in Property and Contract

The area of Roman law regarding matters of indemnity and reparation relevant to *id quod interest* addressed contracts on a particular class of real property loans, known as *commodatum*. These were loans of objects that were fixed (like land), or were unique or varied significantly in their qualities (like houses or oxen). *Commodatum* meant "given for use, benefit, or convenience," neither as a gift nor in exchange; this use of a durable property was lent to another person for a definite period. Ownership was not transferred, and the same article was to be returned to the owner when the time was up. The legal question of *id quod interest* was only brought to bear on real property loans if the contract was disrupted or dishonored, or the property in question was damaged.

---

31. Given the importance of *id quod interest* to the dissemination of this term across Europe, uses of these words were by definition invocations of a Roman legal concept and conveyors of its implications, even if the relation of Roman law to canon law, and to regional and national juridical practices, varied by time and place. Roman law had penetrated European legal systems along multiple vectors by the fifteenth century. It provided a legal grammar disseminated by medieval legal training throughout the Continent and England. Feudal courts turned increasingly to civil law to resolve disputes when customary law fell short. Early modern rulers promoted Roman law because it offered a secular, "universally valid" alternative to canon law. See Peter Stein, *Roman Law in European History* (Cambridge: Cambridge University Press, 1999), 57–65.

Roman law had no strict definition or computational guideline to determine the amount of damages; therefore, the adjudication of indemnity associated with *id quod interest* was regarded as a matter of judgment. A unique valuation was necessary in every case. Such a judgment was also necessarily retrospective because damages could be surveyed only after the fact. For this reason the application of *id quod interest* was not subject to a formula, but rather open to jurists' creative application in individual cases.[32] Wolfgang Orth writes that "it is quite logical [therefore] that in the Roman legal tradition one never uses *id quod interest* for the designation of financial interest [*Zinsen*], especially because financial interest can clearly be calculated according to a formula in each individual case. It is all the more notable that in the Middle Ages *id quod interest* is even turned into the designation of financial interest."[33] But the importance of judgment to determinations of *id quod interest* in medieval Roman law contradicts conceptual histories that, by privileging pecuniary uses of "interest" as an origin, make interest seem intrinsically rational in the sense of calculable. It also complicates the humanist view that (as Hirschman and others have it) sees notions of interest as deriving from self-interest, since jurists figured these damages against the norm of community valuation or the prior agreement, which was itself judged in light of common value.[34] In most instances, common value meant the price that was "common" in the sense of conforming to usual practice, but the judicial doctrine was real and robust insofar as courts used it to prevent extortion and exploitation, particularly during shortages.

Also note that in the legal term, *id* was "the thing" in question, and *interest* functioned as a verb, suggesting the active and dynamic role of contracting parties-turned-litigants, and then jurists, in valuing and realizing the *id* in question. Hegel's exploration of personality in *Philosophy of Right* sheds theoretical light on this matter of realizing and valuing an *id* at a point of conflict. In this work, Hegel theorizes personality among the same matters of Roman law that are home to *commodatum* and *id quod interest*, so his discussion opens a way to think about interest-related subjectivity before and into the period during which "interest" took on financial attributes of calculating rationality.[35] In the sections on property and courts of justice, spanning his consideration of

32. Dieter Medicus, *Id quod interest* (Cologne: Graz, 1962); quoted in Orth, "Interesse," 308; my translation.
33. Ibid.
34. Raymond de Roover, "The Concept of the Just Price," *Journal of Economic History* 18 (1958).
35. Knox, *Hegel's Philosophy of Right*.

abstract right and ethical life, Hegel explores how the exercise of property rights actualizes personality; this exercise happens (*inter alia*) in contexts of conflict and adjudication that arise around contracts.[36] In the midst of his discussion of various types of ownership, Hegel takes up a discussion of permanent ownership and temporary use of real property pertaining to the legal context of *id quod interest*. It's worth noting here that the Latin *id* corresponds to *ein Ding*, Hegel's term for the object to be owned.

The problem Hegel faces in the context of real property loans is that he has just characterized the use of a thing as a more complete form of ownership than the mere taking or marking of it.[37] He must now clarify in what capacity the owner of a thing holds a superior claim to personality in it than does the lessee who uses it. In answer to this question, he writes that "my partial or temporary use of a thing, like my partial or temporary possession of it is . . . to be distinguished from the ownership of the thing itself"—a definition of property loans that, in the context of Justinian's *Institutes* that are Hegel's guide here, corresponds with *commodatum*. Consistent with Roman law, Hegel cites the importance of a loan ending at a specific point in time; indeed, *commodatum* is defined by its temporal restriction. "On the strength of this restriction," he writes, "my abilities acquire an external relation to the totality and universality of my being."[38] For Hegel, this justifies the charging of rent or the payment of reparations: since the loaned object remains the lender's property, it remains the objectification of his freedom. Hegel goes on to say that "only if I have the full use of the thing [am I] its owner" insofar as "the entirety of its use" marks the objectification of the will in the object and therefore the progressive objectification of personality.[39] The entirety of a thing's use, says Hegel, includes its disposal, which is the prerogative of the owner and not of the lessee. Based on this prerogative, Hegel writes that "ownership is therefore in essence free and complete."[40] Confusing partial or temporary ownership for ownership per se would leave the subject "as a positive will at one and the same time both objective and subjective" to him- or herself—"an absolute contradiction."[41] Appeals to and adjudication of *id quod interest* work to avoid this contradiction. Since

---

36. Ibid., §§219, 222; see also Robert R. Williams, *Hegel's Ethics of Recognition* (Berkeley and Los Angeles: University of California Press, 1997), 135–37.

37. Knox, *Hegel's Philosophy of Right*, §§58–59. Hegel does not use the legal terms in question but his discussion pertains directly to *commodatum* and *id quod interest*.

38. Ibid., §67.

39. Ibid., §62.

40. Ibid.

41. Ibid.

ownership is the essence of personality, and since ownership is only real when it's complete, juridical appeals to interest are a means by which possession (i.e., merely having something) is elevated to property (i.e., having it as one's own). A subject's participation in this process, in the face of conflict or damage, is the actualization of his or her personality. This process involves the exclusion of accidentals, like the partial and the temporary, from the definition of property marked by the objectivity of positive will. It is how the state (as the expression of the community) orders positive relations and carves identity out of complexity, space, and time.

Hegel theorizes the historical quality of the state's juridical role in securing identity and ownership against temporary and partial possession, but personality itself is a rather static affair. To see how this is so, consider the adjudication of *id quod interest* in Hegelian terms. Taking contested properties to court under this title was a means toward reconciliation and reparation. The court's judgment organized and consolidated past events to accord with community practices and valuations, and affirmed the juridical process as the means of their final arbitration. Judgment was therefore narrative in the sense of imposing formal coherence upon the messiness and ambiguities of reality.[42] Subsequent to plaintiffs' entering into the legal process, the court's retrospective and compensatory narrative formed a basis for the restoration of community life and articulated the identity of the plaintiff within that narrative, in the face of contests in civil society that threatened personality with contradiction. Of course such a narrative laid a foundation for further action, but it did so by way of assuring that action would not disrupt the steadiness of contracts or their relation to community valuation.

But these considerations applied only to real property; from here, a little further acquaintance with the contours of Roman law is needed in order to appreciate the means by which *id quod interest* first excluded, and later came to legitimate, collecting fees on money loans. Examining a few of these legal terms also shows how seeing these fees as interest connects with the picture of personality.

Medieval scholars tried to systematize Justinian's fragmentary *Institutes* after the rediscovery of his *Digest* in eleventh-century Bologna by subdividing *id quod interest* into ever-finer titles.[43] Significant for my purposes are

---

42. Hayden White, *The Content of the Form* (Baltimore: Johns Hopkins University Press, 1987), 20.
43. The *Digest*'s recovery led to a surge in attention to the *Institutes*, whose brevity and fragmentation had previously frustrated attempts to systematically apply Roman law. See Stein, *Roman Law in European History*, 43.

two pairs of titles among the many they elaborated. First, the scholars distinguished between *interest intra rem* (what matters is in the thing) and *interest extra rem* (what matters is beyond the thing). The former was used to specify the quality of a property, like a horse, considering the physical characteristics that, for example, may have been in need of veterinary mending following an alleged wrongdoing. The latter considered whether, for example, the wrongdoing in question had diminished the horse's usefulness to the owner. This distinction denoted the difference between the property's objectively determined qualities and that which goes beyond those qualities.[44] *Id quod interest* was generally directed toward the *thing* under consideration (the *id* "that matters, is of importance, or makes a difference" to the inquiry); *interest extra rem* introduced an ambiguity as to what had been damaged: the object, or the well-being of the object's owner.[45] This opened the possibility of a shift in the reference of the *id* from the article of real property to the owner of property—in light of this shift, Hegel's connection of personality and the adjudication of real property contracts and indemnity is particularly apposite. *Interest extra rem* turned out to be closely connected to a title that eventually came to cover fees paid on a money loan.

To see this connection, consider a second set of titles under *id quod interest*, namely, *damnum emergens* (damage which occurs) and *lucrum cessans* (gain which ceases). Throughout the late medieval period, scholars attempting to systematize the *Institutes* sought symmetry between this pair of titles and the others mentioned in the previous paragraph.[46] Therefore, *damnum emergens* paralleled *interest intra rem*: damage done to real property corresponded to changes in its determinate characteristics. More important for the story at hand, *lucrum cessans* paralleled *interest extra rem*: diminished future employment of the damaged property corresponded to changes in what went beyond these characteristics, including the well-being (and as Hegel alerts us, the personality) of its owner. Scholars noted by way of warning that this parallel was a route by which the prohibition on usury could be circumvented, but the prohibition retained its power anyway, owing to a formidable distinction between real property loans on the one hand and loans of consumables on the other.[47]

---

44. Orth, "Interesse," 308.
45. Ibid.
46. The coherence of the *Digest* catalyzed scholars' efforts at systematizing the *Institutes*, both internally and in parallel to canon law. See Stein, *Roman Law in European History*, 46.
47. Orth locates this warning in the *Glosse*. See Orth, "Interesse," 308–9.

Medieval or scholastic considerations of commutative justice allowed contracts involving real properties to specify payment in excess of principal, consistent with *interest extra rem*. The lending of real property could be shown to have deprived the owner of the advantage or usefulness of a property that was still his own. By contrast, payment for a money loan was known to Roman law as usury, which signified charging excess return on an altogether different kind of loan called *mutuum*.[48] As distinct from real property, *mutuum* was defined as the giving of consumable items returnable in kind, whose "qualities . . . are fixed by weight, number, or measure, and which are used up in consumption, as are money, grain, wine, oils, and other things of this sort."[49] So the law considered money in its quite physical properties alongside other objects that are alike in quality and measurable in discrete units—it was not seen (in modern abstraction) as a medium of exchange and store of value. Therefore, Augustine's invocation of wine, oil, and grain as illustrating the true properties of money was oft reiterated in the generally monotonous discourse on usury throughout the Middle Ages.[50]

By contrast to real property loans, lent consumables were understood as subject to two distinct transactions, giving and returning. In the time between these transactions, neither the objects themselves nor the quantity exchanged were considered property of the lender, because the borrower returned an equal quantity of grain, oil, or money, but not the *same* grains, fluid, or coins. And so the juridical question of personality, as Hegel sees it, was not at stake. Rather, at the beginning and end of the lending period, the two moments of exchange had to conform to the principles of commutative justice no matter how much time had passed. Any additional payment that rendered this exchange unequal was seen as unjust and immoral; as a result, usury was prohibited.[51] But things began to change in the sixteenth century, as money loans came under the title

---

48. The counterparts of *commodatum* and *mutuum* in English common-law jurisprudence are *letting* and *lending*. These categories are congruent, in part because of the persistence of Law French and in part because of the long influence of ecclesiastical authority over usury. See Eric Kerridge, *Usury, Interest, and the Reformation* (Burlington, Vt.: Ashgate Publishing, 2002), 53–54.

49. Bernard W. Dempsey, *Interest and Usury* (Washington, D.C.: American Council on Public Affairs, 1943), 143.

50. Ibid., 147. On ancient and medieval prohibitions on usury, see Böhm-Bawerk, *Capital and Interest*, chap. 2, and Langholm, *Aristotelian Analysis of Usury* .

51. This prohibition derived at least in part from canon law too, though medieval jurists and theologians increasingly elaborated canon and Roman (civil) law in parallel throughout the twelfth and thirteenth centuries. See Stein, *Roman Law in European History*, 48.

of *lucrum cessans* and therewith entered the formerly forbidden terrain of *id quod interest*. How did this change come about?

Usury and Interest

Hirschman expresses the common view that "interest" entered the terrain formerly known as "usury" as a euphemism designed to make the latter practice appear less morally unscrupulous.[52] He further posits this euphemistic use as a conceptual origin. Although this conjecture is meant to provide a basis for the rationality of interests, it paradoxically acknowledges that the term had a life prior to its newfound servitude but at the same time hides the contribution of that previous life—namely, the adjudication of real property—to the subsequent uses of the term. Aside from the shortcomings of positing a euphemistic use as an origin, how might we conceive of euphemism as a mechanism of conceptual change in the case of interest? Euphemistic uses of the word by merchants and traders, to describe the widespread practice of charging a fee on a money loan, appear early and throughout in the historical record of Medieval Europe. This practice was also carried out under a variety of other names and was roundly supported by humanist scholars.[53]

As Quentin Skinner has shown, rhetorical practices akin to euphemism worried Renaissance moralists for their power to remake discourse; of especial concern was the trope of *paradiastole*, in which actors "attempt . . . to replace descriptions offered by [their] adversaries with a set of terms that picture the action no less plausibly, but serve at the same time to place it in a contrasting moral light."[54] The influence of euphemistic uses on the juridical history of interest lies elsewhere however.[55] Some erosion of the categorical difference between real properties and consumables must have taken place for any such rhetorical move to be legally plausible.[56] Because the distinction between interest

52. Hirschman, "Concept of Interest," 35.
53. Orth, "Interesse," 306. For other titles for a fee on a money loan, see van Houdt, "'Lack of Money,'" 17.
54. Skinner, *Visions of Politics*, vol. 2, *Renaissance Virtues*, 271.
55. Euphemism is a safer characterization of the relation of "interest" to "usury" in light of Skinner's description of *paradiastole* as working within a distinctive feature of Aristotelian moral discourse, namely that every virtue is a mean between two vices (ibid., 274, 83). This criterion of moral discourse does not apply to the legal terrain of "interest" and "usury": while "usury" was immoral, "interest" was *amoral*, and no second vice relates this pair.
56. Historians of political discourse distinguish conceptual changes that are "brought about by action, practice, and intention" in periods of crisis from "unintended structural change occurring in

and usury has not only moral but also broader legal implications, we need to look at the law to understand what shifts were needed to make euphemistic uses effective, and in what broader historical context. In addition to looking at the historical and conceptual conditions that made such a shift legally plausible, in order to appreciate the importance of the shift from "usury" to "interest" in describing the fee on a money loan we need to consider the effects of these conditions and the change on the preexisting uses of the term, especially as they relate to the retrospective and compensatory narrative of personality.

The watershed legal innovations widely regarded as abrogating the early modern legal prohibition on charging a fee on a money loan were articulated by Leonard Lessius (1554–1623), an influential jurist and theologian writing and teaching in Leuven around the turn of the seventeenth century.[57] Given his prominence as a jurist in the Netherlands, which was a center of innovation in banking and other business practices, his work *De iusticia et iure* was an incomparably influential legal text often consulted by businessmen and jurists working to make sense of the period's economic changes.[58] Among the several cases on which Lessius commented in his lectures and writing regarding money-lending practices, one is especially important to the considerations I have just described and has been noted by scholars as a critical development insofar as it signaled a departure from his earlier, more restrictive view on the Roman legal prohibition of collecting fees on money loans.

Discussing a case in which a holder of money made a loan in response to another's need (that is, out of charity), Lessius wrote that the lender was entitled

---

the historical context." See Terence Ball and J. G. A. Pocock, "Introduction," in *Conceptual Change and the Constitution,* ed. Terence Ball and J. G. A. Pocock (Lawrence: University Press of Kansas, 1988), 1, 7, 14; see also Quentin Skinner, "Meaning and Understanding in the History of Ideas," in *Meaning and Context: Quentin Skinner and His Critics,* ed. James Tully (Princeton: Princeton University Press, 1988), and J. G. A. Pocock, "Concepts and Discourses: A Difference in Culture? Comment on a Paper by Melvin Richter," in *The Meaning of Historical Terms and Concepts: New Studies on Begriffsgeschichte,* ed. Hartmut Lehmann and Melvin Richter (Washington, D.C.: German Historical Society, 1996), 48–49. Many focus on intentional change, but Pocock and Ball intimate the importance of long-term change to the success of intended changes when they describe innovation as depending upon the "persuasiveness" of the winning side's argument. Ball and Pocock, "Introduction," 2. Similarly, Skinner's discussion of *paradiastole* (see note 55) shows how plausibility is a precondition for agent-directed conceptual change to have any force (Skinner, *Visions of Politics,* 2:274, 83).

57. Van Houdt, "'Lack of Money,'" 2; see also Louis Baeck, "Spanish Economic Thought: The School of Salamanca and the *Arbitristas*," *History of Political Economy* 20 (1988), and Murray N. Rothbard, *Economic Thought Before Adam Smith: An Austrian Perspective on the History of Economic Thought, Volume I* (Northampton, Mass.: Edward Elgar, 1995).

58. Leuven is in present-day Belgium. Regarding the influence of Lessius, see Roover, "Economic Thought," in *International Encyclopedia of the Social Sciences.*

to a fee for having lent not only the money in question, but also the advantage that comes from holding money.[59] Having given this advantage (as distinct from the money itself), Lessius argued, resulted in *lucrum cessans* (gain that ceases), a title we have already seen was at home in *id quod interest*. Note how Lessius's invocation of *lucrum cessans* draws implicitly on *interest extra rem* (what matters is beyond the thing): the lender may not own the money while it's on loan, but he is entitled to compensation for what goes beyond the sum itself, namely, the advantage that comes from holding it. Consistent with the noncalculable adjudication of *id quod interest*, Lessius's invocation of *lucrum cessans* required lenders to specify a unique claim regarding the fee for each loan. After Lessius's decision, litigants broadly interpreted the notion of a charity loan and began to charge a fee under the title of *lucrum cessans;* over time, jurists gradually dropped the insistence that a new valuation must be argued in every case.[60]

Lessius's legal innovation raises two questions: What made this the title upon which Lessius could rule and to which moneylenders could even appeal? And, in what context is a set price, rather than one newly specified in each case, sensible? Surely, moneylenders' persistent uses of the term "interest" kept the question of the relation of fees charged on money loans and *id quod interest* before the jurists. Given the longevity of this euphemistic practice however, euphemism can hardly account for the change. But two other developments may account for it, in the sense of offering an interpretive context.[61] One is a legal analogy that eroded the categorical distinction between lending money and lending real property. Second is colonialist inflation, a feature of the period widely discussed by economic historians but less so by historians of economic thought. These two factors draw our attention to conceptual conditions and crises that made Lessius's change possible, effective, and perhaps even urgent.[62]

---

59. Lessius, *De iusticia et iure*, 2:20:10; cited in Toon van Houdt, "Implicit Intention and the Conceptual Shift from *Interesse* to *Interest:* An Underestimated Chapter from the History of Scholastic Economic Thought" (paper presented at "Crossroads: Writing Conceptual History Beyond the Nation State," Uppsala, Sweden, August 24–26, 2006). Lessius writes that money is sold (*vendi*) for advantage (*commodum*) but not lent (*commodatum*).

60. In unpublished research, Toon van Houdt explores a notion of "implicit intention" as assisting this development. My argument by contrast explores background changes in light of which the claim to *lucrum cessans* presents a contradiction and in which a market price for the fee makes sense. See ibid.

61. Regarding historical interpretation versus explanation, see Taylor, *Sources of the Self*, 202–3.

62. James Farr explores the "mechanisms" of conceptual innovation as triggered by actors' responses to contradictions. See James Farr, "Conceptual Change and Constitutional Innovation," in *Conceptual Change and the Constitution*, ed. Terence Ball and J. G. A. Pocock (Lawrence: University Press of Kansas, 1988), 14. As Farr suggests and others have realized, describing the historical conditions that set up contradictions is an essential task for rounding out histories of conceptual change.

The first of these considerations came out of attempts to grapple with a formidable restriction on usury aside from the distinction between lending real property and consumables. Money's fundamental unproductivity was a principle in its own right, whose origins, in Aristotle's remarks regarding the unnaturalness of "making barren money breed," medieval jurists and theologians articulated into a doctrine independent of money's status as a consumable.[63] Those opposed to the legalization of fees charged on money loans often appealed to this doctrine. Various analogical arguments were advanced to attack this point of medieval economic philosophy, mostly drawn from among money's fellows among the consumables. But these did not pass muster with jurists. For example, an argument drawn from the principles of agricultural production was that money was "the seed of gain": everyone knew that although grain was considered a consumable, small amounts of it had to be withheld from consumption as the source of next year's planting. The argument along this route was unsuccessful: by this analogy money was said to be fruitful in certain circumstances, but not in itself, just as seed needs fertile soil to grow.[64] Lessius in particular rejected, or rather denounced, this argument, saying that the soil in which money was rendered fecund was "the industry of the greedy."[65]

But a somewhat different analogy found more and decisive success, with Lessius in particular. Drawing upon agriculture and early manufacture, merchants argued that money was a tool of business. Tools (unlike grain) fell under the category of real property, adjudicated according to *id quod interest*. In 1552, Martinus de Azpilcueta (1493–1586), more often known as Doctor Navarrus and writing from the School of Salamanca in Spain, had been the first to acknowledge and reproduce this argument within a work that subsequently circulated among medieval jurists.[66] Dr. Navarrus's approval of this analogy, and Lessius's subsequent reference to it, were crucial developments.[67] While Lessius had rejected the notion that money was productive in itself, he nonetheless accepted that, like a tool which can only be used when it is in the owner's possession, money too had an advantage that the lender relinquished when it was not in his immediate possession. Once recognized, this analogy allowed money to be seen differently than it was when restricted to considerations governing

63. Aristotle, *The Politics* (New York, Oxford University Press, 1958), 1258b.
64. Dempsey, *Interest and Usury*, 159.
65. Lessius, *De iusticia et iure* 2:20:1; cited in Dempsey, *Interest and Usury*, 158.
66. Navarrus, *Enchiridion sive manuale confessariorum et poenitetium* (Antverpieae, 1601), cap. 17, no. 212; cited in van Houdt, "Implicit Intention."
67. In "Implicit Intention," van Houdt notes the importance of Dr. Navarrus's ruling but does not say why it was critical.

consumables, and also brought money into contact with terms formerly related to the adjudication of real property contracts only.

Just as the analogy of money to tools is a precondition for the appeal to interest in the case of money loans, another factor is needed as a precondition of relaxing the requirement that each appeal to *lucrum cessans* required a unique valuation. This factor is inflation, a consideration that will become especially important when we return to the matter of time, narrative, judgment, and interest-related subjectivity. European colonial expansion in the sixteenth century and the trade in expensive consumables like spices, sugar, and coffee increased the number and variety of cases involving consumables before courts of law, particularly in imperial Spain, Portugal, and the Low Countries.[68] But above all, the dramatic influx of African and New World gold and silver into the Spanish, Portuguese, and to a lesser extent, Dutch economies in the sixteenth century is a critical context for this development.[69] The consequent increase in the money supply simultaneously made more specie available for lending and, what was the other side of the same coin, brought inflation at unprecedented levels. After centuries of stable prices, the sixteenth century saw inflation of over 470 percent.[70] Although this is mild by present-day standards, lent money was conspicuously less valuable when returned, especially after a long period.

By midcentury, after at least fifty years of consistent price increases, lenders had ample reason to expect an inflationary future, and to hedge against it. Inflationary conditions would have rendered visible the distinction between a sum of money and the advantage of employing it, since the user of money was capable of employing it in ways that made up for, or perhaps exceeded, the sum's loss in value over time. Inflationary conditions further would have rendered redundant the requirement for a lending party to make a concrete claim in every case regarding how one incurred damage by lending: the damage would be evident, and could be roughly estimated beforehand. Evident too would be what later economists would come to call the time value of money, for inflation rendered it imperative (or, what might amount to the same,

---

68. Dempsey, *Interest and Usury*, 141.

69. For discussion of the contribution of Iberian precious metals imports to the sixteenth-century price revolution, see Pierre Vilar, *A History of Gold and Money, 1450–1920* (New York: Verso, 1991), 146–47, and David Hackett Fischer, *The Great Wave: Price Revolutions and the Rhythm of History* (New York: Oxford University Press, 1996), 82.

70. The figure is for the Iberian Peninsula; the Low Countries experienced only slightly lower rates. See Vilar, *History of Gold and Money*, 78–81. While local and short-term price fluctuations were common throughout the Middle Ages, the sixteenth century saw a long period of dramatically rising prices across Western Europe. See Fischer, *Great Wave*, 4–7.

rational) for the holder of money to put it to gain one way or another, either by investing in business or lending for a fee. In light of these circumstances, the prohibition of usury broadened in practice, intensified in effects, and became more controversial. Given medieval views of just pricing, it would make sense for jurists following Lessius to put this value in the hands of a market—in this case, the meeting of merchants at the local bourse.

Inflation created a crisis for common peoples and treasuries; might it even have influenced Lessius? The steepest inflation of the sixteenth-century price revolution was the period 1595–1602, during which he decisively changed his position on the legitimacy of charging a fee on a money loan by invoking *lucrum cessans*.[71] True, Lessius wrote in Leuven, but his distance from the inflationary extremes of Spain and Portugal do not much lessen the possibility that inflationary pressures are relevant to his change of mind. Not only did inflation affect the Netherlands, but close economic (not to mention political) ties between Spain and the Low Countries in this period erupted as influences in concrete ways: for example, a document written by Spanish merchants residing in Antwerp, justifying *inter alia* their moneylending practices, was partly influential in Lessius's reconsideration of the matter.[72] The observation that jurists did not invoke inflation directly in their writings may be answered by noting that sixteenth-century plaintiffs and jurists did not have our modern notion of inflation, let alone a category or title capable of addressing it separately within the Roman legal framework.[73] Instead, questions of price increases had to be treated as a matter of just prices, which only reinforces the bourse as a location for valuing the advantage of the use of money for a period of time.[74]

Claiming a causal relation between those especially pronounced price increases and Lessius's conceptual innovations would be precarious, but inflation is unmistakably the context in which they would have been and are intelligible. Even to the extent that one should hesitate to conclude that inflation contributed to Lessius's innovation, it is particularly illuminating as a backdrop

---

71. The period 1595–1602 saw inflation of 120 percent. See Vilar, *History of Gold and Money*, 78–81. Regarding the timing of Lessius's decisive change, see van Houdt, "'Lack of Money,'" 4–11.

72. Van Houdt, "'Lack of Money,'" 13–14.

73. In medieval times, people assumed that prices were stable in the longer term; see John W. Baldwin, *The Medieval Theories of the Just Price: Romanists, Canonists, and the Theologians in the Twelfth and Thirteenth Centuries* (Philadelphia: American Philosophical Society, 1959), 81–82.

74. Aspects of just price jurisprudence were developed in response to what would now be termed inflationary pressures in Rome in the third century C.E. See Károly Visky, *Spuren der Wirtschaftskrise der Kaiserzeit in den Römischen Rechtsquellen* (Bonn: Habelt, 1983). Loss of gain by lending in comparison to investment is a common claim taken up by jurists in these disputes; see van Houdt, "'Lack of Money.'"

to the change, given that it was achieved in part by an emerging practice on the part of many litigants and jurists of dropping an individual valuation in the case of each loan. Subsequent to Doctor Navarrus's legal analogy and in light of the inflationary context of the legal changes, the ending of gain came together with consideration of the *id* whose change was viewed as a temporal loss of value.

Categorical Erosion, Inflation, and the Subject of Interest

My presentation of this juridical history emphasizes an origin of interest in the active realization of personality. Recognizing the importance of financial practices to this history, it identifies the categorical erosion that brought money-lending into the legal domain of interest, and notes the intimacy between the newly employed title for charging a fee on a money loan (*lucrum cessans*) and another title that makes judging *id quod interest* particularly relevant to the realization of personality (*interest extra rem*). Last, I look at inflation. Historically, the sixteenth-century price revolution was a crisis that rendered visible the advantage of holding money and was furthermore a condition for the plausibility of fees charged on money loans not needing unique valuations in every case. Conceptually, inflation enters the picture because money suffers temporal devaluation just as it enters *lucrum cessans* and touches the realization of personality. Categorical erosion admits into the adjudication of *id quod interest* a kind of property subject to an altogether alien logic. Formulas are at hand for its adjudication, but money's uneven temporal devaluation introduces future-oriented uncertainty even as its fungibility introduces calculating rationality.

These considerations affirm Hirschman's judgment that financial practices are significant for interest-related subjectivity, but demonstrate that their importance must be interpreted in a broader context than seeing interest mainly as contending with passions. After all, interest is not only a psychological orientation toward benefit, though this is where most political-theoretical attention has been focused. It also denotes a share or stake in something, which implies the question of by what measure or standard that stake or share is determined. The latter question, in turn, implies a "who decides." These two considerations draw our attention to the uses of "interest" as a verb. Although this verb can mean "making curious" or "drawing attention to," it can also denote so doing by giving someone a share or stake in "that which matters" or "is of importance" or "makes a difference"—the very definition of *id quod interest*. These uses of "interest" are inflected with its juridical history, but they are nonetheless political inasmuch as politics does address questions of who has a share and who decides. Insofar as these matters echo juridical interest, how does recovering the juridical history of interest enrich a theoretical appreciation for the concept of interest, particularly in light of how readily interest is invoked (in theoretical, social-scientific, and everyday talk alike) to characterize subjectivity?

To begin, this juridical history offers a way to think about the modern notion of self-interest, and especially of the self as a preexisting or natural backdrop to political institutions. Consider the role played by just prices as a norm in the adjudication of *id quod interest*. Prior to money arriving on the scene, community life was the basis for the court's retrospective and compensatory narrative, and the court articulated the identity of the plaintiff within that narrative. The value under consideration was determined in principle, as Lessius described it, "with the whole town coming together at the voice of the town crier."[75] As this image suggests, Lessius's allowance of charging a fee on a money loan eventually subjected money to a price set *at* the market but it did not yet remand the value of all goods to prices set *by* the market.[76] The crucial difference is that markets, at least as far as Lessius's law was concerned, were still localized in space, time, and activity. Yet even as *lucrum cessans* became a title under which moneylenders could earn licit profits on their activity, common valuation was breaking down at the end of the sixteenth century owing to newly proliferating forms of exchange, like brokerage and auction.[77] Lessius's notion of the market was rapidly becoming quaint; it is alien to modernity. As markets become a more generalized and apparently autonomous part of everyday life, opportunities for the invocation of interest proliferate too. Although these invocations bear elements of the juridical, they are no longer strictly legal.

Given the importance of price to the foregoing story, with inflation being treated under law as a matter of just prices, which are in turn set at the local bourse, personality flows not out of juridical determination but rather from the encounter with universal valuation in the form of price. In modern economic

---

75. Lessius, *De iusticia et iure*, 2:21:76; cited in Dempsey, *Interest and Usury*, 150. For fuller discussions of community valuation and its relation to practice, see Toon van Houdt, "Just Pricing and Profit Making in Late Scholastic Economic Thought," *Supplementa Humanistica Lovaniensia* 16 (2000): 410–11; Odd Inge Langholm, *Merchant in the Confessional: Trade and Price in the Pre-Reformation Penitential Handbooks* (Leiden: E. J. Brill, 2003), 245–47.

76. Van Houdt, "Just Pricing," 20.

77. In addition to new forms of exchange, "common valuation" was eroding as a juridical standard by the beginning of the sixteenth century. See Langholm, *Merchant in the Confessional*, 248–49.

practices, as conceptualized by microeconomic theory, market price represents exchangeable value as the aggregated result of many potential transactions. In the long run, this result indicates the just price, known in the idiom of classical economics as the "natural price." In other words, to modern persons, price is no longer their community's witness of its usual practices in the exchange of useful objects. Instead, price reveals the exchange value of a thing to the community of laborers or consumers as "natural," and community life and the identity of persons alike are revealed by market prices as this norm is ascribed to "nature."[78] In light of such abstract and apparently neutral bases for setting the boundaries of personality, it would be easy to interpret the ascension of money to *id quod interest* as pegging interests to natural persons and their primordial attributes, expressed in neoclassical microeconomic theory as "preferences" and the like.

But the inflationary aspects of interest—particularly given that inflation is a matter of unpredictably rising prices—contravene the apparently natural determination of identity, in two ways. First, the sense of time brought newly to bear on appeals to interest subordinates the present to the future.[79] The incursion of finance shifts the determination of a person's stake or share away from the retrospective and compensatory. Instead, as a norm, financial interest values any principal in a prospective light. Hence interest is closely tied to becoming and to action, suggesting why the appeal to interest is so often a justification for, or an explanation of, an action.[80] The appeal to interest is a claim regarding what course of action (whether political, regarding investment strategy, and so on) rightly promotes the person (or principal) in question. Given uncertainty, however, the future comprises a field of possibilities. Therefore, interest, as a hedge against inflation, is a bet against the future's indeterminacy. This brings us back to a juridical aspect of interest, namely, the role of conflict or contest over the application of a norm and the question of who decides. Attending to conflict or contest is critical, since the picture of interest that emphasizes its rationality, calculability, and basis in ostensibly concrete particulars like natural persons or states cannot account for the disputes regarding in what exactly the interests of persons or states lie. Whole literatures in political theory and international relations are devoted to these as yet unresolved questions. The

---

78. See Karl Marx, *Capital*, trans. Ben Fowkes (New York: Vintage, 1977), 1:164–69.
79. Engelmann describes the futurity of interest as derived from state rationality, stressing its monism rather than seeing the future as a field of possibilities. See Engelmann, *Imagining Interest*, 81.
80. Ball, "Interest-Explanations."

contestability of appeals to interest also appears in political discourse where, for example, the national interest is readily invoked in support of disputed or controversial policies.

Whereas the appeal to interest was first mediated by common valuation, expressed as price and determined by a specific authority, future price as the guide to that determination now escapes specific authority and remains unsettled. So too, in the face of an appeal to interest as a justification for action, another can always argue that it is not in one's interest to follow that course, despite the promise of calculating rationality as the resolution of questions into concrete and unambiguous answers. Thus the uncertainty of inflation keeps contestation relevant to this picture of interests and devalues the present in light of that contestation. It highlights the context in which appeals to interest are often useful, that is, as a justification for action in the face of conflicting possibilities. The connection of interest to juridical determination of personality suggests why calculation of costs and benefits can resolve few, and hardly the most critical, of disputes over the interests of persons (or states, or nations): the dispute is less a matter of calculation than a discussion of becoming. The question is "who" is to be realized by action that promotes what is claimed to already be its "interests." The appeal to interest is still a judgment regarding identity, but owing to the uncertainty and open-ended horizon of the market, no single judgment is complete or authoritative in its own right.

Therefore interest-related subjectivity is paradoxical. Consider two instances of this paradox, drawn from historical documents that are prominent in conceptual histories of interest that have consequently been treated at length by scholars, and which I will reexamine at greater length in Chapters 3 and 5. In 1659, Marchamont Nedham published a pamphlet whose title, *Interest Will Not Lie,* provided seventeenth-century England with a political catchphrase.[81] On the title page, Nedham promised to illustrate England's interest against another writer's contrary (and "treasonable") picture of England's interest, thus giving the impression that the pamphlet's author punned on the ability of "lie" to mean both "deceive" and "stay put."[82] Could each of these author's visions speak to a different England and call upon his readers to realize his vision by means of action? To but mention a second example, note how interest can be seen either as a banner under which Jeremy Bentham sought a monistic

---

81. J. A. W. Gunn, "'Interest Will Not Lie': A Seventeenth-Century Political Maxim." *Journal of the History of Ideas* 29, no. 4 (1968): 556.

82. Marchamont Nedham, *Interest Will Not Lie, or a View of England's True Interest* (London, 1659).

account of motivations on the one hand, or as a term that ultimately stymied his attempts, on the other.[83] Herein lies the paradox: the term "interest" bears the possibility, if not the imperative, of calculation when it comes to matters involving interest, including those connected to real property and personality. Nedham, Bentham, Hirschman, and Holmes have taken this aspect of interest as an assurance that it is unified and rational. At the same time, the uncertainty of an inflationary future means that the benchmark against which questions of identity must be measured becomes uncertain too. As the sites of appeals to and judgments regarding interest proliferate with money's transgression of these categorical boundaries, so do conflicting possibilities among the identities at which appeals to interests aim. Even as appeals to interest attempt to hedge against the uncertainty of identity, such appeals signal the intrusion of uncertainty into the question of subjectivity.

The paradox of appeals to interest raises doubts about the "simple fact," cited by Hirschman, "that each person is best informed about his or her own [interests]," even if he or she *is* "best informed about his or her *own* desires, satisfactions, disappointments, and sufferings."[84] Hirschman's claim may reflect a liberal prejudice regarding "who decides," but it does not reflect a conceptual feature of interests. Although Hirschman and others take the rationality of financial interests as securing the acceptance of individual, self-regarding reason in early modern and modern discourses, particularly liberalism and social science, its juridical history illustrates how subjects' interests are inflected by rationality, but more importantly by an effort in the present to hedge an identity in the face of an uncertain future.

Interested Agency

A conceptual history of interest illustrates how juridical practices extend and affect other areas of life by means of the transit of terms through different areas of language, enabling and activating novel forms of subjectivity along the way. It enables us to see how emerging modern subjectivities draw from and reflect older categories even as these subjectivities exceed them. The insights for interest talk in politics generated by a recovery of juridical discourse suggests the incompletion and variety of notions of subjectivity, and how related notions

---

83. See Engelmann, *Imagining Interest*, and Hanna Fenichel Pitkin, "Slippery Bentham: Some Neglected Cracks in the Foundation of Utilitarianism," *Political Theory* 18, no. 1 (1990).

84. Hirschman, "Concept of Interest," 36.

(e.g., the person) have a role to play in thinking about political agency—a question for which no single category (subject, person, and so on) will provide a complete account.

Taking into consideration the juridical roots of interest and the significance of those roots to subjectivity, we must hesitate before assuming, on the basis of its conceptual history, that interests are a marker of freely exercised calculating rationality on the part of actors whose identities form a backdrop to political institutions and power. Instead we must consider how appeals to interest echo juridical scenes of contestation and judgment regarding the identities in question, even as these identities shift from retrospective and compensatory to prospective, inflationary, and uncertain. These origins of interest—juridical determination of quality, character, kind, personality, and identity—direct our attention to features of interest that a focus on rational individuals predisposes us to overlook. We now see how appeals to interest take different and indeterminate subjects as their points of departure; how appeals to interest invoke rationality at the service of temporal, uncertain, and contingent identities; and how appeals to interest remain open to contestation.

A history of interest that includes its legal side also enables us to think about the relation of the juridical to the political outside its usual equation with sovereignty, particularly those aspects of the juridical that its usual equation with sovereignty tends to obscure. These aspects include the importance of contestation on the one hand, and the extent to which rendering a decision is at the same time to acknowledge, however tacitly, the norm and the contestation in question, on the other. In this case, the norm includes the suitability and effectiveness of appealing to interest as a means of provoking the identity in question. To this end the conceptual history of interest in particular shows legal language escaping the confines of judicial institutions, extending into financial life, and from there into commercial and eventually into moral and political discourses, bringing with it elements of juridical practices. The transit of a once-juridical term, "interest," into politics is therefore a particularly rich site for exploring the effects of this term's and its entailments' crossing into matters pertaining to representation, constitution, and the state.

3 APPEALS TO INTEREST IN SEVENTEENTH-CENTURY ENGLAND

Medieval Provocations

Geoffrey Chaucer's short poem "Fortune, *Balades de Visage sanz Peinture*" (c. 1374) depicts a dialogue between Fortune and a person named only as *le pleintif* before a princely judge.[1] In the opening remarks of the poem, *le pleintif* laments:

> This wrecched worldes transmutacioun,
> As wele or wo, now povre and now honour
> Withouten ordre or wys discrecioun
> Gouerned is by Fortunes errour.[2]

In response to *le pleintif*'s many complaints, Fortune reminds the princely judge that she rightfully governs earthly life, and that for the security of "resoun" (reason), *le pleintif* must wait for death. She closes with the remark:

> The heuene hath proprete of sykyrnesse,
> This world hath euer resteles trauayle;
> Thy laste day is ende of myn interesse
> In general, this reule may nat fayle.[3]

---

1. Geoffrey Chaucer, "Fortune: *Balades De Visage Sanz Peinture*," in *The Riverside Chaucer*, ed. Larry D. Benson (Boston: Houghton Mifflin, 1987), 652–53.
2. "This wretched world's transmutation, / As well or woe, now poor and now honor / Without order or wise discretion / is governed by Fortune's error" (ibid., 652).
3. Heaven has the property of security, / The world has ever-restless travail; / Your last day is the end of my interest. / In general, this rule may not fail" (ibid., 653).

Fortune implores the prince not to allow *le pleintif* to blame her for his troubles, as though her influence is unwarranted, but to conclude instead that her influence is rightful in light of her argument that she is "beste frend of his noblesse / that to some beter estat he may atteyne"—an appeal especially relevant to the aspirations of a prince.[4]

The appeal to interests as a general rule and the rhyme of *sykyrnesse* (security) and *interesse* (interest)—a rhyme subsequently lost in English if not in common sense—suggest various modern associations. Even so, Fortune's appeal to *interesse* sits uneasily with the dominant tradition of writing conceptual histories of interest, which see origins of the term's political relevance in Renaissance, humanist, reason-of-state literature. Fortune's claim implies neither intrinsic rationality nor concern for security (quite the opposite!). Neither is her claim tied narrowly to the usual terrain of *id quod interest*. She does not allege to own the fate of earthly life; nor is that fate specifically financial or related to damage or loss, even if her remarks bear, at least incidentally, on considerations of wealth. Rather, despite the legal setting, Fortune's appeal to *interesse* is an occasion to connect property with political matters more broadly. While the prince is called upon to adjudicate Fortune's *interesse*—that is, he has some power to determine its scope and effects—he must nonetheless bear in mind Fortune's power to reciprocate his decision when it comes to the intrinsic in-*sykyrnesse* of earthly holdings. And particularly notable in that regard is the power that Fortune claims to substitute the prince's current "estat" for another, perhaps "beter" one. It is this that the prince must bear in mind when deciding *le pleintif*'s case; Fortune argues that acknowledging a broad scope of her *interesse* is itself the means to the betterment of the prince's "estat."

"Fortune" is a fitting beginning point for examining the ancient and nuanced connections between juridical practices and politics in that it makes contestation over property, and ambiguity regarding who decides, into a matter of princely decision—and speaks to the contingencies that confront that decision. While the legal (and French)[5] framing of the dialogue in "Fortune" partakes of the "mirror of princes" genre of political writing, whose eventual association with Machiavellianism and humanism has overdetermined most historical accounts of interest, the appeal to interesse in "Fortune" connects

---

4. Ibid.
5. Chaucer's usage here reflects a world whose daily language remained vernacular forms of English while the legal medium of exchange was Norman French. See Pocock, *The Ancient Constitution and the Feudal Law*, 34. That "interesse" was primarily a legal term is suggested by the fact that Chaucer uses it nowhere else in the body of his work.

to politics in ways that are not reducible to these later tropes. And influential though Machiavellianism and humanism have been in political language, the older associations are still audible in our present-day idiom. Chaucer's use of *interesse* in "Fortune" befits the legal uses of the term familiar from Roman law and shows how this legal imagery could be extended to the broader concerns of social life represented in vernacular literatures. Moreover, it hints at elements that will later contribute to the development of early modern notions of the state, in that juridical interest is brought to bear on determining the "estat" of a prince—while at the same time acknowledging the contingencies that impinge, for well or ill, upon this determination.

Though "Fortune" contains Chaucer's only known invocation of *interesse*, his usage is not merely antiquarian or idiosyncratic; his successors also implicitly or explicitly connected interest to the active realization of "estat." Fifteenth-century legal documents, for example, show *interesse* (or *enteresse*, another common variant) used in the legal sense of "the right to enter or pass though," especially to take possession by so doing. This sense may be seen as a blending of *interesse* with a French vernacular term, *entress,* meaning "entry," at a time before standardized spellings combated homophonic cross-reference and equivocity. Connections to possession, property, and exchange in fifteenth-century examples suggest, in a quite physical register, the active quality of realizing proper personality in one's "estat." So when a medieval judge rules that "whanne he to whom the forseid tenement was devised be comyn in to countre, have he *interesse* and his sesyn with oute eny lettyng or withseyeng of him to whom the sesyn was takyn in his name," he indicates that a newly landed lord takes (seizes) proper possession at the moment when he physically enters the parcel.[6]

Such a juridical connection of interest to property-related personality was deeply political in late medieval and early modern England, as the close connections between freeholding property, privileges, and liberties throughout that period would suggest.[7] And while "the state" is anachronistic to the fourteenth century, the anachronism lies in the fact that the person of a prince was not linguistically or conceptually distinguished from notions of dominion expressed in terms of estate or status. In this regard, Niccolò Machiavelli's

6. "When he to whom the aforesaid tenement was promised comes to the country, he may have interesse and seisin without any leasing or withholding of him from whom the seizure was taken in his name." *Ipswich Domesday* 2, vol. 1, c. 1436.

7. Ewart Lewis, *Medieval Political Ideas*, vol. 1 (New York: Alfred A. Knopf, 1954), chap. 2.

sixteenth-century advice to princes, *mantenere lo stato*, enjoined them to maintain their estates and their statuses as one and the same—while singling out these *stati* as a matter of special concern.[8]

It's well-known that the proliferation of "Machiavellian" pamphlets occasioned the dramatic expansion of the uses of "interest" in seventeenth-century England. For this very reason, Renaissance humanism as typified by Machiavelli is generally taken as the origin of interest's importance to political discourse. But Chaucer and the preceding examples show a precedent for the relevance of the term's legal uses to matters political. In other words, the bearing of "interest" upon the relation of a prince to his or her political status long predates Renaissance humanism. And since "interest" circulates in English as a legal term even today, much as it did in the seventeenth century, it would be astonishing if the long-standing political patterns of this usage were entirely swept aside and quarantined from political discourse by a reason-of-state import from the Continent. Therefore, the view that the legal side of interest was displaced by humanist intellectual and political developments demands close scrutiny.

Opening seventeenth-century English political discourse to this scrutiny is the aim of this chapter. In Chapter 2, I traced the connection between juridical interest and personality in the broadest sense. I examined how the application of the legal title *id quod interest* to financial matters significantly changed how personality proper to interest might be determined. Bringing the insights of that change to the seventeenth century in this chapter will enable us to see these effects on the level of politics, where juridical interest goes without final determination. Political interest, in other words, is intrinsically plural, or contested. The contestation at the heart of juridical interest becomes all the more important because it is in the seventeenth century that interest takes up a close relation to important foundational concepts, like the state or the nation. Therefore, rather than the language of interest being a faithful tool of sovereign agency (whether it be of the state or any other person), as its supposed origins in reason-of-state discourse might suggest, we see that the intrinsic plurality in the language of interest erodes this picture of sovereignty. When examining the persistence of juridical themes in the language of interest, we will see how appeals to interest lend an agonistic and democratic cast to the language of politics, because of its intrinsic and irreducible plurality.

---

8. Niccolò Machiavelli, *The Prince* (New York: Oxford University Press, 2005), chap. 7.

Recovering Interest as Conflict, Action, and Constitution

Machiavellianism and Renaissance reason-of-state literatures dramatically transformed seventeenth-century English political discourses, including the novel prevalence of the language of interest.[9] Given the complexity of changes during the seventeenth century, wide variation in scholarly perspectives on the place of interest in these changes is no surprise. English republicanism is one often-examined development of this period; the politics of interest is noted to have emerged alongside republicanism, possibly as its competitor.[10] Steven Pincus describes the emergence of a self-conscious commercial society of the 1650s as pressing the language of interest to the defense of the Commonwealth and the promotion of commercialization. He argues that this, rather than republicanism, is the dominant and historically most significant development of the period.[11] This perspective supports the widely held view that the rise of political interest enabled the development of liberal democracy and even of capitalism.[12] Mary Poovey sees "self-interest" as matter of partiality and bias—and thereby as a problem for the strivings toward objectivity of early modern politics and science.[13] Stephen G. Engelmann describes the incursion of reason-of-state arguments into a millennial context as underwriting the transformation of "interest" into a broadly economic term (as opposed to a narrowly financial one), thereby inaugurating all-encompassing notions of the public interest that dominated political discourse into and through the eighteenth century.[14] By all accounts, the roles played by the language of interest in the intellectual, cultural, and political transformations of the seventeenth century have much to tell us about the emergence of political discourses—like republicanism, utilitarianism, liberalism, and even neoliberal government—that continue to frame political debate and theorizing today. All of these accounts fit a larger narrative that emphasizes the intellectual and

---

9. Felix Raab, *The English Face of Machiavelli* (Toronto: University of Toronto Press, 1965), 95.

10. J. G. A. Pocock, *The Machiavellian Moment* (Princeton: Princeton University Press, 1975); Quentin Skinner, *Liberty Before Liberalism* (New York: Cambridge University Press, 1998); Steven Pincus, "Neither Machiavellian Moment nor Possessive Individualism: Commercial Society and the Defenders of the English Commonwealth," *American Historical Review* 103, no. 3 (1998).

11. Pincus, "Neither Machiavellian Moment nor Possessive Individualism," 708–9.

12. Hirschman, *The Passions and the Interests*, 4–5; Holmes, *Passions and Constraint*, 4, 26–66.

13. Mary Poovey, *A History of the Modern Fact* (Chicago: University of Chicago Press, 1998), 70–71.

14. Engelmann, *Imagining Interest*, 122.

cultural displacement of scholasticism, of which juridical discourse was a part, by humanism in myriad forms.[15]

While these stories illuminate a great deal about the languages of politics in seventeenth-century England, even when taken together they are nonetheless incomplete as an account of the language of interest and of early modern political discourse, because they miss the contribution of interest's juridical side to these changes. The undeniable novelty of Machiavellian arguments has tended to overshadow older connections in the language of interest and their contribution to the unprecedented ways of talking about, and living, political sovereignty and subjectivity as the seventeenth century progressed. Some commentators ignore the legal side of interest altogether;[16] others note an earlier legal language of interest but see English political discourse of the mid-seventeenth century as decisively turning away from the older associations.[17] When the term's financial uses are discussed, it is as if these pertained strictly to the activity of making money, and were not themselves legal.[18]

Those who have taken the humanist break as a point of departure for historicizing and conceptualizing interest see the confluence of interest talk and reason-of-state discourse as suggesting that interest is a kind of reasoning that

---

15. "Humanism" is a complex term that connects a variety of intellectual movements and cultural attitudes. I will use it in reference to a family resemblance among movements and attitudes in the early modern period, recognizing that the term itself is of nineteenth-century vintage. Renaissance "humanism" begins with the study of pagan sources. While in itself not a direct attack on the authority of the Church, the conviction of many scholars that pagan authors had reached an apotheosis of human achievement eroded respect for church authority and scholasticism, and promoted secularism. And their writings modeled a study of human things for which the Church was not central. Civic humanism, as it was developed in Florentine thought, premised citizen participation on incipient notions of man's intrinsic autonomy. And early modern humanism after the Renaissance, as it spread throughout Europe, took the shape of the study of human nature by observation rather than by scriptural and doctrinal authority. The intellectual tradition that emerges from these movements—that man can be understood as autonomous, and understood independent of the authority of the Roman Church—is the one that I will call humanism.

16. Hirschman, *The Passions and the Interests*; Hirschman, "Concept of Interest"; Holmes, *Passions and Constraint*; Pincus, "Neither Machiavellian Moment nor Possessive Individualism."

17. Gunn, "'Interest Will Not Lie'"; Raab, *The English Face of Machiavelli*. Stephen Engelmann notes the significance of residual juridical elements in the language of interest, which he calls "interest pluralism," in English political discourse, but his concern is primarily to trace the seventeenth-century origins of a monistic "interest theory" prevalent in the eighteenth century. See Engelmann, *Imagining Interest*, 122.

18. "Interest" has a long history as a legal term related to finance, and questions of financial regulation, that obviously continues to the present day. See John M. Houkes, *An Annotated Bibliography on the History of Usury and Interest from the Earliest Times Through the Eighteenth Century* (Lewiston, N.Y.: Edwin Mellen Press, 2004), 429–30, and William Blissard, *The Ethic of Usury and Interest: A Study in Inorganic Socialism* (New York: Charles Scribner's Sons, 1892).

takes the state—and later, individuals—as its object. They therefore forget, or even ignore, the immediate juridical connection between interest and state. Remaining attuned to the ancient connections of interest to notions of *estat*, as we saw in "Fortune," can correct this bias. Notions of the state were very fluid up to and throughout the seventeenth century. The notion of the state as a seat of sovereignty and agency, independent of communities and monarchs, is a particularly notable seventeenth-century development.[19] Part of my task of renewing our appreciation for the juridical side of interest in this chapter is to show how the language of interest contributes both to the independence of the state from the person of the monarch and, concomitantly, supports contestation regarding what *counts as* that state.

The closeness of "estate" and "state" brings us to a second term whose older range of meanings we must bear in mind when tracing the importance of the juridical for the new language of interest in seventeenth-century England. That term is "property." The two senses of this term are familiar to present-day speakers of English: beyond positive exclusive right to an object, "property" also means the characteristics of any thing. The equivocity of these senses was quite salient to early modern writers. It was even crucial to their way of confronting political matters.[20] This equivocity can be drawn out by focusing on the ambiguity in saying that some body "has properties." On the one hand, this body has characteristics; on the other, it may own something. The equivocity lies in the fact that this ownership is, of course, itself a characteristic of the body in question. To press the equivocity a bit further, we might say that a body that has properties has characteristics that are its own. A dispute over ownership shades into a dispute over essential characteristics; a judgment regarding one becomes a judgment regarding the other.

Both changing conceptions of the state and the equivocity of "property" are crucial to the language of liberty in seventeenth-century England. Liberties were closely tied to offices that were themselves defined in terms of estate, status, and property. Contests over the proper relations of persons to their official status, and the proper attachment of liberties and privileges to estates, were central to the political conflicts and changes in England during the civil war,

---

19. Skinner, *Visions of Politics*, 2:379, 86, 91–99.
20. Tully, *Discourse on Property*, 33–34. The extension of this entitlement to actions is apparent in the close connection between the terms "property" and "propriety," which were not orthographically differentiated until the late seventeenth century. The close relation appears to derive from both words' common root in the Latin *proprietas*. Tully does not comment on early modern distinctions between "property" and "propriety."

the Protectorate, and the Commonwealth.[21] When appeals to interest meet these conflicts, their juridical inflections—as sites for the contested provocation of personality—come to bear on a range of political personages, from monarchs to states and citizens, in ways that a humanistic picture of interest as a kind of rationality cannot encompass. When we foreground this picture, juridical interest is hard to see because it is a language of action, not of contemplation; because it is a matter of constituting persons, not of psychological motivation; and because conflict and contestation are its crucial context, even as room for contest is what an appeal to interest disavows and denies. And so we miss how throughout the seventeenth century, political appeals to interest became a means of contesting and remaking the contours of liberty and action pertaining to the "who" or "what" that is said "to have an interest" and "to be interested"—state and citizens alike.

In order to bring life to these conceptual, historical, and philosophical arguments, in this chapter I examine the explosion of the language of interest in seventeenth-century English political discourse in a way that recovers the role played by the contested, identity-provoking side of interests. This recovery is aimed both at enriching the historical record and at shedding light on the meaning of seminal historical developments to us. I proceed in three stages. I principally examine the writings of Henri, duc de Rohan, and Marchamont Nedham, two authors whose arguments became catchphrases that played critical roles in changing English political discourse during and after the civil war. Along the way, I trace the juridical, antihumanist (and often, Counter-Reformation) provenance of the language of interest in the debate that set the stage for Rohan's, and then Nedham's interventions. To those who see interest as a form of rationality, the emerging language of interest appears to subjugate sovereigns or other political actors as a form of knowledge. In other words, the agency of these persons appears to be circumscribed by the "way of knowing" proper to their state or status. I find that the juridical side of interest precludes the idea that in the seventeenth century interest was a kind of knowledge. Instead it is a means of provoking and contesting the very contours of the state or status.

From there, I explore how interest escapes final determination even in the context of religious millennialism familiar from seventeenth-century England. In the sway of these movements, the righteousness of England and the true conscience of citizens were argued to offer the final determination of the

---

21. Conal Condren, "Liberty of Office and Its Defense in Seventeenth-Century Political Argument," *History of Political Thought* 18, no. 3 (1997): 468.

interests of the polity.[22] To see how appeals to interest nonetheless remained contested, I examine the record of the debates at Putney, between members of the New Model Army and their leaders. Even in a context where "the people" are said to be the final arbiters of interests, these debates reveal that appeals to that interest remain contested because who counts as the people is itself a contested matter. Here we see how interest, owing to its juridical and plural side, relates to democracy in ways that are distinct from the formal egalitarianism of individuals and their aggregation in popular representation. The debates at Putney reveal a language of interest that animates practices of democracy as both constituting and contesting collective identity.

I close this chapter by reflecting on the present-day language of interest to see how it bears traces of the seventeenth-century language of interest revealed in Rohan, at Putney, and elsewhere. These resonances of juridical interest bear on how we theorize the legacy of seventeenth-century politics, as reflected in conceptions of sovereignty, subjectivity, and democracy. I show how present-day ways of speaking of interest, even those that appear to refer to what's "psychological" in the sense of subjective and individual, nonetheless reflect the power to constitute and contest the contours of personality and selfhood. This power, I contend, is the core contribution of the language of interest to politics. In the seventeenth century, this language became a means by which constitution and contestation were made integral to political agency, in forms as apparently diverse as the state, the citizen, and the nation.

"Machiavellian" Reason-of-State and the Citizen

The explosion of interest talk in politics is, by all accounts, attributable to two principal figures: Henri, duc de Rohan (1579–1638), and Marchamont Nedham (1620–1678). Their writings, which were clearly "Machiavellian" in tone and, to a degree, in substance, catalyzed English political discourse by their radically innovative ways of invoking "interest." So it's not surprising that scholars have emphasized the influence of Machiavellian humanism in early modern England and to see the language of interest as among its newest and most potent conveyances.

But the emphasis on the novelty of these men's arguments has gone a step too far. When they rendered their arguments in the language of interest, they also drew the juridical aspects of this language into the mix in significant ways.

---

22. Engelmann, *Imagining Interest*, 127.

Recovering the importance of juridical and plural interest to political language can begin, then, by reexamining their contributions. I read Nedham's and Rohan's arguments from interest through a lens that draws out the persistence of juridical inflections, particularly regarding contestation over proper identity. The juridical backdrop of interest in their writings, I contend, reveals the importance of plural interest in opening and sustaining contestation regarding the identity of state and citizen. I shall begin by introducing them and their works in ways broadly consistent with how they have been discussed by my predecessors. Then I shall go on to explore their contributions with a distinctive view to the politics of contested identity and action.

Marchamont Nedham was among the earliest professional journalists. He was also a strikingly unscrupulous character who wrote and published ostentatiously inflammatory and only apparently principled treatises on behalf of whoever could pay him—pay being the "professional" side of his journalism. So his career was something of a scandal. In 1647, he penned a royalist tract titled *The Case of the Kingdom Stated: According to the Proper Interests of the Severall Parties Ingaged*.[23] Therein Nedham surveyed the major factions (or "parties") of contemporary English politics, according to their "interests": all of which, one way or another, turned out to support the king. Nedham continued to support the royalists through 1648; in 1649, after a short imprisonment for his royalism, he switched sides and wrote for the regicides. Though his support for the Protectorate varied through the middle years of the 1650s (writing occasionally on behalf of republican causes, for pay), he was on Cromwell's payroll as a spy all the while the Lord Protector was fighting in Scotland. Nedham lost his pension in 1659 when the Rump parliament was restored, so he switched sides again, and wrote *Interest Will Not Lie, or a View of England's True Interest*, in support of the Rump and against a Stuart restoration.[24] Nedham's new book again surveyed the major parties of the day, this time arriving at a pro-Parliament—or more to the point, an anti-Catholic—"interest of England." His pension (and his privilege to publish) was promptly restored. He was exiled upon the Restoration. He later returned to England as a medical practitioner, but he still managed to write on behalf of Charles II (and against the Earl of Shaftesbury) before his death.[25]

23. Henri, duc de Rohan, *Of the Interest of the Princes and States of Christendom*, trans. Henry Hunt (Paris, 1641); Marchamont Nedham, *The Case of the Kingdom Stated, According to the Proper Interests of the Severall Parties Ingaged* (London, 1647).
24. Nedham, *Interest Will Not Lie*.
25. J. B. Williams, "The Beginnings of English Journalism," in *The Cambridge History of English and American Literature*, ed. A. W. Ward et al. (Cambridge: Cambridge University Press, 1921), 50–54.

The two texts of Nedham that I have mentioned are notable for the prominence they give to the language of interest. Because of Nedham's visibility (not to say notoriety) as well as his political and rhetorical flexibility, his writings both reflected and shaped trends in the political discourse of the day. Nedham himself described these two works as greatly inspired by Rohan's "little, but weighty book," *On the Interest of the Princes and States of Christendom*.[26] This 1638 treatise was known in England, both in its original French and (especially) in Henry Hunt's 1641 translation. Rohan's book was a compact reflection on European international affairs that offered pithy advice to rulers regarding what courses of action best served the aims of security and influence, in light of the precarious balance of power between Spain and France in its time. Rohan's argument was innovative in terms of its future orientation, its treatment of government as a matter of proper knowledge, and for how thoroughly it parsed the contours of princely power.[27] It is also innovative for the prominence it gives to the language of interest as a means of developing these insights.

After a preface devoted to extolling *l'intérêt* as the category proper to his analysis, Rohan offers a picture of each major and several minor nations and principalities. He draws conclusions for each regarding what present-day observers might describe as optimal foreign and domestic policies, considering both the bipolar international scene and domestic factions. While Rohan's tract was but one example of a prolific genre, Rohan's ambitious reputation as a fiercely successful Huguenot statesman and military strategist particularly recommended him to the English, and especially to those English Protestants opposed, like Nedham in 1659, to Charles's proximity to Catholicism. (The Nedham of 1647 may have instead appreciated the royalist overtones of Rohan's work—or at least, its emphasis on kings and princes.)[28] Perhaps owing precisely to the flexibility of arguments that could be made on the basis of interest, the English went on to transform political discourse with Rohan's slippery watchword.

Rohan's tract is conspicuously concerned with reason-of-state; Nedham's appropriation of its terms models political action on calculations that heed no moral precepts. As seminal contributors to the rise of interest talk in politics, then, it's no surprise that these texts, and the language of interest they promoted, are seen primarily in Machiavellian terms and as reflecting humanism

---

26. Rohan, *Of the Interest;* for Nedham's reference to Rohan, see Marchamont Nedham, *Christiandus, or Reasons for the Reduction of France to a More Christian State in Europe* (London, 1678).
27. Engelmann, *Imagining Interest*, 101.
28. Gunn, "'Interest Will Not Lie,'" 553–54.

more generally. The reason-of-state genre of Rohan's contribution in particular is argued to suffuse the newly political language of interest with humanist, realist, or rationalist preoccupations and to make this language a vehicle of tensions among them. Regarding these tensions, commentators have noted two problems in particular. The first is the question of whether arguments from interest are tautological—whether, to paraphrase Thomas Macaulay, they can only tell us that a man (or state) had rather do what a man (or state) had rather do.[29] The second is whether appeals to interest in reason-of-state arguments erode the very sovereignty that the arguments are supposed to advance, by means of limiting (to a knowable interest) the scope of a sovereign's decisions and actions. Each of these questions can be answered, or more aptly put, dispelled, when the juridical inflections in the language of interest in Rohan's and Nedham's arguments are given their due.

In what follows, my first task is to draw out the juridical side of these authors' appropriation and deployment of the language of interest in political argument. Considering juridical interest as a contested claim regarding personality that is troubled with futurity and uncertainty, we see how Rohan and Nedham extend the juridical power of appeals to interest to state, nation, and citizen in novel ways. My second task is to consider how rethinking the seventeenth-century development of the language of interest contributes to overcoming the dilemmas that arguments from interest present when viewed in a humanist frame. As I see it, appreciating the power of juridical and plural interest in these authors' texts illuminates a politics of interest that exceeds the broadly liberal perspectives on sovereignty and autonomy underwriting these theoretical tensions, in that appeals to interest are provocations of political identity, rather than rationalizations on the basis of identities given in advance.

Juridical and Plural Interest in Rohan and Nedham

The legal language trailing Nedham's invocations of interest is so obvious that the standard view of Nedham as breaking with juridical uses of the term is quite curious.[30] The very title *The Case of the Kingdom Stated* suggests a legal proceeding; this language reappears in *Interest Will Not Lie*, where Nedham asserts that "if a man state his own interest aright, and keep close by it, it will

---

29. Thomas Macaulay, "Mill's Essay on Government: Utilitarian Logic and Politics," in *Utilitarian Logic and Politics*, ed. J. Lively and J. Rees (Oxford: Clarendon Press, 1978), 125.

30. Gunn, "'Interest Will Not Lie,'" 551–52.

not lie to him or deceive him, in the prosecution of his aim and ends of good unto himself."[31] Interest, then, is a claim to be stated and prosecuted in the court of action. Moreover, Nedham explains, "if you can apprehend wherein a man's interest to any particular game on foot doth consist, you may surely know, if the man be prudent, whereabout to have him, that is, how to judge of his design."[32] It may be too much to speak of Nedham "apprehending thr subject," but the intimation of counsel and references to prosecution, prudence, and judgment bear, superficially at least, juridical inflections even outside a strictly legal domain. They suggest from the outset that whatever we will find in Rohan's appeals to interest, Nedham's appropriation of Rohan's work as an idiom of citizen action will reflect something of the long-standing juridical uses of the term in English.

Perhaps the juridical side of Nedham's appeal to interest has escaped scrutiny because *Rohan's* concern—international affairs—is one in which the rule of law is mostly irrelevant. And so the story goes that rather than emphasizing external authority—legal or otherwise—Rohan and then Nedham promote a radically new style of reasoning to politics, namely, interestedness, that emphasizes rational calculation. Rohan is said to have elucidated the calculating conduct appropriate to a prince, and Nedham is seen to have extended this style of reasoning to individuals on the one hand, and to parties on the other.[33] As a calculating style of reasoning characteristic of all political action, interest is seen mainly as a force contending with passions in the interior landscape of each human being—as distinct from external authorities, which were proved and reproved as insufficient as a basis for order. In other words, the kind of interest that readers have seen at work in Rohan, Nedham, and many others, is what we moderns would like to call a psychological faculty, modeled on individual awareness and the individual pursuit of benefit or gain. The striking opening of Rohan's *Of the Interest of the Princes and States of Christendom*, "the Princes commaund the People, & the Interest commaunds the Princes," would appear to exemplify the insertion of interest, as a style of reasoning, into political discourse.[34] When the supremacy of "interest" was brought to the realm

---

31. Nedham, *Interest Will Not Lie*, 3.
32. Ibid.
33. Regarding Rohan, see Hirschman, *The Passions and the Interests*, 36. Regarding Nedham, see Gunn, "'Interest Will Not Lie'"; Hirschman, *The Passions and the Interests*, 36n; Pincus, "Neither Machiavellian Moment nor Possessive Individualism," 729; and Engelmann, *Imagining Interest*, 183 n. 82. Nedham's innovation would in particular be congruent with James Tully's description of newer juridical modes of governance, though Tully does not mention him. See Tully, "Governing Conduct."
34. Rohan, *Of the Interest*, A1.

of everyday action by the likes of Nedham, the power of conscience, with its antinomian unpredictability, could at last be denied.[35]

But Rohan's inaugural invocation of interest sits uneasily with an account that sees interest as an internal motion contending with passions and virtues. Instead it speaks to an external power, force, or influence of some kind—one that subjugates and activates, rather than rationalizes and liberates, its object. To this end, Rohan's subordination of princely conduct to the imperatives of interest is clear. He declares that "the *Interest* commaunds the *Princes*," and goes on to write that "the knowledge of this Interest is as much raised above the Princes actions as they themselves are above the *People*"—"the Interest" commanding the prince's actions rather than the prince commanding them directly.[36] Staying with the "countervailing passions" reading, we may be tempted to see the prince as somehow divided here, and Rohan's argument merely aiming at identifying what passion has the upper hand. But there is good reason to consider, for a moment, ways that the prevailing power comes from without.

Rohan's invocation of "the Interest" complicates the usual story of interest as a rational faculty. One way to begin seeing this is to allow the translator's provision of a definite article to provoke us away from the modern, psychological notion for which such an article is not idiomatic.[37] But the article does suit a juridical notion, like a stake or a share. Whatever sense we may make of it, in the seventeenth century, "the Interest" also evoked the power or influence one person exercises over another or a group—by means more authoritative than drawing attention. Such a sense could also be expressed in the now unusual phrase "to make interest," which meant something like "to bring personal influence to bear."[38] Such "making interest" could itself be formal and legal,

---

35. Tully, "Governing Conduct," 12–13.
36. Rohan, *Of the Interest*, A1.
37. Gunn, "'Interest Will Not Lie,'" 553 n. 9. Gunn reads "the Interest" as simply a too literal translation. Also, it may be tempting to read the difference here as a distinction between "objective" and "subjective" interests. But this temptation is better resisted, since this philosophical distinction is an anachronism for the seventeenth century. I discuss some present-day theoretical problems this distinction presents in Chapter 6.
38. *Oxford English Dictionary*, s.v. "interest." The *Middle English Dictionary* records the sense from 1456, and the *OED* provides myriad examples of its use from the end of the sixteenth century until the early eighteenth century. At this same time, the *OED* records a "new" sense of "power to attract attention or concern." Of course, lexicons like the *OED* and the *MED* are insufficient as sole bases for conceptual-historical investigation; for a discussion of the lexicons' problems in that regard, see Richter, *History of Political and Social Concepts*, 147–57. The dictionary's entries are useful, however, as a reminder of the diverse uses of words, particularly those which are no longer the most familiar in most dialects of English.

such as the liberty that a superior enjoyed by virtue of office.[39] We may also hear it in Edward Blount's translation (1600) of Gerolamo Franchi di Conestaggio's *Historie,* where we find complaints that certain magistrates "were mechanicke men, in whom feare hath a more interest, then the respect of a King."[40] In its alignment with fear in this passage, our first thought is to follow Hirschman in seeing interest contending with a passion. But the proper source of juridical influence, Conestaggio seems to be saying, resides in subordination to political authority. Even at the cusp of interest's legibility as an independent motivation, internal to the political agent, we are alerted—by Rohan, by Blount, and by others—to how the language of interest is caught up in relations of domination and subordination.

Of course, all of this raises the question of how that language dominates, subordinates, or "subjectivates," and what it means to bring "interest" to bear on a prince, state, or other political actor. At a more theoretical level, it raises the question of the bearing of interest on sovereignty—a problem that is most acutely illustrated by invocations of interest in reason-of-state literatures.[41] Drawing out the contested, action-oriented, and identity-provoking side of "interest" that exceeds modern psychological notions offers a path through some of these questions. It points not only to the emergence of the state as distinct from the monarch (and the concomitant emergence of the citizen as distinct from the subject), but more particularly to the role of appeals to interest in provoking action on behalf of states (and citizens) toward their realization.

Interest and Improbable Knowledge

To the extent that humanism has provided patterns by which the language of interest enters political argument, one would expect that interest would subjectivate the way that humanism does: as a form of knowledge.[42] The dominant tradition's way of seeing interest as a kind of reason, namely, calculating self-regard, gratifies this expectation, and both Nedham's and Rohan's writings

---

39. Condren, "Liberty of Office," 466.

40. Gerolamo Franchi di Conestaggio, *Historie of the Uniting of the Kingdom of Portugall to the Crowne of Castill,* trans. Edward Blount (London, 1600), 202. Gerolamo Franchi di Conestaggio is thought to be a pseudonym for Juan de Silva, conde de Portalegre (dates unknown).

41. Engelmann, *Imagining Interest,* 101. The erosion of sovereignty indicated by the delimitation of princely action in reason-of-state literature leads Engelmann to see reason-of-state as antijuridical. Appreciating the juridical side of interest suggests instead seeing competing tendencies in juridical language, in which sovereignty and personification are in some ways at odds. Cf. Engelmann, *Imagining Interest,* 78, 90.

42. Ibid.

appear to fit this pattern. Rohan remarks that "according as [the Interest] is well or ill understood, it maketh *States* to liue or die"—here we see might see interest as a knowledge essential to reason-of-state.[43] Nedham's writing, legal imagery aside, appears to treat the study of interest as a kind of practical knowledge: "If a man state his own interest aright," he writes, "and keep close by it, it will not lie to him or deceive him."[44]

Seventeenth-century standards for what counted as knowledge emphasized the probable over the certain and the future over the past. In this light, humanist scholars' legal gains in bringing money under the Roman legal category of *id quod interest* would also appear to support interest as an object or a kind of knowledge.[45] In legal practices more generally, this conception of knowledge as probable manifested in the development of evidentiary standards. Overall, probabilistic knowledge directed action in ways that earlier humanistic catalogs of historical anecdotes—as are familiar from Machiavelli's *The Prince*— did not.[46] Probable knowledge cultivates not a prince's (or theoretician's) acumen in correlating a predicament with a historical precedent and distilling its principle, but instead promotes attention to more general relations of cause and effect. An emphasis on probability reduces (if it does not eliminate) the scope of a political actor's *virtù* in confronting the play of uncertainty. Rather, it advises a definite course of maximally prudent action. With all of this in mind, producing knowledge regarding reason-of-state in the seventeenth century, therefore, does appear to be a quite paradoxical development: it would, after all, subject the sovereign.[47]

Striking as the confluence of these humanistic elements might be, the juridical remains a key and distinctive aspect of the language of interest throughout these transformations of political discourse. For commentators who acknowledge a legal past to "interest" at all, the appearance of this term at the confluence of discourses saturated with humanism, like reason-of-state and fees on money loans, would seem to be evidence enough that Rohan's language of interest is severed from its previously retrospective and compensatory role in Roman law. But the appeal to interest—as one among a variety of tropes humanist writers employed in reflecting upon matters of state—fits poorly with late Renaissance standards of knowledge in other ways when it comes to political argument. The

43. Rohan, *Of the Interest*, A1.
44. Nedham, *Interest Will Not Lie*.
45. Barbara J. Shapiro, *Probability and Certainty in Seventeenth-Century England* (Princeton: Princeton University Press, 1983), 5; Tully, "Governing Conduct," 27–33.
46. Engelmann, *Imagining Interest*, 92.
47. Ibid., 99.

kind of uncertainty that pertains to agency is less a matter of probability, than it is a matter of action and becoming; appeals to interest, we shall see, speak decisively to the latter. The end to be achieved is itself subject to dispute, rather than being a given object whose attainment is in some way aleatory. Reading Rohan and Nedham, we will see that appeals to interest draw on the pretense to interests as an object or form of impartial knowledge, but as a means to another end—staking a claim regarding what counts as the state or the nation, in light of multiple and conflicting possibilities.

Herein the pretense lies. Nedham's seventeenth-century journalist colleagues drew heavily on notions of impartiality that were also newly current in scientific and legal discourse.[48] In Nedham's case such a posture—"England's True Interest" revealed by the confluence of all truly English parties' interests—was merely a heady (and, given the ire he stirred in his contemporaries, evidently transparent) cover for partisanship. Nedham's treatise proceeds as an exploration of the heterogenous elements—"parties"—from which a picture of England emerges. This England is known by observing the concord of attachments among many, but not all, of these parties. This concord lies not in their shared future destiny, but in patterns of injury and grievance, suffered by each, at the hands of Roman Catholic monarchs and their allies and advocates. In a richly juridical vein, this interest is illuminated at the site of the deep wounds and grisly conflicts adumbrated by Nedham throughout the work. But extending this juridical power into the political context, we see him inveigh against one party in particular—calling it "papist," he reveals it as treasonous rather than English—whose designs, Nedham argues, would certainly bring more of the same. To that end, his discussion of "England's True Interest" is largely a polemic against John Fell, the "treasonable" author of *The Interest of England Stated*.[49] In sum, then, Nedham's aim is to provoke the actions of all Englishmen worthy of the name away from those suggested by Fell (i.e., a Stuart restoration), on pain of treason to the nation and its consequences. The complex and controversial question of what counts as "England" is more revealed than settled by Nedham's intervention. If Nedham seeks to adumbrate "what's knowable" about political action at all, it is only as a cover for staking a claim to what counts as England in this contested field.

Looking back from Nedham to his inspiration in Rohan, there too we see the author staking a claim, in the guise of imparting knowledge, on a complex

---

48. Shapiro, *Probability and Certainty*, 264–65.
49. John Fell, *The interest of England stated: or, A faithful and just account of the actions of all parties now pretending* (London, 1659).

and undecided thing. And here, the language of interest provides a ready connection to such a thing in the state. As we have seen, this connection is as old as Chaucer. We can also see it in some of Rohan's more immediate precursors. And here, complexity regarding what counts as the state begins to emerge, alongside the language of interest, in fine detail. Consider the works of Francesco Guiccardini (1483–1540), Giovanni Botero (1544–1617), Federico Bonaventura (1555–1602), and Traiano Boccalini (1556–1613). All of these men are identified with reason-of-state argumentation and noted for having used the language of interest. It's also worth noting that all of these men were Counter-Reformation authors, adding yet another reversal to the Huguenot Rohan's appropriation of their lexicon.

Guiccardini discussed *interesse* as legally recognized estates; Bonaventura and Boccalini criticized the turn toward *interesse* in reason-of-state reflections as tearing at the moral fabric of Christendom, but nonetheless saw a proper basis of *interesse* in canon and Roman legal orders.[50] Bonaventura, Boccalini, and Rohan alike drew inspiration from Botero's *Della Ragione di Stato* (1589), a Catholic and critically negative discussion of *The Prince*.[51] Its quick mention of *interesse* introduces a long work that elaborates the role of virtue and religion in guiding a prince's affairs.

Botero's opening remarks are strikingly modern, and routinely invoked as heralding the discovery of interest as a deductive principle of reason-of-state.[52] "It should be taken for certain," he writes, "that in the decisions made by Princes, interest will always override every other argument; and therefore

---

50. Orth, "Interesse," 322. These authors' critical references to *interesse* were consistent with those of contemporary Spanish and Italian mystics who condemned *interesse* as a species of self-love. Ignatius de Loyola implored his readers to do away with self-love and *interesse* alike in turning toward Christ—suggesting these were related but nonetheless distinct ideas. Other mystics, like Domingo de Soto, Teresa d'Avila, and Juan de la Cruz used *interesse* to denote whatever countered a soul's love of God. Such a notion of *interesse,* was originally sinful, negative, and marked a soul as outside the community of grace—associations dire enough that describing princely action as "interested" becomes a stinging critique. Such a notion of *interesse* is quite the opposite of a single, unifying force of action, speaking rather to dispersion and loss. See Lewis, *Medieval Political Ideas,* 1:94, and Orth, "Interesse," 319.

51. Victoria Kahn, *Machiavellian Rhetoric: From the Counter-Reformation to Milton* (Princeton: Princeton University Press, 1994), chap. 3, especially 76–78. *Della Ragione di Stato* is therefore a critical discussion *of* reason-of-state; the usual English translation of its title as *Reason of State* is therefore misleading. Dropping *della* gives the impression that Botero's writing is a contribution to, rather than a critique of, the discourse named in the title. To the extent that Botero's writing in *Della Ragione di Stato* does elaborate on good statesmanship, the work's title might be better translated *Of the Principle of State,* in keeping with its positive, rather than deductive, argumentation.

52. Peter Miller, *Defining the Common Good: Empire, Religion, and Philosophy in Eighteenth-Century Britain* (Cambridge: Cambridge University Press, 1994), 36.

he who treats with princes should put no trust in friendship, kinship, treaty, nor any other tie which has not basis in interest."[53] True, Botero's definition of state as "a stable rule over people," and *reason of state* as "the knowledge of the means by which such domination may be founded, preserved, and extended," may seem to have marked reason-of-state discourse as a template for emerging Renaissance models of knowledge with interest at its center.[54] Yet taken alone, Botero's opening says nothing at all beyond the tautology that has dogged interest explanations, because it says nothing substantive regarding the prince's interest: only that he had better do what he had better do.

The rest of Botero's book, only seldom examined in discussions of interest, is devoted to the substance of a prince's interest.[55] It offers a long discussion of the prudent ruler's submission to, *inter alia,* the authority of canon law, the advice of bishops and the pope, and other authoritative parameters of virtuous action.[56] Unlike friendship, kinship, or treaties, these authoritative parameters were "interests" beyond the creation and control of the prince him- or herself. For the most part, Botero offered the authority of the Church as the only sure means of forging successful political ties; no basis under the king's own control could be regarded as a worthy one for alliances or negotiation.[57] And so when Botero says that "interest will override every other argument," he may well have in mind that interest overrides other arguments by virtue of its institutional authority, that is, in its rightness, rather than in its realism. Consistent with the linguistic observation I drew from Blount, Botero appropriates the power of "interest" to subjugate its object; not in terms of probabilistic knowledge but rather in terms of its being embedded in institutional life. With this in mind, we see that interest's inaugural appearance in a reason-of-state argument seems more to have contravened than to have endorsed a humanistic sense of interest that readers have seen in Rohan.

Botero saw interest not as reason, but rather as the delimitation of a proper sphere of action. Indeed he writes that "reason of state" encompasses "such

---

53. Giovanni Botero, *Reason of State* (London: Routledge & Kegan Paul, 1956), 41.
54. Botero, *Reason of State,* 3; cited in Kahn, *Machiavellian Rhetoric,* 90.
55. While Engelmann examines the elements upon which Botero's discourse must be brought to bear, he does not consider what *interesse* these elements are meant to serve. His reading of Botero's work as a contribution to reason-of-state rather than an immanent critique of it is fair nonetheless in light of how Engelmann shifts our perspective on what reason-of-state arguments entail and achieve. See Engelmann, *Imagining Interest,* 81, 95–97.
56. Botero, *Reason of State,* 64.
57. Orth, "Interesse," 322. For Botero's effects upon reason-of-state literature aside from his reference to *interesse,* see Engelmann, *Imagining Interest,* 81, 95–97.

actions as cannot be considered in light of ordinary reason."⁵⁸ Discussing the elements that make up this proper compass of action, he says that "because the reputation of a Prince consists in the opinion and in the conception that the people have of him, the material which he ought to occupy himself, to acquire so great a good, should be such as the people would have an interest in [*a che il popolo vi habbia interesse*]."⁵⁹ *Interesse* here is share in property, territory, or power, as opposed to reasoning or knowledge.

Bonaventura and Boccalini followed suit, though like the substance of Botero's argument, this has gone unrecognized lately. I say lately, because it seems that our disposition to see the juridical connection between interest and the state has attenuated relatively recently, as interest masquerades more as a psychological faculty of reasoning.⁶⁰ Friedrich Meinecke, whose genteel *Ideengeschichte* has long been superseded by Cambridge school and *Begriffsgeschichtliche* research methods, noted that for Bonaventura, Boccalini, and their contemporaries, "in the end, *ragione di stato* differs little from *ragione d'interesse.*" In other words, Meinecke sees these authors aligning interest in parallel to state and status as an object of their account, rather than interest being a form of reasoning specific to that status.⁶¹ Meinecke noticed that, for these Counter-Reformation writers, *interesse* substituted not for reason but instead for the *stato* whose outlines were broadly contested, variously comprehending status, territory, and other factors.

---

58. Botero, *Reason of State*, 3.
59. The English text is taken from Giovanni Botero, *Practical Politics*, trans. George Albert Moore (Washington, D.C.: Country Dollar Press, 1949), 233; the Italian original is from Botero's *Della riputatione del prencipe,* in *Della ragione di stato libri dieci . . . accresciuti da diversi Discorsi* (Venice, 1659), 36. Both of these sources are cited in Kahn, *Machiavellian Rhetoric,* 77.
60. Hirschman's text is particularly marked with erasures of juridical interest. For example, he excises historian Felix Raab's mention of legal uses of interest when he cites Raab as an authority for the extent of the pre- and extra-Machiavellian uses of interest. According to Hirschman, "Raab writes at the end of a long bibliographic footnote on 'Interest': 'It was at the end of this period [that is, in the last decade of the seventeenth century] that 'interest' acquired a specifically economic . . . meaning.'" Hirschman, *The Passions and the Interests,* 37. Raab, by contrast, acknowledges that economic uses are an offshoot of legal uses, not a wholesale replacement of them: "It was at the end of this period," he writes, "that 'interest' acquired a specifically economic, *as distinct from its original legal* meaning." Raab, *The English Face of Machiavelli,* 237 n. 6; my emphasis.
61. "Schliesslich ragione di stato wenig anderes ist als ragione d'interesse." See Friedrich Meinecke, *Die Idee der Staatsräson in der neueren Geschichte* (Berlin: R. Oldenbourg, 1924), 85. As another example of calculating self-regard overwriting other possibilities in the language of interest, Hirschman (citing Meinecke's passage) describes Boccalini and Bonaventura as instead using the "twin, initially synonymous terms *interesse* and *regione di stato*" in elaborating realist principles—in other words, treating interest as the principle of reason-of-state as a whole. Hirschman, *The Passions and the Interests,* 33. For consequences of this shift, see p. 88.

These Counter-Reformation writers gestured to interests as something knowable, and made known in their writings: the authority of the Church and its laws, or domain, territory, and estate. Rohan's seventeenth-century appropriation of interest—as a means of elucidating the person of the state, and distinguishing this person from the natural understanding of the prince—draws and builds upon what he found in the sixteenth: the intimacy that Botero, Boccalini, and Bonaventura see between "interest" and the state. His innovation lies less in rendering these reflections consistent with late Renaissance criteria for knowledge than in drawing juridical interest in all its facets as a means of advancing his own conception of in what the state consists. Juridical interest allows him to elaborate this personality out of contested materials, within the conceit of an incontrovertible statement. Rohan masterfully brought these elements to bear on the most conspicuous and controversial genres of political argument in his day, namely, the sphere of action proper to a preeminent leader.

Just as the modern view of interest takes the conceit of "interest" to be the final statement of affairs as the whole story, the pretense of interest to be a kind of knowledge is an essential part of Rohan's and Nedham's appeals to interest—but given the object of their reflection (i.e., the state, England), it is only a pretense. While the uncertainty of financial interest can be turned into probability (or risk) by means of interest rates, juridical interest, when brought to political affairs, remains a language of personality, and therefore of prerogatives of action, and therefore of becoming. Action and becoming cannot be reduced to parameters of risk and chance, because they qualitatively change—or, it may be said, "realize"—the agent in question. Juridical interest, when brought to the domain of politics as a provocation to act in the face of possibilities, was futuristic and uncertain, but not probabilistic; it is a contested claim, but not one to be decided solely on the basis of evidence.[62] Therefore political interest is not knowledge by the standards of any time.

The conceptual change involved in "interest" becoming a term of finance may have supported the apparent epistemic authority of interest throughout shifting standards of knowledge. This apparent authority—captured in the

62. While the mode of juridical governance appropriate to interest may have been displaced by the early modern ideas of probabilistic knowledge, appeals to interest remained at their core akin to the dispositionist's argument that the individual will tend to act toward what is good. And like dispositionists' arguments regarding the good, appeals to interest were ultimately arguments of persuasion masquerading as a kind of knowledge. Could it be that Locke's relative reticence on the subject of interest may well reflect awareness, on the part of the master theorist of probable knowledge, that appeals to interest are in fact covers for something like the dispositionist view? For a discussion of Locke and probable knowledge, see Tully, "Governing Conduct," 27–33.

catchphrase "interest will not lie"—plays an important supporting role. Its combination with the older juridical determination of personality, engendered by all of these authors' drawing the language of interest from strictly legal territory into political discourse, promoted equivocity in the language of interest that is the key to its vogue in political discourse. Interest's appearance as an object or form of knowledge screens its power to provoke action and thereby to shape agents. As a rhetoric of persuasion, the appeal to interest is warranted in the face of multiple and conflicting possibilities. But like any such claim, it is effective in large part because it disavows the alternatives. This disavowal is particularly evident in the way Rohan presents interest as singular or monistic.

Plural Interest and the Work of Singularity

Plurality and contestation are critical to Rohan's way of giving content to the person of the state as distinct from the prince. Yet the role of plurality in Rohan's and Nedham's appeals to political interest, and in the vogue of interest talk they inaugurated, goes unnoticed. Nedham, after all, speaks to the true interest of England, united against the papacy. Rohan's interest argument is monistic to the point of straining the idiom. His most prominent term, "the Interest," unifies and encapsulates the aims and ends of reason-of-state, presenting a kind of internal monism. Indeed that definite article where we moderns are apt to use a possessive pronoun or an adjective—a national chief executive claims to pursue "the state's interest" or "the national interest," not "the Interest"—further asserts the independence of "the Interest" from anything: state, nation, or whatever. It is a picture of sovereignty toward which all political things ought to aim, though which very few political things may achieve.[63] Opening by declaring that "the *Interest* commaunds the *Princes,*" Rohan displaces God—let alone Botero's concern to establish Rome as His earthly representative—in the ineluctable order of subordination by naming "the Interest" alone as a single principle girding successful rule.[64] Stressing a nearly Platonic power of this unity, Rohan avers that "the Interest alone can never fail."[65]

Rohan retains the singularity of interest, even in the face of the conspicuously irreducible complexities of international affairs. Consider his discussion

---

63. Stephen Engelmann develops the concept of monism as applied to interest; see Engelmann, *Imagining Interest*, 3. He goes on to show how the monistic moment of arguments like Rohan's are the basis for later imaginings of global economies premised on monistic interest.
64. Rohan, *Of the Interest*, A1.
65. Ibid.

of how the numerous small states of Europe are situated with respect to France and Spain. He writes that "the other *Princes* are annexed to the one, or to the other, according to their *Interest*"—as if to stress that their hand in the play of sovereignty, rather than the peculiarity of their situation, is what really matters. He continues: "But forsomuch as this *interest* (as it hath beene well or ill followed) hath caused the ruine of some, or the greatnesse of others, I haue purposed to publish in this present Treatise."[66] Rendering reason-of-state in terms of "the Interest" therefore appears to be a unique vehicle for monism to enter broader political discourses and to dispense altogether with the plurality of interest's old juridical side, with its differences that matter and points of contestation. When interest monism is taken up by observers of citizen action in domestic affairs, like Nedham, a humanist plank appears to be set in the platform of liberal subjectivity: persons capable of (and responsible for) the organization of their own multiple desires and obligations into a single, autonomous end.

As usual we can turn briefly to Nedham to see, not only how saturated with legal tropes his appropriation of Rohan's idiom is, but also how the force of plural interest lurks in Rohan's account. We see how the pretension of appeals to interest to be knowledge supports the juridical aim of realizing the proper person, of the state or of the citizen, from the messy ambiguities confronting men and women as monarchs or as subjects. The subtitle of Nedham's *The Case of the Kingdom Stated,* for example, promises to illustrate the "proper interest" of the parties in question, rather than their interest *simpliciter,* thereby suggesting an improper interest—a competing claim—that needs to be ferreted out by some means. Speaking of various parties, Nedham (unlike Rohan) notes their "interests" in the plural. Nedham's explicit gloss of Rohan's writing shows the difference most clearly: "I shall commend to [all]," Nedham writes, "what the Duke of *Rohan* saith of the States of *Europe,* that according as they follow their proper *Interests,* they thrive or faile in *Successes,* so the *Parties* now on Foot in the *Kingdom,* must looke to stand or fall upon the same Ground."[67] Rohan, as we have seen, takes no care to address the propriety of "the Interest" or to write of princes' "Interests" in the plural, even when he recognizes that they conflict, and that two opposing interests are the basis for everyone else's.

What accounts for the difference? Nedham recognizes that Rohan's appeal to interest is an argument regarding propriety, even when it comes to the state;

66. Ibid., A2.
67. Nedham, *The Case of the Kingdom Stated,* dedication.

but what Nedham fails to grasp, despite his asseverations that interest is true and does not lie, is how much more shrewdly Rohan denies the very plurality that calls for an account of interest in the first place. And so Nedham unwittingly shows the contestation and plurality intrinsic to the juridical side of "interest." After all, while both Rohan's and Nedham's discussions appear to explain events on the basis of interests, they are in effect calls to action. Laying the groundwork for such an action requires adding formal coherence to the messiness and ambiguities of reality, drawing at least apparent unities from a probably irreducible heterogeneity. That this is the logical form of Rohan's task is both achieved and rhetorically masked by his following Botero in naming "the Interest" as the principle sine qua non of princely action.

Rohan's first step in elucidating the actionable form of this principle shows that plurality is everywhere and fundamental to his effort. The object whose elaboration becomes Rohan's opportunity to reduce contingencies to proper form appears to have been quite evident to the typesetter, at least, if his italic handiwork is any indication. "According as [the Interest] is well or ill understood," reads the text, "it maketh *States* to liue or die ... and as it always aimeth at the *augmentation,* or leastwise the *conservation* of a *State.*" This "*State*"—as vexingly complex and abstract as any political formation—is a deeply contingent creature. Following its elaboration in Rohan's account reveals the intrinsic plurality that is at the heart of Rohan's appeal to interest.

On one level, the contingency of the state, essential for Rohan's argument, is supported by the centrality of conflict to its articulation. As I have noted, the present in Rohan's account is marked by a central conflict: "There be two Powers in *Christendom,*" he writes, "which are as the two *Poles,* from whence descend the influences of peace and warre vpon the other states, to wit, the howses of *France* and *Spaine.*"[68] This conflict structures but does not exhaust the conflicts which occasion the elucidation of interest; each prince's interest is examined opposite the others' and in light of groups opposing one another and the prince within his or her domestic purview. And so even as Rohan appeals to "the Interest" as a settled, univocal, and unified guide to the prince's action, contest and fluidity are prime occasions for its explication. A rhetorical strategy that did not have its origin in conflict and contestation would inhibit Rohan's space to intervene with his own construal of affairs regarding how a prince should choose among courses of action in the face of a contested situation. And so in spite of the apparent singularity of "the Interest," the space for Rohan's

68. Rohan, *Of the Interest,* A2.

intervention and even his agency in this text lies in his noting that "the Interest" of the state "ought to varie according to the times."[69] Giving an account of "the times," as bipolar, lays the groundwork for his narration of "the Interest." Locating the variance here comports well with the inherent temporality of interests—and the space for action, change, and uncertainty that the open horizon of the future promotes.

Properties of the Person of State

The contingencies of the state appear on a second level in Rohan's text, namely, in *what counts as* the state whose conservation and augmentation Rohan elaborates. With this in mind, recalling the complexity of and changes in the notions of the "state" in Rohan's time is crucial for grasping the significance of his use of "interest." We have already seen the old connection of "interesse" and "estat" in Chaucer, Botero's attempt to spell out the *interesse* of a prince's *stato* in canonical and territorial terms, and the frequent offhand association of Machiavelli's *mantenere lo stato* with interest among political theorists. Separately and together, they reveal the relevance of "interest" to the conceptual amalgamation of status and estate into a distinct person of "the state." The proper contours of this person were still very much unsettled in the middle of the seventeenth century, as the turns of the English civil war so vividly attested.[70]

As a legal matter, person and man (or woman) were distinct, though the latter was sometimes known as a "natural person"—the supplemental term serving mainly to reinforce the difference. This distinction carried into matters of office: the person, not the man or woman, was attached to the office composed of its state, estate, or status. Interest, consistent with its legal provenance, attends to the former. Rohan's writing reflects this distinction and its priorities. Though "the *Interest* commaunds the Princes"—consistent with its powers to subordinate—"it maketh *States*," not princes, "to live or die."[71] This conceptual separation of the state from the agent or agents of its realization was fundamental to the seventeenth-century language of political action, for it opened a space for contestation and resistance to individual "natural persons" without risking charges of rebellion or treason.[72] The state in the seventeenth century may have comprised many, possibly contradictory elements. Older models, such as

69. Ibid., A1–2.
70. Skinner, *Visions of Politics*, 2:391–99.
71. Rohan, *Of the Interest*, A1.
72. Condren, "Liberty of Office," 466.

the treasury, arms, family ties and aristocratic relationships, standing in papal esteem, compete with newer ones like territorial integrity, natural resources, and population, for relevance and primacy.[73] Given the possibilities, specifying what's proper to a state and therefore fundamental to sovereignty is a complex, unsettled, and unsettling affair. And fidelity to the person of the state, as opposed to fidelity to a natural person or group, can be a tricky and uncertain affair when this office is itself ill-defined and contested. In order for the prince, or anyone for that matter, to conserve or augment a state, he or she must first know what that state properly is. In Rohan's work, the appeal to interest becomes a point for articulating the identity of that state, as distinct from the natural person of the prince, from the complex and heterogeneous possibilities of its determination, and promoting the actions that lead to its realization.

Rohan's elaboration of "the Interest," in the substantive work that follows his opening chapter, mainly regards what "makes a difference" between a prince and his or her state. Even if a prince may be presumed to know him- or herself, knowing his or her state is another matter, with plenty of room for competing views. Knowledge of the former is not Rohan's to impart; knowledge of the latter is where his intervention may lie. His discussion of Queen Elizabeth exemplifies how he enters into this contested field and deploys the power of "interest" to shape the state, by delineating Elizabeth's proper action as a prince from her personal attachments. Using her relationship to King Philip of Spain as an example, Rohan specifies "the Interest" of a state as derived from a source more authoritative than the prince's own inclinations. Rohan writes that "although [Queen Elizabeth] professed her selve very much obliged to *Philip*, towards whom shee bare ever a speciall regard, neverthelesse she had so carefull a consideration of the Interest of her *State*, that she believed it was never fit to conclude a peace with him."[74] Elizabeth rightly distinguishes her state from affections that interest excludes. Although Rohan's directing princes to the state as matter of concern distinct from their natural affections and inclinations preserves, in some respects, a prince's autonomy over his most intimate affairs, what exactly becomes of a prince whose state has died is a matter that surely gave pause to the mighty.[75]

Although we may be tempted to see Rohan's exclusion of amorous attachment as the paradigm of substituting reason for passion, excluding a prince's

---

73. Michel Foucault, "Governmentality," in *The Foucault Effect: Studies in Governmentality*, ed. Graham Burchell, Colin Gordon, and Peter Miller (Chicago: University of Chicago Press, 1991).
74. Rohan, *Of the Interest*, 55–56.
75. Ibid., A1.

"speciall regard" does not in itself secure the rationality of what Rohan does endorse. All the other possibilities that vie for priority in the determination of the state are still at play. Reducing this complexity, Rohan finds religion—or, more specifically, sectarian allegiances and ties—to be decisively proper to the state, and therefore to princely power, however much it may depart from the prince's other attributes and ties. It is this element, more than territorial integrity, arms, or treaties, to which the prince must attend to secure his or her power. Here too we see Rohan's real departure from Botero, who similarly sought to ground the proper identity of the state and compass of its actions. Both disdained purely secular accounts regarding territory or arms. But whereas Botero sought it in the preestablished authority of the Church, Rohan looks to patterns of confessional allegiance and factionalism. So, for example, Rohan counsels King Philip of Spain to establish an "apparent amitie" by which "he may the more easily render himself *Protector* of the *Catholikes* of *England*." This will make potential martyrs of those Catholics, and will thus serve "the greatness of Spaine, at the cost of [Englishmen's] King and Country." Though religious affiliation is a vector of action properly commensurate with the state, it is not itself the end. Rohan urges Philip to give Rohan's fellow Huguenots "underhand courage and assistance . . . to stirre vp there a Civill warre, which might so much the more weaken the Kingdome" of France.[76] Whereas Botero sought to tie a prince's interest to church authority, Rohan draws state power from sectarian factionalism.

Rohan goes on to recommend courses of princely action in the case of each European power, regarding intelligence, diplomacy, the treasury, and arms, each of which merits a short paragraph. All are found to serve or to align with the course of action recommended in the first instance by the religious affiliation of each prince and the patterns of confessional alliance and factionalism within his or her realm. To secure the boundary between the state and the prince as holder of its office, Rohan points to religion as the difference that, to return to the etymological roots of "interest" in *id quod interest,* "makes a difference." This is all the more clever, not to mention ironic, in light of the fact that the "two *Poles,* from whence descend the influences of peace and warre vpon the other states, to wit, the howses of *France* and *Spaine*" were both Catholic countries.[77] In other words, religion is what makes a difference—not

---

76. Ibid., 6–7.
77. Ibid., A2.

between two countries, but among all the possibilities that vie as the crucial element in the identity of the state. Whereas Botero sought the unity of interest in the ordered canons of the Church, Rohan sees the essence of state power in dispersion and difference.

In sum, appeals to interest in *Of the Interests* subordinate princely conduct to the imperatives of the state, as Rohan has defined it, from a complex, unsettled, and contested field. Masquerading as modern knowledge, oriented to the future and to probable outcomes, his appeal to interest in this tract is, substantively, a judgment regarding the identity of the state, wherein its power lies, and the actions that should be taken in light of that power and identity. So when we see that Rohan, and other reason-of-state authors, subordinate princely conduct to interest, we must also see in the prescriptions for action that attend this subordination a particular vision to be realized. When it comes to princes, status, and estate—captured in terms like the Italian *stato* or Chaucer's "estat"—appeals to interest outline what properly guides a prince's conduct, in ways analogous to how earlier Roman legal determinations of *id quod interest* delineated the personality of a litigant at a site of conflict over real property. The appeal to interest contributes to reason-of-state discourse by providing an opportunity to articulate what, among the myriad attachments of any particular prince or monarch, "makes a difference" to the exercise of princely power. Given conflict and contest as a precondition for determining the state—as a paradigm of political agency more generally—interest need not, and perhaps cannot, coincide with the self-determined ends of the natural person and his or her presumably privileged knowledge of the natural self. Therefore, the confluence of juridical interest and reason-of-state is a potent tool in the process of developing ideas of the state as person independent of the man or woman who holds its office at any point in time—a tool deployed by Botero, Rohan, and many others. And, as the debates at Putney will reveal, this tool does its work also in developing ideas of the citizen as independent of the subject.

But before turning to the Putney debates, we have a bit of unfinished theoretical business. I mentioned earlier in this chapter that commentators who have interpreted Rohan and Nedham through a primarily humanistic lens have raised some apparently intractable questions regarding the language of interest in political argument. These questions regard, first, whether arguments from interest are tautological, and second, the relationship between interest and sovereignty. Having explored the juridical inflections in the language of interest in Rohan's and Nedham's arguments, we may now approach these questions anew.

Theoretical Reflections on Self and Sovereignty

Recovering the role played by juridical interest in the explosion of political interest talk is of clear historiographical importance. But modern oblivion regarding the power of appeals to interest—whether pertaining to the state or of other personages—has rendered the force of arguments from interest enigmatic for present-day political inquiry as well.[78] Readers of Nedham and Rohan have reflected on these problems along the way to interpreting these authors' significance; having explored the contribution of juridical interest to them, we may return to these questions as well. On one hand, their arguments appear implausibly forceful: rendering reason-of-state arguments in terms of interest, some have argued, paradoxically renders a sovereign subject to a body of knowledge. On the other hand, these arguments appear implausibly weak: arguments from interest appear to tell us only that a person had rather do what a person had rather do. Reorienting the study of "interest" to give proper compass to the juridical sheds light on each of these objections, revealing them as too quickly naturalizing the very identities that appeals to interest provoke and contest.

Appeals to interest rely on contingency for their point and their effect, but part of their appeal is their claim to incontrovertibility. After all, contest is the context in which legal claims are animated in the first place, yet the very point of a legal claim is to deny the plausibility of an alternative to the claim's picture of "what matters" or "is of importance" to the conflict. Bringing this peculiar rhetoric to political discourse, both Rohan and Nedham explicitly deny that, however contested the context of their appeals to interest may be, their own contribution is similarly contestable. But such asseverations are needed even more urgently, given the rich layers of contingency that each exploits to make a case for the interest of persons or of states as he sees it. Viewing appeals to interest as such, a rhetoric can refigure tensions between juridical "interest" and sovereignty, and push theoretical reflection on interests beyond the appearance of arguments from interest as tautological.

---

78. Constructivists in the field of international relations have explored the ways that state agency is shaped by social forces, though their treatment of state interests still by and large sees interests as following from identity. Alexander Wendt follows this pattern, and in fact deepens the modern psychologizing of interest, associating it closely with desire. Interests then are what states desire on the basis of an identity that is formed in a social context; see Alexander Wendt, *Social Theory of International Politics* (Cambridge: Cambridge University Press, 1999), 115–19, 231.

State Interest and Sovereignty

Had interest conformed to emerging seventeenth-century standards for knowledge, the specification of interests in reason-of-state literature would, indeed, make subjects of sovereigns by closing the field of plausible and effective decision. But just as the juridical and plural side of interest defies probabilistic standards of knowledge by relying upon—and denying—a more fundamental contestation, appeals to interest bear a more complex relationship to sovereignty. Rohan's language of interest makes sovereignty an attribute of the state, rather than an attribute of a prince; the prince becomes its executive, rather than its origin.[79] The prince is subjected to the sovereignty of his or her state. The decisive—and more threatening—development in Rohan is the contestability of the very contours of that state, a contestability that even Rohan takes pains to deny. But with the state as sovereign, the prince is subjected to his or her office, perhaps even becoming incidental to it—as the fate of Charles I attests.

Therefore, Rohan's appropriation of "interest" for reason-of-state discourse reorients sovereignty away from terms familiar from Jean Bodin and Louis XIV ("l'etat, c'est moi") and toward the person of the state as distinct from the prince. Insofar as the absolutist reason-of-state associated with Bodin presupposes a modern notion of the interiority of the person of the sovereign,[80] the distinction advanced by Rohan between the monarch and the sovereign person of state casts the sovereignty of such interiority into doubt. Of course, the new formulation of sovereignty that we see in Rohan reached its famous apotheosis in the writings of Thomas Hobbes.[81] But as I argue in the next chapter, Hobbes constructed sovereignty in terms of representation, not interest, because he prefers the univocal language of subjection—representation is always of a subject—over the contestation and plurality that underwrite and are promoted by appeals to interest.

To the degree that appeals to interest intervene in arguing for, and acting upon, the proper state, the sovereignty of the state becomes paradoxical in a different way. The delimitation of sovereignty is not at stake. On the contrary, owing to the contestability of claims regarding the identity of the state that gives shape to a prince's prerogative, the decisions of that prerogative remain incomplete. Arguments regarding what counts as the state are always subject to revision, in light of changing circumstances and in light of the complexity

---

79. Skinner, *Visions of Politics*, 2:391–93.
80. On sovereignty, atomism, and interiority, see Taylor, *Sources of the Self*, 195.
81. Skinner, *Visions of Politics*, 2:368.

and incompatibility among the many candidates for being counted as among elements of the state. Seeing interest as *reason*-of-state errs in supposing that political knowledge is the elaboration of a scientific epistemology on the basis of a state whose contours are already complete; seeing interest as reason-of-*state* reveals political knowledge as the contingent enforcement and realization of what that state is. A sovereign "decider" therefore finds it not only not inimical, but even useful to appeal to "the national interest" in pursuit of policies. Such an appeal serves well to shape the very nation his voice is said to represent. George W. Bush, like so many presidential candidates before him, promised on the campaign trail in 2000 that his administration would promote policies that were in the "national interest." In the immediate wake of attacks on the Pentagon and New York's World Trade Center in September 2001, he urged Americans to continue shopping, construing the national interest (in part) in terms of an expanding economy driven by household consumption (abetted by a weak dollar and easy credit). A nation urged to defend fiercely its civil liberties in the wake of these attacks may have tolerated a different range of government policy in subsequent years than those that the Bush administration pursued, like warrantless wiretapping or designating an American citizen an enemy combatant, who therefore could be held indefinitely without trial. This is not to say that a leader's invocation of national interest results in a unified nation, or that these policies will succeed in a longer run, though even here the question remains as to who defines success, and we are reminded that no nation is sovereign over its economy. Rather, it is to note that that patterns of citizen action that such an appeal encourages and discourages change, over time, the nature of the nation so that it more resembles this vision.

Tautologies of Interest

Hirschman's picture of interest as a rational, internal motion of calculating self-regard leaves humanist interest—and liberal theories predicated on it—at a theoretical impasse. Even as humanistic interest pervades political, economic, and other social discourses with its universalist appeal, rational and calculating interest also appears "meaningless" as a category for analysis and explanation of action because it lacks the moral texture that lies at the core of notions of agency.[82] In the face of this problem, Hirschman argues that the "widening use of the concept [of interest] turned out to be a disservice" to moral and

---

82. Taylor, *Sources of the Self,* 27–28, 33, 41–42.

social thought, in that it diluted the value of an interest explanation to the point of tautology.[83] In his 1829 critique of James Mill's theory of government Thomas Macaulay encapsulated the emptiness of liberal interest theory when he quipped that the politics of interest "means only that a man had rather do what he had rather do."[84] According to one historian, seventeenth-century commentators anticipated Macaulay's jibe in their distress that an interest explanation of human action "withheld judgment pending the outcome of events," which, he says, they found "most distressing in a maxim purporting to say something new."[85] But while this shortcoming has long been—and continues to be—pointed out by critics of interest explanations in politics, the "tautology" critique neither disables interest explanations nor moves beyond them. To the contrary, both the appeal of "interest" as a term of political discourse and charges of its tautological quality display remarkable, and perhaps mutually reinforcing, staying power. The mistake of Hirschman, Macaulay, and others, however, is to have missed how interest is a rhetoric of persuasion and provocation that plays on the malleability of the person whose interests are in question.

The "tautology" critique derives from thinking about "interest" through the modern lens of the distinction between descriptive and normative modes of analysis, or the "is-ought" distinction.[86] On the one hand, people are said to be driven by interests, in which case, interest *is* the motivation of a person. On the other hand, persons are exhorted to follow their interests; in other words, interest is what *ought* to motivate the person. Each side needs the other: the latter exhortation would be pointless if the first view were reliable. Macaulay's complaint codes this distinction and relation of "is" and "ought" in the equivocal phrase "had rather," which after all can mean either what a person prefers or what a person should prefer. But the appearance of tautology in the language of "interest" derives from an impoverished understanding of what the language of interest does in political discourses—how the appeal to interest is itself an action whose contingent effect is provoking action toward the realization of personality from a contested field. Just as a legal claim has contest as its context while denying alternative plausible statements of affairs or applications

---

83. Hirschman, "Concept of Interest," 48.
84. Macaulay, "Mill's Essay on Government," 125.
85. Gunn, "'Interest Will Not Lie,'" 556. Gunn does not offer evidence of seventeenth-century contemporaries voicing this concern, leaving open the possibility that the appearance of tautological interest is a later development.
86. Regarding is-ought and the example of "justice," see Pitkin, *Wittgenstein and Justice*, 177–80, 219–22.

of principle to the case at hand, the interest claim simultaneously partakes of and denies conflict or contest over what makes a difference.

Nedham's polemics in *The Case of the Kingdom Stated* and *Interest Will Not Lie* not only present the much-lamented tautology but point beyond it substantively. In them Nedham elaborates a means for predicting a person's actions in terms redolent of legal attachments, but he also acknowledges throughout that persons have nonetheless acted wrongly from the point of view of these interests. Which is to say, Nedham wants his readers to act otherwise. Nedham shows that articulating one's proper attachments, legally and otherwise authorized, is crucial to action. His pattern of argument is consistent with a seventeenth-century context in which liberty is always articulated in relation to estate or office.[87] His treatises are open letters to all parties regarding how they should act, in the form of predictions regarding how they will act if they see their interests truly—namely, as he sees them. Yet the rhetorical flexibility of "interest" across Nedham's career illustrates the wide latitude for construing such attachments, and therefore the diversity of courses of "free" action. Since the opposite of "true interest," for Nedham, is "treason," a course of action that accords with "true interest" will necessarily change with the times. What counts as "true interest" will, like treason, be as irreducibly contested as the identity of the state. Reading Nedham's wily tracts as elucidating actions as inwardly self-determined puts liberal prejudices regarding the origin, stability, and knowability of interests in the place of the very flexibility and openness that rendered "interest" so useful—and dangerous—in the early modern political idiom.

Therefore we should hesitate before concluding that, at the threshold of its seventeenth-century vogue in political discourse, "interest appeared so self-evident a notion that nobody bothered to define it precisely."[88] To the contrary, precise definition was quite beside the point for those whose aims were best served by equivocation. Defining "interest" is not merely beside the point, but rather inimical to it. Indeed, rather than search for a definition *of* "interest" in Rohan's or others' works that shared in the vogue of political interest, we must instead see the appeal to interest *as* definition. The is-ought dichotomy of "interest," and hence the tautological character of interest explanations, is dissolved by considering this power of appeals to interest to provoke action in the service of identity. By means of action, "ought" becomes

---

87. Condren, "Liberty of Office."
88. Hirschman, *The Passions and the Interests*, 43.

"is" as identity is realized from a field of possibilities. Yet this power is hidden in the appearance of a tautology as the appeal to interest deflects awareness of the open horizon of identity. It makes fundamentally contested articulations of proper action appear not contested but instead essential, and it makes the horizon of identity appear not temporal and open but instead spatial and bounded—Nedham's proper Englishman acting in opposition to Fell's "treason." Early modern appeals to interest only appear tautological to us moderns for whom the identity of the body said to have an interest, be it *homo economicus* or the modern state, is no longer acknowledged to be an open and vital political question.

Interesting England

The ascension of the action-provoking power of appeals to interest in political discourse following Rohan's popularity and Nedham's notoriety had far-reaching implications for conflicts over the state in the period during and after the English civil war. In the remaining sections of this chapter, I move from considering the complexity inherent in Rohan's and Nedham's enormously influential political writings to examining how the incursion of the language of interest in political discourse more generally reflects juridical and plural interests. This incursion, I argue, opened democratic possibilities that are invisible to the view of interest as a faculty of calculating self-regard.

The importance of the juridical side of interest should not be surprising given that the personification of the state remained closely tied to questions of property. The dramatic and novel proliferation of "interest" in political discourse shows how powerfully even the most basic juridical association of interest with property held sway with parties on all sides of a variety of debates.[89] One writer, a contemporary named Charles Herle, saw the multiplicity of interests in Parliament as serving the public interest, and the monarch, being one person, as serving only a private interest. Herle explicitly connects "self-interest" to "privileges and properties."[90] John Cook, a prosecutor of Charles I, argued that landholding Parliamentarians could grasp the "true policy interests" of the state because "if the Kingdom suffer, they suffer in their private estates."[91] Still others contended that the shared burden of taxation, which itself resulted from

89. Cf. Engelmann, *Imagining Interest*, 117, 80 n. 36.
90. Charles Herle, *A Fuller Answer to a Treatise Written by Dr. Ferne* (London, 1642), 12.
91. John Cook, *Redintegratio Amoris, or a Union of Hearts* (London, 1647), 45.

holding property, gave Parliamentarians a common interest, if anything did.[92] Even national security was justified in terms of propertied interest: pamphleteers argued that landholding men were less likely than those without property to flee the country in case of a national calamity.[93]

But even though these invocations of interest gestured in the direction of a (more) democratic politics, political writers also expressed a connection between property and interest in the negative. Excluding the poor from participation was necessary, in the view of one, because "seeing men are by innate and hereditary distemper biased toward wicked practices, indigent people who are not restrained from injustice by any self-interest, but on the contrary, tempted to rapine and perfidiousness, are altogether unfit to manage the public affairs of a nation."[94] Property, therefore, was not only a sufficient condition for "having an interest"; it was in this author's view a necessary one. And so while seeing early moderns' appeals to interest as a motivation capable of bridling passions and therefore rendering people more fit for public duty is congruent with these examples, overlooking the connection of this term to property obscures how *indigence* was seen as a critical source of the political deficiency of the poor. It also obscures how authorized attachments, more so than the *doux commerce* of reason, were held to make the propertied capable of dispassionately exercising power. The passionate were not to be restrained *merely* by an "element of reflection and calculation with respect to the manner in which . . . the totality of [their] human aspirations were to be pursued," but also by their attachments to the prevailing social order, mediated in part by the distribution of interests.[95]

But even as the language of interest became a potent means for disciplining reason in the Commonwealth, at a deeper level its contestability promoted the conceptual separation of the monarchy from the office of the state—an ultimately more fateful development of the period. Distinguishing the man or woman from his or her office or status was particularly significant to the English during the civil war because, as I already intimated in my discussion of Rohan, it provided what we might call a language of resistance without advocating rebellion.[96] The contribution of reason-of-state is to articulate that office

---

92. Gunn cites eight pamphlets debating this point, noting that even "those who favored keeping rich men out of Parliament" still "assumed that property would be the main criterion in choosing representatives." J. A. W. Gunn, *Politics and the Public Interest in the Seventeenth Century* (Toronto: University of Toronto Press, 1969), 9–10.
93. Ibid., 9.
94. L. S., *Nature's Dowrie: Or, the People's Native Liberty Asserted* (1652), 13.
95. Hirschman, *The Passions and the Interests*, 32.
96. Condren, "Liberty of Office," 466.

in terms of interest; congruent with the contestability of interests, this office too became a site of contest, as the conceptual and legal separability of the office or state and its interest from those who occupied it rendered the properties of that state contestable.

In terms of what *authorizes* the person of the state, a variety of answers presented themselves as possibilities in the seventeenth century, and in England in particular: *salus populi,* the ancient constitution, and God all vied for authority after the king lost his head. Religious nationalism provided an originally alternative language and substance for "England" to have interests distinct from those of the Stuarts.[97] With England conceived as an entity capable of action, "England" personified could be itself a subject of reason-of-state speculation. Once the object of this speculation, the "estat," no longer belonged to the monarch but rather to the God of England, this was no longer the prerogative of the king or the learned statesman, but rather was known in the community of the elect.[98] In light of this development, Rohan's appropriation of "interest" may be seen as having moved the term from its former association with "cupiditas"—as seen in Bonaventura and Boccalini—to a virtual stand-in for religious notions of redemption.[99]

By bringing its constitutive power to bear not only on the persons of men and states, but now also on the body of the nation, the language of interest entered competitive and well-precedented terrain. Throughout the seventeenth century, England was variously defined in reference to apocalyptic and chiliastic mythologies.[100] How to know what counted as England was therefore increasingly subject as well to the Dissenters' contentious language of "true conscience."[101] The language of interest entering into this terrain was therefore made to speak to these matters of constitution, at once both political and confessional. To either of these languages, however, the juridical side of interest makes a distinctive contribution. Regarding confessional matters, the language of interest as an analogue to conscience could figure relations of subjection to God on the model of subordinates to an estate. The sermons of Reverend (and prominent Independent) Joseph Symonds, for example, model conscience (and self-consciousness) explicitly upon the legal relationships of persons to

---

97. Pocock, *Machiavellian Moment,* 343; Gunn, *Politics and the Public Interest;* Engelmann, *Imagining Interest.*
98. Skinner, *Visions of Politics,* 2:388–411.
99. Engelmann, *Imagining Interest,* 125.
100. Pocock, *Machiavellian Moment,* 346–47.
101. Engelmann, *Imagining Interest,* 125; see also Pocock, *Machiavellian Moment,* 336–37.

estates.[102] True knowledge of the self, as Symonds has it, accords with a picture of personality as indistinguishable from the authoritative ascription of property—and meditation upon interest as this ascription is his model for ecclesiastical authority wherein men have an interest and a propriety in God. His discussion of hierarchy and subjection in terms of interest therefore speaks to the relevance of juridical to the so-called psychological senses of "interest" which have generally been presumed to reflect a primordial interiority.

In a less lofty, but apparently no less contentious register, appeals to interest as a constitutional matter provided rhetorical openings for the promotion of a commercial culture that most commentators have seen as based on interest as a faculty of reason—since commerce is among the attributes that can be said to "matter" and to "make a difference" to England.[103] To the extent that commerce captures this picture of what counts as England, appeals to interest organize the conduct of citizens within the rubric of such a state.[104] Yet across all of these domains, even as combatants appealed to interest to give England identity, the contestability of "interest" holds open a conduit for political contestation, be it in the shape of civil war, a beheaded king, a republic, a commercial society, or a restoration. The sheer cacophony of perspectives on the interest of England that followed the entry of appeals to interest in English political discourse alone demonstrates that although the *conceit* of the appeal to interest is that it was beyond dispute, the outcome of such an appeal was neither certain nor complete. Even the religious backdrop to "England," in its chiliasm or millennialism, could not stem the free fall that attends the open-ended horizon of interests in a time when its authoritative ascription was in doubt. Doubt and contest over this ascription is displayed nowhere as vividly as the debates at Putney—where appeals to interest as a means of contesting the state and citizenship reveal its democratic potential.

Democracy of Interest: The Putney Debates

The Putney Debates illuminate both how interest was connected to the political importance of property in early modern England, and how it exceeds this connection in the service of a democratic possibility. True, the religious notion

---

102. Joseph Symonds, *Three Treatises, Being the Substance of Sundry Discourses, Namely the Principal Interest, or the Propriety of the Saints in God, on Micah 7.7, and God's Interest in Man, Natural and Acquired, on Psalms 119.4* (London, 1653).

103. Hirschman, *The Passions and the Interests;* Pincus, "Neither Machiavellian Moment nor Possessive Individualism."

104. Engelmann, *Imagining Interest*, 2, 114–16.

of "true conscience" in part underwrites the turn to interest as a "shared language" in the debate, if only because it broadly distributes the matter of who is entitled to even speak to the matter of what counts as England. Yet interest becomes a point at which notions of property and privilege intersect those of franchise, empowerment, and foundations. Bringing the contestability of interest to bear on the constitution of the polity, the debates at Putney reveal the democratic power of appeals to interest in that such appeals claim a collective identity for the citizens in a language that does not foreclose, but rather promotes further contest regarding that identity. In other words, "interest" is democratic not because of its egalitarianism, but because of how it constitutes, distributes, and contests power. Last, appeals to interest are a vehicle for the reciprocal means by which contests around the constitution of a polity in turn constitute its citizens.

In the fall of 1647, the victors in the First Civil War—including members of Oliver Cromwell's New Model Army—began to work on a constitutional settlement with the shared aim of ensuring that the restored king would be unable to rule arbitrarily in either civil or ecclesiastical affairs. But factional differences that had been suppressed during the campaign against a common enemy resurfaced in the face of this constructive task. The intersection of property and franchise was a key point of contention. General Henry Ireton, General Oliver Cromwell, and other Grandees of the New Model Army belonged to a party of Independents who, like mainstream parliament-party Dissenters, were fiercely committed to the notion that only those who owned a substantial amount of fixed property should be given the franchise. Major William Rainborough, Colonel Nathaniel Rich, and a few others represented a heterogeneous group of "Levellers," Agitators, and rank-and-file members of the New Model Army who supported an expanded franchise—though various records suggest disagreement among these groups over the basis of such a franchise.[105] Conflict among these positions revealed the extent to which the long-standing institution of private property was not a basis for, but rather a result of, a narrow basis for participation among already vested interests.

The record of the debates at Putney have been revisited by scholars not only as a record of early modern radicalism, but furthermore as embodying "crisis political theory," wherein "participants attempt to come to terms" with new

---

105. C. B. Macpherson, *The Political Theory of Possessive Individualism* (Oxford: Oxford University Press, 1962), 117–36. Levellers and Agitators are names given to these political movements by their opponents, but in both cases the movements eventually and defiantly adopted the names for themselves.

circumstances "under dangerous and fluid conditions."[106] Most discussions of these debates focus on the arguments of the Levellers. By virtue of being the radical underdogs, their audacious demands—a broad suffrage, equal protection of the law, the right not to be conscripted into the army—offer an appealing proto-liberal-democratic model of broad participatory inclusion, and of constraining institutional power.[107] The Levellers' willingness to bring such demands forward in the face of institutional intransigence has even broader appeal.[108] But turning to these debates with "interest" in mind directs our attention mainly to the Grandees' position, as offered by General Ireton in particular.

The Grandees' appeals to interest unwittingly demonstrate how interest, when invoked as a foundation for political order, supports contestation regarding the share in that order. This paradox appears despite the fact that Ireton is concerned to maintain a constitution that circumscribes *who* could have an interest in the kingdom by ensuring (the unequal distribution of) private property. Reflecting Rohan's innovation, its imbrication with legal tropes as reflected in Nedham's writing and the broader, property-saturated English political discourse of the day, the language of interest in the Putney Debates show the state (and "England") to be an unsettled, contested, and malleable site for subsuming diverse particulars into a body to be achieved by means of action. This language reflects the possibility for a contested and unsettled politics in which persons are "interested" in the sense of being made to have interests by virtue of their own collective makings and doings. Ireton's claim to present a final and secure foundation of the kingdom by means of an appeal to interest—always the conceit of such an appeal—is undermined by the inevitability of contestation that the Levellers' dispute with the Grandees reveals, but which they ultimately do not exploit.

At a meeting of the General Council of Officers at Putney on October 28, 1647, John Wildman read a paper, the "Agreement of the People," presenting

---

106. Engelmann, *Imagining Interest*, 124. Reading these debates, Engelmann remarks on how potentially destabilizing the language of interest becomes, but also as helping to forge a future-oriented, newly "constitutional" public interest that is potentially stabilizing (124–25). In what follows, I examine how claims to interest destabilize, and how the democratic potential in the language of interest is revealed in that destabilization.

107. See, for example, Leon Friedman, "Conscription and the Constitution: The Original Understanding," *Michigan Law Review* 67, no. 8 (1969): 1500. See also Macpherson, *Possessive Individualism*, 150–59; Pocock, *Machiavellian Moment*, 375–76, 81, 90; and Sheldon Wolin, *The Presence of the Past: Essays on the State and the Constitution* (Baltimore: Johns Hopkins University Press, 1989), chap. 8.

108. A. S. P. Woodhouse, ed., *Puritanism and Liberty, being the Army Debates (1647–9) from the Clarke Manuscripts with Supplementary Documents* (London: J. M. Dent & Sons, 1951), 443–44.

the Levellers' vision of a new political constitution for the revolutionary English government. The first article of the paper declared that "the people of England, being at this day very unequally distributed by Counties, Cities, and Burroughs, for the election of their Deputies in Parliament ought to be more indifferently proportioned, according to the number of the Inhabitants; the circumstances whereof, for number, place, and manner, are to be set down before the end of this present Parliament."[109] Ireton and the Grandees understood the Agreement's call for representation proportional to the numbers of inhabitants as a move to broaden the franchise—an interpretation that the Levellers did not dispute. Habitation as a requirement worried Ireton most of all because it represented to him a novel—indeed, revolutionary—foundation for the kingdom. He therefore opposes broadly construing the franchise under the Agreement, arguing that to take this position, one must "fly for refuge to an absolute natural right, and . . . deny all civil right" (Woodhouse, 53). Civil right was crucial, according to Ireton, because it respects "the right of the people of this kingdom, . . . as they are people of this kingdom, distinct and divided from other people" (53)—a requirement that habitation somehow fails to procure. Natural right, argues Ireton, cannot respect the distinction of "these people" from "other people" and is therefore to be denied.

Rainborough and the Levellers invoke their birthright as Englishmen as a basis for participation that can distinguish "these" from "other people." Ireton in turn disputes that birthright reaches political voice. He argues that "no person hath a right to an interest or share in the disposing of the affairs of the kingdom, and in determining or choosing those that shall determine what laws we shall be ruled by here—no person hath a right to this, that hath not a permanent fixed interest in this kingdom, and consequently are also to make up the representers of this kingdom, who taken together do comprehend whatsoever is of real or permanent interest in the kingdom" (53). The legal valence of Ireton's first two invocations of interest in this passage is clear as day—interest is a "right" and a "share." The third, however, seems to be a point at which this interest is transformed into a matter of reason or conscience—as though the debates were an opportunity for the "representers" to discover, realize, or understand the kingdom's interest. But once again, imputing to psychological interest a status distinct from the legal obscures both the work of the appeal to interest in political argument and the conceit of that appeal. It turns out that

---

109. C. B. Macpherson argues that for Levellers and Grandees alike, property qualifications remained the fundamental basis for manhood suffrage; see Macpherson, *Possessive Individualism*.

by "comprehend," Ireton means less to know than to make up, to comprise, to grasp, to hold, to bear, and most of all to enclose within limits—a comprehension that his articulation of interest as a civil right is meant to secure.

Ireton's explicit argument is that real property, which is fixed, local, and permanent, is the proper basis for a right to "dispose of the affairs of the kingdom" (67). Just as "a freehold cannot be removed out of the kingdom," Ireton argues that the "interest of the kingdom . . . is not able to be removed anywhere else" (55). The question, therefore, is not one of "these people" as distinct from "others" after all, but rather of England as a physical, material place (a notion abetted by its island imperialism), and of its state as representing its estates rather than the status of its citizens as political agents. In this regard, Ireton's turn to articulate a civil right in terms of real property hews closely to the old restriction of *id quod interest* to *commodatum* in Roman law, but (in a quite modern register) makes this restriction a matter of constituting a nation. Discussing the property qualification for the franchise, Ireton insists that even money cannot be the basis of an interest since "money is as good in another place as here; he that hath money hath nothing that doth logically fix him to this kingdom" (67). Hence the traditional forty shillings as a requirement for the franchise must be the annual revenues of real property in land and trading corporations, which make up the "interest of the kingdom" because they—unlike the revenue itself—are "fixed and permanent" in the realm. On this basis, Ireton argues it is necessary "to restrain . . . the bounds of those who are to be the electors . . . still to men who have a local, a permanent interest in the kingdom, who have such an interest that they may live upon it as a freeman, and who have such an interest as is fixed upon a place, and is not the same equally everywhere" (62). But Ireton's attempt to comprehend this constitution by reviving interest's (already contested) juridical tie to *commodatum* and by establishing the state of the kingdom as a collection of estates, rooted in time and place, is doomed already in this passage by his tacit admission that interest exceeds the freehold. This tacit admission is the backdrop, not only for his increasingly frantic modification of "interest" with "fixed" and "permanent," but also for his outright admission that the matter at hand is to restrain, rather than to recognize as obvious, "the bounds of those who are to be the electors."

Political power, according to Ireton, includes the right to "dispose of land, and of all things" (54). By the power "to dispose" of England Ireton most evidently does not mean to orchestrate its destruction or abandonment, but rather "to assign or deliver authoritatively" and "to place things in proper distances and positions with regard to each other"—including, it seems, the ability to distinguish who's in from who's out. The appeal to interest is therefore particularly well suited to the disposal of the kingdom in that it is a language of organizing relationships and assigning identity. Rainborough recognizes the intimate relation between power and interest implied in Ireton's argument, paraphrasing it as saying that "a man, when he hath an estate, hath an interest in making laws [but] when he hath none, he hath no power in it" (56). Ireton's worry that to establish the franchise on basis of birthright alone is to "take away all the property and interest that any man hath either in land or by inheritance, or in estate by possession, or anything else" (55) belies his awareness of the crucial fact of these debates. In the face of well-organized (not to mention well-armed) soldiers, the civil institution of real property reflects the juridical power of appeals to interest to determine the properties of the kingdom. Those properties are not themselves primordial foundations of interest, since it is the business of appeals to interest to determine those properties at points of conflict.

Democratic Interest: Contest and Critique

The contested and contestable side of "interest" deployed by Rohan, Nedham, and others—a means toward refiguring the persons of political agents, be they states, nations, or citizens—opens an alternative that Rainborough explores when he departs, if only momentarily, from the Leveller script of arguing from conscience and birthright. Over the course of the debate, rather than property foreclosing the contestation of participation in citizenship, interest as a language of constitution becomes the means by which participation, in the form of franchise, itself is revealed as a constitutive "property." Rainborough begins his reply to Ireton by expressing concern that "I do very much care whether [there be] a king or no king, lords or no lords, property or no property; and I think, if we do not all take care, we shall all have none of these very shortly" (54). One might take this statement, as C. B. MacPherson and others have done, to be evidence of a Leveller commitment to "possessive individualism" as a basis for political order. But it is not clear what kind of property Rainborough has in mind. This property may be a power one exercises or disposes rather than an object one possesses—a possibility that the progress of the debate supports. As Rainborough follows the slide of the kingdom's interest from comprehension by property to contestation and power, he begins to explore a notion of property that includes participation. By this means, Rainborough ultimately uses the Independents' appeals to interest against Ireton, by making a property out of a man's right or share in the franchise.

Examining "the thing itself—property" (60), Rainborough turns to the matter of franchise, and then inquires as to how this property was first acquired. Ireton does not reply. Instead he reaches for material evidence—his own estate—to prove that "[he has] an interest in choosing burgesses of the parliament," though "choosing" itself is hardly a material constituent of the kingdom (60). Even as Ireton frankly opposes "introducing an equality of interest in this government, among those who have no property in this kingdom, or who have no local permanent interest in it" (62), in so saying he acknowledges that "interest" can represent the share, right, or privilege in "disposing of the affairs of the kingdom" not already bound to freeholds (54). Query by query, Rainborough and Edward Sexby press Ireton to recognize—and nearly to admit—that England is not a merely physical place, a collection of freeholds and corporations, to be represented, but rather a power to be disposed. Therein lies Ireton's anxiety that this power will be disposed wrongly by the victors in this stage of the civil war.

The Levellers, grasping their moment in the slippage of Ireton's argument from interest, step up to their most compelling argument—and evidently the one most threatening to the Grandees—regarding how their action of fighting in the New Model Army, drafting the Agreement, and bringing it forward for debate (with guns in hand) redeems their rights. And so when Rainborough and Sexby each argue that the Levellers' participation in the Army, and their having reconstituted England by that means, redeems their birthright, namely, their voice in government, Ireton offers a high-minded but palpably weak reply. He say that the soldiers fought so that "those who have an interest in the kingdom," and not merely the will of one man, shall have the right to make laws. It may come as news to the soldiers—many of whom are said to have carried small printed copies of the Agreement in their hatbands while charging into battle—that such an arrangement is to their benefit in that they too may one day be, as Ireton puts it, "capable of trading to get money, to get estates by; and therefore have a great deal of reason to build up such a foundation of interest to themselves.... Here was a right that induced men to fight, and those men that had this interest, though this is not the utmost interest that other men have, yet they had some interest" (69). This argument falls flat. Ireton's offer of interest as a reason for obedience and subjection is evidently not convincing for the men who have now heard interest lauded as a basis for participation in power. The emphasis Ireton places on interest as both a foundation and an outcome of participation brings with it the aspect of interest that exceeds the representation of propertied vestments but instead distributes power, including property. While Ireton supposes interest to be local, permanent, and connected to real property, by his own usage it also represents a right or a share that, like property, is granted and secured by political decision—and that is in some ways built up, through political action.

The Levellers and their allies have plenty of opportunities to adopt the Grandees' appeals to interest on behalf of the commoners' participation, but they do not do so. Perhaps they are reluctant to spring for bait that Cromwell laces conspicuously with venom: "Is there any bound or limit set if you take away this limit [i.e. forty shillings a year in land and corporations]," he asks, "that men shall have no interest but the interest of breathing shall have voice in elections?" (59). Though the very debate of this day is premised upon and dedicated to how political participation can be granted (by themselves, through an expansive reading of the first article of the paper), the Levellers forgo the opportunity that this realization offers by returning, programmatically, to a "natural" source—birthright—to justify why participation should be widely inclusive.

The difficulty Ireton faces in refuting the Levellers' position by appealing to interest reveals the real situation of the constitution of England: interest constitutes the kingdom, but interest is also contested. It does not respect, but instead determines the kingdom's properties. The power of interest as a positive right to dispose exceeds material constituents, since England itself is more than a merely physical realm, and is itself more contested. Interest is not then something that everyone has in the sense that everyone is seen as having reason or conscience, even if equality on these bases were planks in the Levellers' platform for broadening suffrage.[110] Interest is not a language of exclusion or of inclusion. Rather the Levellers' program of suffrage raises the specter for the Grandees that everyone has an interest by virtue of having the power to constitute and reconstitute England. Against interest as a notion upon which political order can be sustained once its foundations in ancient constitutions and times out of mind are secured, in the Putney Debates we see appeals to interest as a means by which communities are remade at points of contestation. We also see the inherently provisional quality of that remaking, given that the polity is never made once and for all. If interest must be construed as a "foundation" to

110. For discussions of democracy that draw in various ways on such a definition, see Jacques Rancière, *Disagreement: Politics and Philosophy*, trans. Julie Rose (Minneapolis: University of Minnesota Press, 1999), chap. 5; Jacques Derrida, "The Politics of Friendship," *Journal of Philosophy* 85, no. 11 (1988): 103–4; Sheldon Wolin, "Norm and Form: The Constitutionalizing of Democracy," in *Athenian Political Thought and the Reconstruction of American Democracy* (Ithaca: Cornell University Press, 1994); and Sheldon Wolin, "Fugitive Democracy," *Constellations* 1, no. 1 (1994).

political order, it is one that reflects the paradoxical essence of democracy, in that it retains spaces for contestation at its very core.[111]

Democratic Traces in the Language of Interest

Throughout my discussions of Chaucer, Rohan, Nedham, and Putney, I have been concerned to recover a crossing point of subjection and contestation in the language of interest that is foreclosed by a modern prejudice to see only reason and desire, psychology and interiority. While reopening the seventeenth century in this way invites us to revisit the past, it also may alert us to how present-day appeals to interest sit uneasily with the notion of interest as calculating self-regard that informs some liberal theorizing and social science, and that characterizes neoliberal politics more generally.[112] Both the affinity of "interest" with the constructed, the contested, and the civil on the one hand, and the power to shape agency that was so evident and vital in the seventeenth century on the other, are alive in the word's uses today. The echoes of interest's first incursion into political language in today's political discourse link the seventeenth-century vogue of "interest" to our time in ways that are generally unrecognized. Of course, it takes little investigation or imagination to see how the juridical side of interest lives on in the uses of the term to describe a stake or a share. And while political theory has tended to overlook these uses, even the most libertarian observer of political life can see how such stakes and shares are guaranteed by, if not products of, community and even state authority. Even so, the more mysterious and magical force in the recent political imagination has been the kind of interest that seems to make the others matter: the ability of political agents to know what is best for themselves, and to plot a course for achieving it from among the stakes and shares provided by community life and government surety. This is the force of interest said by Hirschman and others to be the signal achievement of modernity, represented by the explosion of interest talk on the seventeenth-century English scene.

Yet traces of the juridical and plural language of contested and agent-shaping interest reside in myriad uses of the word "interest"—even, and perhaps especially, in those uses of the term which appear most saturated with the psychological. And here the modern-day lexicographer's and philosopher's tactic of

---

111. Engelmann, *Imagining Interest*, 1–3; see also Wendy Brown, *Edgework: Critical Essays on Knowledge and Politics* (Princeton: Princeton University Press, 2005), 41–43.

112. Taylor, *Sources of the Self,* 191; Taylor, "Philosophy and Its History," 18, 26–27.

dividing senses of the term—objective versus subjective, or individual versus aggregative—is the most misleading. In Chaucer we saw interest as causing someone to have a personal share; in Rohan, as the power or influence a person exercises over another—a power that Blount extended by metaphor to the means of one passion overpowering another. Each of these senses invokes the kind of action expressed by a verb. Yet the verb senses of "interest" apparently come closest to the psychological functions of attention and concern, diverting our attention from the collective means and ends of provoking interest and the language of interest as itself an activity of promoting and achieving collective ends.

Close attention to the language of interest suggests that "interest" as a feeling of concern nonetheless bears traces of "interest" as the power of influence, suggesting how even a language of interest that is supposed to most intimately reflect and respect the autonomy of political agents—by virtue of their privileged knowledge of their concerns—resists the division of interests into subjective and objective senses. The word "interest" differs from the other words associated with desires, drives, or motives in that while one "feels interested (in)" something in much the same way as one "feels concerned (about, by)," something, the past participle "interested" does not correspond to an analogous emotional state: one "feels concern" but does not "feel interest." When we speak of something being "interesting" to someone, the adjective form is the same as the gerund, suggesting an active role for the external object upon the body said to be interested—much like such an object may be said to be moving, changing, or transforming it. In other words, unlike such psychological terms as "desire," "concern," or "attraction," "interestedness" wears its quality as provoked or influenced from the outside on its sleeve. Similarly, if something is "of interest," it is also "interest*ing*," the gerund form suggesting an ongoing, if not dominant activity on the part of what interests. (By contrast, something that is "of importance" is simply "important.") Within these differences lies a philosophical point: some body said to be interested is subject to, rather than sovereign over, its interests.

This point is further illustrated in the relation of a body to its object of curiosity, desire, drive, need, or passion; this relation is reversed when expressed in terms of "interest." So, for example, "John desires wealth" becomes "wealth interests John"; "Californians want campaign finance reform" becomes "Campaign finance reform interests Californians." What were the grammatical subjects in these examples—John, Californians—become the grammatical objects of the thing previously needed or desired—wealth, campaign finance reform. Or, to speak philosophically, John and Californians are subjected, by "interest," to wealth and campaign finance reform. Even the prepositions idiomatic to the language of interest suggest the intimacy of interest over supposedly synonymous expressions of desire: "Maia is passionate (or curious) *about* the new hybrid convertible car" becomes "Maia is interested *in* the new hybrid convertible" or "The new hybrid convertible interests Maia." One has a concern or desire *for;* one can be concerned *about* or benefited *by;* but when it comes to "interest," the preposition is always *in.* One has an interest in a job, a movie, or a potential suitor; *in* relates its objects not merely in proximity—it is a relation of enclosure or comprehension. Therefore, translating relations of need, curiosity, or desire into the language of interest not only troubles the stability of relations between subjects and objects in the language of interest, but the divide itself comes into question. Quite contrary to the usual Cartesian way in which we think about persons related to their interests (including their stakes and shares) as subjects related to their objects, interest is therefore not something a person has simply by virtue of having a *cogito.* Rather, interest is a relationship in which the object that interests quite possibly enjoys the upper hand.

Noting how the usages of "interest" disrespect the subject-object distinction warns us also against the temptation to see the body said to "have interests" or "to be interested" as *wholly* constituted by external articulations. Not only is the interested body in some way affected by the object of its "interest"; it also can be active about its interest in a way that has no parallel in the vocabulary of concern, need, or desire. So, for example, one does not "take a desire" (or a concern, or a need), but one *does* "take an interest." This suggests that while some body said to be interested or to have an interest does not have sole or even privileged access to its interests, every body is nonetheless capable of actively recruiting interests, even if these recruitments remain subject to some kind of contestation, and the object of interest, once taken, reciprocates this power. Even the present-day usages of interest at its most apparently and intimately subjective therefore harbor a pre-Cartesian notion of the self.

To conclude, my case for suspending the attribution of psychological interest to the seventeenth century entails tracing conceptual continuities where others have emphasized conceptual change. But however plausible tracing continuities from the opening to the closing decades of the seventeenth century may be, do I not merely replicate the error I have been keen to correct by seeking seventeenth-century conceptions in today's language? The answer is no. The language of interest, rendered richly equivocal by centuries of linguistic innovation, bears the traces from more than one epoch. The danger lies in our blindness to the heterogeneity, past and present, in the language of interest, and how the various strands from different periods come together in today's idiom. This danger is all the more acute when it allows notions of self-originating interest to mask the powers of language in the power of interest to provoke action and to incompletely realize subjectivity.

What Rohan formulated as a means of provoking a prince to action toward realizing and consolidating a contested notion of the state, Nedham followed as a means of provoking citizen action toward a contested notion of the nation. The Putney Debates show how this picture of interests becomes available as a democratic one about participation in politics, given that determinations of interest are revealed as political rather than as reflections of pregiven forms of political agency. Interests are democratic in that they can become and remain contested, if democracy is understood as permanent contest. The language of interest may have been subsequently transformed into a commercial and liberal language, but the juridical side contributes a contestability and contingency to this language that rides in perpetual tension with its governance of conduct.

4 CONTESTING SOVEREIGNTY

Interest in Thomas Hobbes

Reading Interest in(to) Hobbes

The seventeenth century left many things to us moderns. One is a political idiom saturated with the language of interest, and the sense—equal parts cynical and scientific—that any claim can or even must be rendered in its terms. Another is the deeply puzzling, darkly insightful, but ever rigorous philosophy of Thomas Hobbes. It seems natural beyond a doubt that to bring light to the puzzles of his work, with a realism and rigor worthy of his own, we must understand it, politically, as a claim regarding interest. We might even hope to find liberation at the point where the most unrelenting of absolutist philosophers set interests at the foundation of sovereignty.

Leviathan, Hobbes's most widely read text, could reasonably be expected to have given interest a political-philosophical home, not only in light of this work's composition during Hobbes's self-imposed civil war exile, but also for its appearance in English vernacular as a giant contentious pamphlet on behalf of monarchy. Indeed this text appears innovative to many readers in part because it imagines a political order with interests at its foundation. As one commentator has it, *Leviathan* exemplifies how in the seventeenth century, "the satisfaction of interest came to be considered the foremost objective of politics."[1] Hobbes's work might be seen as a harbinger of modernity for this reason alone.

And yet Hobbes's relation to the language of interest in the politics of his time has not only been poorly understood, it has been positively obscured.

---

1. Wolin, *Politics and Vision*, 280.

Readers have made Hobbes out to be a seventeenth-century forebear of what are, in truth, very recent liberal and social-scientific commitments to finding interests at the basis of political order. These readings are not merely proleptic. They import notions of interest to Hobbes that are impossible to square with his own references to interest—references that have led Quentin Skinner (no doubt one of the most prominent interpreters of Hobbes) to note that Hobbes was opposed to interest.[2] But leaving the matter at that, Skinner's reading joins its proleptic others in obscuring Hobbes's distinctive treatment of interests. For reading Hobbes's remarks about interest, rather than reading interest into (or out of) his theory, we are led to significant and fertile insights regarding the role of appeals to interest in contesting, rather than constituting, political arrangements. My central argument in this chapter is that if we theorize the politics of these, Hobbes's own references, we shall discover Hobbes to be not simply "against interests," but the consummate *anti-interest* theorist. He is concerned to exclude a politics of interest from his theory of sovereignty, precisely because appeals to interest have the power to contest and remake political agents in ways that more recent liberal and social-scientific perspectives on politics are inapt to recognize. Taking Hobbes at his word, we see how he reveals interests to be impediments to sovereignty—they can serve neither as its foundation, nor as its result.

Descriptions of Hobbes's philosophy as based on or promoting self-interest are legion in both historical and philosophical literatures of political theory.[3] The pervasive sense that interest holds a central place in Hobbes's thought, particularly among scholars and students who do not specialize in the study of Hobbes, is easy to understand. An impressive lineage of historical interpreters of political thought offhandedly identify Hobbes as among the first theorists of interest (Machiavelli generally being the other), even though their conclusions about Hobbes's theory differ widely.[4] The ability of a common starting point to yield myriad readings becomes more puzzling, however, when it comes to those which focus explicitly on interests. The self-evidence of this concept as Hobbes's starting point is quickly belied by the difficulty these readers face in

---

2. Quentin Skinner, *Reason and Rhetoric in the Philosophy of Hobbes* (Cambridge: Cambridge University Press, 1996), 429.

3. Gunn, *Politics and the Public Interest;* Tully, *Discourse on Property,* 30; Holmes, *Passions and Constraint;* John Rawls, "The Idea of an Overlapping Consensus," in *Collected Papers,* ed. Samuel Freeman (Cambridge: Harvard University Press, 1999), 422.

4. Michael Oakeshott, "Introduction," in Thomas Hobbes, *Leviathan,* ed. Michael Oakeshott (Oxford: Oxford University Press, 1947); John Plamenatz, "Mr. Warrender's Hobbes," *Political Studies* 5, no. 3 (1957); Macpherson, *Possessive Individualism.*

settling on exactly *what* interests Hobbes sees as foundational, and how his theory accounts for or deals with these interests. Indeed, the heuristic flexibility of "interests" as a rubric for the interpretation of Hobbes's political theory is astonishing. Those who see Hobbes as a "theorist of interest," in the sense that his philosophy is based upon or accounts for natural or prepolitical interests of persons, have proffered a bewilderingly wide variety of readings.[5] Others propose that Hobbes's theory of sovereignty remakes subjects' interests. These readers present Hobbes as a "theorist of interest" in the sense that he pursues a program of forming or reforming subjects' interests. Viewed from this angle, Hobbes's account is based on persons' interests not as they are in the state of

---

5. Bernard Gert and Gregory Kavka each use "interest" as a catchall for Hobbes's various depictions of egoism. For these commentators, whatever can rightly be described as Hobbes's picture of egoism is foundational to his argument and rightly called "self-interest." See Bernard Gert, "Hobbes's Psychology," in *The Cambridge Companion to Hobbes,* ed. Tom Sorrell (Cambridge: Cambridge University Press, 1996), 168, and Gregory S. Kavka, *Hobbesian Moral and Political Theory* (Princeton: Princeton University Press, 1986), 42. Some approach the relationship of interest and egoism more narrowly; for W. H. Greenleaf, the "rational pursuit of self-interest" is equated with "the motion of appetite and aversion." See W. H. Greenleaf, "Hobbes: The Problem of Interpretation," in *Hobbes-Forschungen,* ed. Reinhart Koselleck and Roman Schnur (Berlin: Duncker & Humblot, 1968), 9–10. David Gauthier extends the logic of this pursuit into the contract, seeing short-term self-interest transformed into long-term self-interest as the institution of the sovereign circumvents a prisoner's dilemma. I engage Gauthier's later arguments in *Moral Dealing* later in this chapter. See David Gauthier, "Hobbes's Social Contract," in *Perspectives on Thomas Hobbes,* ed. G. A. J. Rogers and Alan Ryan (Oxford: Clarendon Press, 1988). Jean Hampton takes a more utilitarian (and even evolutionary-biological) view, locating self-interest in "enhancing pleasure and decreasing pain" with the ultimate aim of self-preservation. See Jean Hampton, *Hobbes and the Social Contract Tradition* (New York: Cambridge University Press, 1986), 23. A. E. Taylor equates "interest" with immediate inclination, which he in turn equates with benefit and desire; see A. E. Taylor, *Thomas Hobbes* (London: Archibald Constable, 1908). Howard Warrender defends Taylor's reading of Hobbes from critics by equating "interest" instead with benefit and self-preservation; see Howard Warrender, *Political Philosophy of Hobbes* (Oxford: Oxford University Press, 1957), chap. 9. A realist reader, Laurie Johnson, says that according to Hobbes, "human begins are universally and always motivated by interest," though as the foregoing survey indicates, just in what those interests consist is not altogether clear. See Laurie M. Johnson, *Thucydides, Hobbes, and the Interpretation of Realism* (DeKalb: Northern Illinois University Press, 1993), 3. S. A. Lloyd takes a similar commitment to the foundation of "interests" to Hobbes's political thought in the argument that it is transcendent interest, namely religion and belief, as opposed to material interests or faculty psychology that lies at the basis of Hobbes's political theory. As applied here to religious belief, Lloyd too intends "interest" to emphasize the primacy of religious beliefs as motivational. Lloyd takes a further step that places one of her feet in another camp. Part of Hobbes's program, according to Lloyd, is the reformation of transcendent interests by means of education in such a way as to solve the problem original posed by these interests. S. A. Lloyd thereby joins William Connolly and others, in holding that Hobbes has a program, rather than a theory of interests. See S. A. Lloyd, *Ideals as Interests in Hobbes's Leviathan* (New York: Cambridge University Press, 1992).

nature, or as consistent with egoism, or as indicated by a mechanistic psychology, but rather on persons' interests as defined by the sovereign or as an outcome of sovereignty.[6] Yet another view straddles the line: Hobbes is concerned with appetites and egoism, natural law, and anxiety about salvation as interests—yet he refigures the content of these interests so they become a foundation for a civil state.[7] And so on.

The stakes for political philosophy in situating Hobbes as a theorist of interest go beyond—perhaps inevitably—the hope of "getting Hobbes right." The backdrop of these discussions frequently is that Hobbes's work—which he himself promoted as setting a new *scientia civilis* on the foundations of geometry—is a precursor to the present-day ambitions of a political science founded on the geometries of our own time, be they behavioralist or rational choice. The assessment of Hobbes as having made a compelling case for a scientific study of politics goes hand in hand with his critical role in uncovering self-interest as a regular building block of political order. From this point of view, Hobbes's theory reveals something essential not only about human interests, but also about how these interests—now seen as fitting objects of study—buttress the relationship of scientific knowledge and politics.[8] Interest is what makes a science of politics possible. And yet elucidating Hobbes's role as an authority in both critical and celebratory discussions of this relationship cannot evade the bewildering variety I have mentioned. Even so, as a result of the intersection of present-day liberal and social-scientific certainty that interests are an orderly foundation of politics with Hobbes's own claim to have put a *scientia civilis* on a firm footing, Hobbes has become a theorist of interest as these authors debate not whether, but *how* Hobbes saw interests as a fundamental solution to the problems of knowledge, right, and order. Given the apparent chorus of agreement that Hobbes has something fundamental to tell us about interest, a

---

6. William Connolly, *Political Theory and Modernity* (Ithaca: Cornell University Press, 1993), 28 and chap. 2. Stephen Engelmann approaches this view as well, noting that for Hobbes, when confronting danger and disorder, "the self-interested self is not the problem for political order, but instead part of the solution." Engelmann goes on to argue that the later development of monistic interest theory was developed in large measure in response or opposition to Hobbes, who is "not a philosopher of interest." See Engelmann, *Imagining Interest*, 23–25. Gauthier's theory can also be seen as a program-theory, on the view that long-term interest is qualitatively different than short-term interests; see Gauthier, "Hobbes's Social Contract."
7. Lloyd, *Ideals as Interests in Hobbes's Leviathan.*
8. Wolin, *Politics and Vision;* but see also Sheldon Wolin, *Hobbes and the Epic Tradition of Political Theory* (Los Angeles: William Andrews Clark Memorial Library, University of California, 1970). The latter text does not bear directly on interests.

reader today may conclude that the centrality of the concept to his thought is self-evident—even if the thought itself remains an enigma.[9]

A brief, though necessarily schematic and incomplete, sketch of Hobbes's philosophy as it unfolds across *Leviathan* illustrates why Hobbes's theory is capable of such diverse interpretations in terms of interest in the first place. Telling this story without using the word "interest" is also a fitting way to begin thinking about what layering the idiom of interest over these points may conceal in Hobbes's thought. This, in turn, hints at what the effort to locate interest in Hobbes's text reveals about modern liberal and social-scientific preoccupations. Hobbes begins with an examination of cognition, noting how imagination is founded in sensation and the memories of sensation.[10] These sensations and memories come to bear on appetite and aversion, which Hobbes describes in mechanistic terms, yielding passions (*Leviathan*, chap. 6). The various manifestations of these appetites and aversions are further mediated by language, a system of signs for memorializing and communicating original sensations (chaps. 4 and 6). Language also becomes the basis for deliberation and, ultimately, reason (chaps. 5 and 7). But the ability to reason rightly is impeded by egoism—the desire for and pursuit of power to the point of conflict with others (chaps. 8 and 9). This is particularly the case where appetites turn toward the same object (chap. 13). Hobbes posits a natural right of each human being to everything necessary to preserve him- or herself. Conflicts over objects of such a natural right means that human beings are naturally in a state of war (chaps. 13 and 14). But reason points to a law of nature, namely, to seek peace; the problem faced by Hobbes is that reason is poorly understood and so is seldom followed (chaps. 4, 5, and 14). Hobbes's task, therefore, is to lay out right reason. Yet such reason is truly possible only under the condition of sovereignty, which emerges from a contract that each person makes with all the others to invest one artificial person with the power of each (chaps. 13, 16, and 18). But sovereignty and right reason can truly emerge only when all threats to the commonwealth are removed (chap. 31).[11]

---

9. The influence of this idea can be seen as far and wide as economics, marketing, and psychology. See, for example, Dale T. Miller, "The Norm of Self-Interest," *American Psychologist* 54, no. 12 (1999). Dissent on this point is rare; Engelmann notes that Hobbes ought not to be read as an "interest theorist" in any sense. See Engelmann, *Imagining Interest*, 23.

10. Thomas Hobbes, *Leviathan*, ed. Richard Tuck (Cambridge: Cambridge University Press, 1991), chaps. 1–2.

11. This sets the stage for a long discussion that reveals Hobbes's radical Christian theology (chaps. 32–43). The centerpiece of this theology, intrinsic to confining overriding fear to the disobedience of civil authority, is the nonexistence of hell (chap. 44). See Lloyd, *Ideals as Interests in Hobbes's Leviathan*, 36–47.

Hobbes's exposition of this theory contains a number of recursions, signaled by all the "yets" and "buts" in the account I have just given, which reveal the problems of politics in richly nuanced ways. So, for example, right reason points to a law of nature, but right reason does not seem possible unless sovereignty is established. Hobbes thereby paradoxically shows the law of nature to be a human construct by virtue of the need of reason for its revelation. Even so, Hobbes himself models right reason by providing a series of definitions (e.g., of "passions," "honor," "right," and so on), thereby positioning himself as a Moses figure or epic theorist and raising the possibility that once these foundations are secured, a sovereign would have little more to do than to keep his or her subjects in awe.

The present-day reader can redescribe any or several of these main points of Hobbes's text in the language of interest. After all, appetites (and perhaps even aversions) are interests in a sense we recognize as psychological, as is egoism. So, too, the law of nature, to seek peace, is undoubtedly in one's interest, though perhaps in another sense altogether. Last, one's duties to God, religion, and one's own soul are interests in yet another, perhaps "transcendental," sense.[12] Possibly it is the sheer number of points in Hobbes's argument that can be described in terms of interest that makes this concept so attractive, for it promises to unify these elements, rendering them—and therefore interpretations of Hobbes's philosophy—seamless, logical, and sensible.

"Interest" is all the more attractive as a term to employ to give a coherent account of Hobbes's thought because he himself uses the term only rarely, and never does he define it, the way he defines others that are indeed central to his theoretical edifice. Therefore, redescribing the points that I have noted in terms of interest will not run afoul of Hobbes's own definitions. Precisely because Hobbes had relatively little to say explicitly about interests per se, there is all the more room for disagreement—and creative intervention—regarding just how Hobbes is distinctive for having made interests central to his work.

But Hobbes did use the term, even if he did not define it. His own invocations of "interest" point to an altogether distinct place for interest in his theory, one that must be reckoned with if we are to grapple with Hobbes as a theorist of interest and with interests as integral to political knowing and acting. For surely a reading of Hobbes's theory as based on interest cannot ignore how Hobbes himself depicts interest and still be an accurate depiction of "how Hobbes views interests" or the role of interests in his theory. And while Quentin Skinner has

12. Lloyd, *Ideals as Interests in Hobbes's Leviathan*, 51–52.

set himself apart from the readings I have briefly surveyed by noting the negative importance of interests for Hobbes, even he does not engage these uses, to the detriment of his speculations as to their provenance and importance.

Skinner conjectures that Hobbes came to reject interest after having been exposed to imitators of Rohan's *The Interests of the Princes of the States of Christendom*, which I examined in Chapter 3.[13] Skinner does not examine, however, the apposite question of whether Hobbes's uses of "interest" are congruent with the French discourse around *intérêt*, associated with Rohan, that he says motivated Hobbes's turn away from interests—a question that is beyond the scope of my account as well. More to the point, however, Hobbes's frequent association of interest with attachments in civil society, including estates and dominion, rather than with the aims and achievements of statecraft, suggests that the juridical inflections of English discourse, rather than the reason-of-state inflections reflected in the French debates around Rohan's work, underlie Hobbes's "discovery" of interests as a political problem. Exposing this juridical (i.e., legal and property-related) family of associations in Hobbes's uses of interest, I would argue, also attends more closely to the audience for whom Hobbes was presumably writing and the context into which *Leviathan* was received.

That Hobbes says little about interests and never explicitly defines the term is consistent with his view that appeals to interest are the root of inconstant signification, reflecting difference and rendering counsel inapt—including the counsel that Hobbes himself offers readers in the form of *Leviathan* and his other works. Hobbes demonstrates appeals to interest as the kind of claim that makes language, self-understanding, and human intentions messy and unreliable from the point of view of sovereign power. Therefore, as a key source of trouble with words, interest strikes at the foundation Hobbes wishes for his theory of sovereignty in secure definitions. Hobbes *is* concerned with interests, but in a way that contradicts the view that his theory of sovereignty succeeds by the machinations of interest. Seeking to quarantine interests from sovereignty and law, Hobbes's philosophy signals the transformation of the juridical side of interest into plural interest; Hobbes shows "interest" to be unfit for the task of articulating proper personality in modern sovereignty, owing to the indeterminacy and contestation at the core of appeals to interest in politics. Interests are a threat to sovereignty: they cannot be its foundation.

---

13. This influence, Skinner argues, accounts for the differences between *De Cive* and *Leviathan*; see Skinner, *Reason and Rhetoric*, 428–30.

Readings that have obscured the fact that Hobbes is an anti-interest theorist are of recent vintage: interest as a category for interpreting Hobbes emerged only haltingly in the 1930s, and became central to interpretations of his thought only in the 1960s. Which is to say, reading Hobbes's philosophy as being based upon or otherwise promoting interests has been self-evident only to modern readers. And so the self-evidence of modern interest in this text reveals something about the preoccupations of our era even as it obscures Hobbes's insights regarding appeals to interest in politics. Reading Hobbes's own uses of "interest" as a means of generating a Hobbesian political theory of interest therefore is an opportunity to meditate upon the modern preoccupation with interests, by examining what insights regarding the politics of interest are denied by the self-evidence (to present-day students of politics) of interest as rational, calculating self-regard. For the modern view of interest elides the power of sovereignty in the making of subjects as proper persons and, more important, obscures the power of appeals to interest to disrupt this proper personality—a democratic power revealed in the debates at Putney and still alive in the uses of "interest" today.

In the next part of this chapter, I examine Hobbes's invocations of interest to illustrate what role they play in his overall theory of sovereignty. My reading points in particular to the close ties among Hobbes's concern about interests, the multitude, opinions, and conflicts regarding one's "own"—that is, conflicts over persons' actions and goods. Hobbes's concern, I argue, is to replace interests and other improper notions of one's "own" with propriety, which reflects subjection under the rubric of authorized personality. In the third part of this chapter, I turn to an episode in the history of Hobbes scholarship to examine why, how, and to what effects interests became a prominent rubric for the interpretation and systematization of Hobbesian thought in the middle of the twentieth century. Noting how the modern language of interest came into contact with and eroded a key Kantian distinction between desire and duty, I turn to liberal social science by way of examining how two otherwise disparate readings—Sheldon Wolin's critique of Hobbes in *Politics and Vision* and David Gauthier's rational-choice reconstruction of the contract in *Moral Dealing*—follow this erosion by equating desire and self-preservation. I then look at elements of Hobbes's arguments that these readers' notions of interest connect, namely, desire and self-preservation, but whose connection in Hobbes's theory depends not on interest but rather on sovereignty. Any reading that attempts to bridge desire and self-preservation by means of interest, I argue, will always be haunted by the side of interest that Hobbes warns against:

instability, fragmentation, and protean identity. Viewing Hobbes as a theorist of interest subverts a critical aspect of Hobbes's theory, namely, his attempt to quarantine, by means of a rubric of sovereignty, the power of appeals to interest to both provoke and disrupt subjectivity.

Theorizing Interest in the Idiom of Hobbes

My recovery of juridical interest in the foregoing chapters—in which we see interest as a legal term pertaining, inter alia, to the execution of contracts—suggests another route, though one not explored in the literature on Hobbes, by which his theory could be seen as basing sovereignty upon interests. After all, although Hobbes is not the first to see sovereignty as a matter of performing contractual obligations, he is certainly among the best-known innovators in that regard. And indeed Hobbes's own references to interests in *Leviathan*, *De Cive,* and *Elements of Law* support the thesis that interests bear traces of the term's legal past regarding contracts, as I will show in a moment. But although Hobbes is attentive to the objects of these interest-related contracts being matters of estate, dominion, or one's own, he sees the relevance of interest to these matters less as one of performing contracts or covenants regarding these properties than as one of conflict or contestation around the performance—and this is why interest is an impediment to, rather than a model for, sovereignty that is rooted in the performance of contract. When it comes to politics, Hobbes shows the importance of interest's juridical side to lie in its contestability and intrinsic plurality, particularly as these qualities contribute to how the inconstancy of language strikes at the basis of sovereignty. Hobbes's emphasis on the conflicts at the root of appeals to interest leads him to reform people's attachments and their sense of their "own" in a way that shuts down the contestation that is interest's most striking feature.

From this point of view, Hobbes's concern about interests appears close to his view of egoism. But to equate these terms would be to miss the peculiarities of interest that exceed people's "restlesse desire of Power after power" (70), including the conventionality of interest and its effects on language. Moreover, several of Hobbes's references to interests pertain to multitude, so theorizing Hobbes on interest directs our attention to people in this condition, and to the special problems Hobbes faces in reaching an audience so situated.

Like Hobbes's explicit references to "interest," the peculiarities of people in the liminal state of multitude, between outright war and commonwealth, are seldom noticed by commentators. Perhaps Hobbes's own insistence that life without a true commonwealth is a state of war *simpliciter* leads present-day readers to overlook the distinctive attachments of multitude and the attractions, however apparent, that Hobbes at least recognizes. People in multitude, it seems, have made provisional and apparently stable arrangements to meet their wants—their lives may seem far from being "solitary, poore, nasty, brutish, and short"[14]—and therefore Hobbes is at pains to show that these provisions remain contingent so long as they are not yet secured by sovereignty. "Being distracted in opinions concerning the best use and application of their strength," he writes, "[men in multitude] do not help, but hinder each other. . . . When there is no common enemy, they make warre upon each other, for their particular interests. For if we could suppose a great Multitude of men to consent in the observation of Justice . . . without a common Power to keep them all in awe . . . then neither would be, nor need to be any Civill Government, or Common-wealth at all; because there would be Peace without subjection" (118–19). Attending to multitude is critical because the condition of multitude represents a range of inevitably social attachments that exceed naturalistic determinations of desire and egoism, both in their complexity and in the temptation they present (say, to Dissenters) as a suitable foundation of politics exclusive of sovereignty.[15] Though such a condition may be sunny, Hobbes is quick to point out the clouds of insecurity on the horizon. "For as the nature of Foule weather," he writes, "lyeth not in a showre or two of rain; but in an inclination thereto of many dayes together: So the nature of War, consisteth not in actual fighting, but in the known disposition thereto, during all the time there is no assurance to the contrary."[16] Although multitude

---

14. Hobbes, *Leviathan*, 89. Hobbes's readers find themselves in the condition of multitude, with its vexing ambiguities. They live under a kind of government, and ought not to try to change it (233–34), but they also face elements of the state of war, because they cannot be assured that there will be no violence (88–89). This suggests that the commonwealth has yet to be formed. Even so, they may have (and the English in the seventeenth century did have) the elements of "commodious living" Hobbes says are impossible in the state of war (89). Meanwhile, Hobbes shows readers that they must recognize their duty as subjects as a means of perfecting the civil law and the commonwealth.

15. Other scholars have noted the importance of multitude for Hobbes. See, for examples, Michael Hardt and Antonio Negri, *Empire* (Cambridge: Harvard University Press, 2000), 102–3; Michael Hardt and Antonio Negri, *Multitude: War and Democracy in the Age of Empire* (New York: Penguin, 2005), 238–39; and Mary G. Dietz, "Hobbes's Subject as Citizen," in *Thomas Hobbes and Political Theory*, ed. Mary G. Dietz (Lawrence: University Press of Kansas, 1990). But few have focused interpretations of Hobbes upon it; see, for example, David Boucher, *Political Theories of International Relations: From Thucydides to the Present* (New York: Oxford University Press, 1998), 155, citing Hobbes, *Leviathan*, 67–68.

16. Hobbes, *Leviathan*, 88–89.

passes for government, in that it comprises institutions and imparts a sense of order, it lacks the unity and cohesion that Hobbes argues is possible with a right understanding of sovereignty and subjection. To the extent that Hobbes's remarks about multitude can be said to represent his rejection of democracy, the close association of interests and multitude directs our attention to the democratic side of interests, as we have already seen it active in the debates at Putney—revealing at once its constitutive power and its instability. As Hobbes sees it, only the formation of the commonwealth, the subjection of the populace, and the suppression of dangerous difference can overcome the effects of the insecure attachments of interest.

Although Hobbes wishes to escape from the condition of multitude, knowledge of interests is just as crucial to Hobbes as is knowledge of human nature—but these are not one and the same. Warning of the illusions and enchantment to which human beings are prone, he writes that "such is the ignorance and aptitude to error generally of all men, but especially of them that have not much knowledge of natural causes, and of the nature and interests of men, as by innumerable and easy tricks to be abused."[17] Hobbes figures knowledge of interests as distinct from knowledge of human beings and the natural world—a distinction that thinking of self-interest as a part of human nature is apt to miss. Consistent with their pertinence to multitude and unlike nature, interests are thoroughly conventional. Given their conventionality, they are all the more appropriately and urgently in need of replacement with conventions that are consistent with right reason. From the very beginning, then, Hobbes sees interests as set apart from the basic foundations of sovereignty—except perhaps in that they are a complex problem that a theory of sovereignty must urgently address.

Reasoning "One's Own" Against Interest

Hobbes's association of interests and multitude suggests interest's potential inadequacy as a form of subjectivity and the foundation of sovereignty. His reflections on the effects of interests in public discourse take his concern a step further: Hobbes sees interests as prone to dissolve people's common endeavors because they render their speech inconstant.[18] Interests impinge deeply on the fitness of speech for reason and science; they thereby not only contribute to

---

17. Ibid., 304.
18. It is from this concern of Hobbes that Quentin Skinner briefly notes interest as a matter of negative concern, but the larger context of Hobbes's other uses of "interest" remain unexamined. See Skinner, *Reason and Rhetoric*, 429.

the myriad failures of multitude but threaten to erode and disrupt civil society. Hobbes's reflection on the ways interests impinge upon language suggests how clearly he saw what more recent theorizing of interests has failed to grasp: the role of language as a critical, if not primary, medium for the work of interests in politics. To see how this is so, consider Hobbes's discussion of language in *Leviathan*—and his first reference to interest in this text. After describing speech as the foundation of human community and discussing its abuses, Hobbes sorts words into four classes, each of which has proper uses; good argument will use words appropriately, according to their proper kinds. Reason, he notes, will particularly exclude words that fall into a category he calls inconstant names:

> The names of such things as affect us, that is, which please and displease us, because all men be not alike affected with the same thing, nor the same man at all times, are in common discourses of men, of *inconstant* signification. . . . When we conceive the same things differently, we can hardly avoyd different naming of them. For though the nature of that we conceive, be the same; yet the diversity of our reception of it, in respect to different constitutions of our body, and prejudices of opinion, gives every thing a tincture of our different passions. And therefore in reasoning, a man must take heed of words; which besides the signification of what we imagine of their nature, have a signification also of the nature, disposition, and interest of the speaker; such as are the names of Vertues and Vices. (*Leviathan*, 31)

Though inconstant names cannot be given proper definitions, they signify nonetheless; an inconstant name refers not only to its ostensive object, but also to the interest of the speaker, which in turn reflects ineluctable differences. Because Hobbes adds "interest" as a third term, distinct from the other two, this passage begins to hint at how these differences exceed those attending the constitution of the body and the prejudices of opinion. And evidently, the influence of a speaker's interest is particularly dangerous, because Hobbes's warning against the intrusion of interests is more serious than the warning he offers against "Metaphors, or Tropes of speech," even though the latter are intended to deceive (26). Metaphors are "less dangerous" than the names whose inconstancy is generated by interest, he writes, "because they profess their inconstancy, while the others do not" (31).

Such inconstancy openly saturates the moral discourse of multitude. Although Hobbes's identification of interest as a root of this inconstancy appears as a simply cynical maneuver, it speaks to the vulnerability of moral discourse to the vagaries of life in such a condition. Because inconstant names signify disparate things when uttered by various people or even by the same person at different times—which is to say, because interests are intrinsically changeable—Hobbes declares that "such names can never be the true grounds of any ratiocination." Alluding to the Corcyraean revolution as depicted in Thucydides' *Peloponnesian War*,[19] Hobbes remarks in *Leviathan* that inconstant "are the names of Vertues, and Vices; For one man calleth *Wisdome,* what another calleth *feare;* and one *cruelty,* what another *justice;* one *prodigality;* what another *magnanimity;* and one *gravity,* what another *stupidity*" (31). Hobbes's allusion to Corcyra serves to disqualify the scholastic moral discourse of the "Schoolmen," who expound a moral philosophy upon these terms as a form of reason appropriate to political philosophy. For whatever the Schoolmen may offer by way of definitions, their terms can never do the work of moral philosophy proper because they will always be intruded upon by speakers' interests. The moral discourse of the multitude, Hobbes suggests, is a cover for appeals to interest analogous to the diffidence, invasions, and violence that plague the state of war. Given an English civil war that was being fought in part with an avalanche of pamphlets that were filled with conflicting invocations of "interest," could Hobbes's insistence that interests contravene reasoned discourse be an exile's dig at the bewildering vogue of this word in the partisan papers of his contemporaries? Civic virtues may play an important role in Hobbes's philosophy, but moral and political discourses alike are prone to the inconstant signification brought on by this newfangled language, and are therefore all the more wanting as bases of reason.

Even appeals to reason Hobbes reveals as inconstant—that is, to be in essence appeals to interest—as long as people are in the condition of multitude. Those living in multitude are prone to "receding from custome when their interest requires it" at times, but interest will also step in to bolster custom as a rationale for action. To that end, Hobbes cites interest (alongside, but distinct from, ambition, profit, and lust) as what "disposeth a man to make Custome and Example the rule of his actions" (73–74). That Hobbes consistently sees reason and interest as opposed to each other is further illustrated by Hobbes's dedication of *The Elements of Law* to William, earl of Newcastle. "From the two principle parts of our nature, Reason and Passion," writes Hobbes, "have

---

19. Thucydides, *The Peloponnesian War,* trans. Thomas Hobbes (Chicago: University of Chicago Press, 1989), 205–6.

proceeded two kinds of learning, mathematical and dogmatical. The former is free from controversies and dispute, because it consisteth in comparing figures and motion only; in which things truth and the interest of men oppose not each other. But in the later," he continues, "there is nothing not disputable, because it compareth men, and meddleth with their right and profit; in which, as oft as reason is against a man, so oft will a man be against reason."[20] Although this remark might seem to support the notion that people have a common interest in reason, Hobbes does not go so far; rather he says that they do not oppose geometry and mathematics, because this kind of learning does not bear on their interests. "Dogmatical" learning speaks to the positive differences from which people seek to profit. This is not to say that Hobbes therefore finds interests a sound basis for adopting reasoned discourse; he complains in *Leviathan* that people "appeale from custome to reason, and from reason to custome, as it serves their turn; receding from custome when their interest requires it, and setting themselves against reason, as oft as reason is against them."[21] Here Hobbes seems to imply that interest can lead people to reason. If so, this passage would support at least those readings of Hobbes that see him offering a program of interest. But the passage says merely that interest governs whether people choose reason or custom, which choice Hobbes would rather were steadied upon the mode of reasoning and reasons offered in *Leviathan* and his other works.

Hobbes's concern about interests in politics returns naturally from right reason to the public discourse of the multitude. Here, Hobbes's particular concern with the effects of interests suggests their legal and proprietary genesis. In the preface of the 1651 English translation of *De Cive*, Hobbes describes his prudence in having shielded many of his thoughts from exposure to "publique interest," so that "if anything appeared erroneous, hard, or obscure, I might correct, soften, and explain them."[22] Hobbes's Latin reads *publici juris*, which may as easily have been rendered "public judgment"; Hobbes's choice of "interest" for *juris* echoes a seventeenth-century context in which "interest" was still often associated with legal claims—the fitness of which as a model for public life Hobbes rejects. More important, and consistent with the particularities of juridical interest, the claims themselves originate in attachments to dominion and other goods: he locates interest in "domestique affairs," where, he says, one's "particular interest is concerned" (*De Cive*, 37); "interest" appears

20. Thomas Hobbes, *The Elements of Law* (Cambridge: Cambridge University Press, 1928), xvii.
21. Hobbes, *Leviathan*, 73.
22. Thomas Hobbes, *De Cive* (Oxford: Clarendon Press, 1983), 37.

analogous to the "great private estates" (159); and he associates "interest" and "dominion" (74). To the extent that interests have a material basis that underwrites their corrosive effects upon language, they are tied up not with appetites or passions, or even the more general "perpetuall and restlesse desire of Power after power" (70), but rather with holdings and attachments, and their only apparently principled and orderly claims thereto.

These interests are of particular threat to political philosophizing not only because of how they contravene reason but also in that they present themselves as a model basis for associational life; people in multitude, Hobbes notes, form "Systemes" on the basis of estate and dominion. And it is in their relation to systems that interests further depart from appetite, passion, and egoism. "Systemes," says Hobbes, comprise "any number of men joyned in one Interest, or one Businesse" and characterize the subordinate parts of a commonwealth, "which resemble the similar parts, or Muscles of a Body naturall" (155). These interests—such as churches, corporations, clubs, and other institutions of society organized for gain and perhaps self-preservation—are among the sinews of life in the condition between outright war and commonwealth. They connect the legal recognition of people as persons representing households and estates in matters of business and the associations of everyday life—the various relationships, holdings, and offices that make up property. The problem raised by Hobbes is that these systems are not effective as models for government. Examining this problem, Hobbes discusses the adjudication of an individual's "private interests" by an assembly on the question of whether buying votes is just or unjust (164). Hobbes thinks that it is just if there is no law forbidding it; however, in a court of law, a defendant may exclude a judge "whose interest maketh him suspect" (168). The problem here, as Hobbes sees it, lies in the difference between the person authorized as a public minister to judge, and the judge as an individual with particular attachments impeding reason and judgment. Mere systems cannot secure this distinction, which is partly why Hobbes urges his readers to look elsewhere.

Hobbes addresses the inconstancy and conflict that follow from the incursions of private attachments to the duties of offices and persons by substituting for these interests a notion of propriety that defines "one's own" and, therefore, delimits proper personality. Hobbes's turn from interests to propriety explains why, for all his references to dominion and estates as the attachments of multitude that appear as interests, as well as his awareness of the juridical context of interests, Hobbes does not mention interests in connection to propriety—the juridical context of interest claims alone is an insufficient basis for commonwealth. A theory of sovereignty independent of interests is needed. Hobbes's substitution of propriety for interests is critical because instead of connoting material goods and attachments in themselves, propriety further indicates one's worthiness of ownership (90, 101, 112, 125). Hobbes's turn to propriety is, moreover, an opportunity for him to address the problem of the goods whose scarcity he cites as a primary cause of conflict in the state of nature—a problem insufficiently avoided by people following their interests in multitude.

Hobbes's specification of propriety as the proper authority and boundary of actions and attachments replaces contested and inconstant interests with propriety as a measure of one's own. Propriety, according to Hobbes, is "the Rules, whereby every man may know, what goods he may enjoy, and what Actions he may do, without being molested by any of his fellow Subjects" (125). Being the rules, rather than the goods and actions in themselves, propriety is unique to the commonwealth constituted by sovereignty: "for before constitution of Sovereign Power," Hobbes reminds the reader, "all men had a right to all things; which necessarily causeth war; and therefore this Proprietie, being necessary to Peace, and depending on Sovraign power, is the Act of that Power, in order to the publique peace" (125). Closely connected to propriety is the notion of one's own, a notion I shall follow closely as I examine the relation of interest and subjection later on. "Where there is no *Own*," he writes, "that is, no Propriety, there is no Injustice; and where there is no coercive power erected, that is, where there is no Common-wealth, there is no Propriety" (101).

Unlike estates, dominion, and interests, a person's propriety can never come into conflict with the sovereign and its civil law; nor, under conditions of sovereignty, can one's propriety conflict with another's. And so the problems related to judgment that Hobbes saw threatened by the intrusion of interest are removed. Moreover, propriety admits of one person's claims against another only in cases of injury, which itself is a concept relevant only within a commonwealth. And under no circumstances can propriety serve as a claim against sovereign power. The implication that proprietary relations are harmonious while interests threaten the opposite is a critical one, for Hobbes believes civil society to be corrupted to the extent that it is lacking in reason. So interest is to multitude as propriety is to sovereignty, and Hobbes's concern is to move from the former relation to the latter. Even to the extent, then, that we may recover Hobbes as a theorist concerned with possessive individualism,[23]

---

23. On the recovery of Macpherson's reading of Hobbes as a theorist of possessive individualism, see Michael Bray, "Macpherson Restored? Hobbes and the Question of Social Origins," *History of Political Thought* 28, no. 1 (2007).

we should also see how Hobbes aims to capture for sovereignty the power to distinguish proper holdings and doings from the myriad attachments found in multitude. The vainglory and pride of the emerging aristocratic (and even commercial) gentry are controlled in part by moral reeducation, but also in part by reestablishing the power of the state to set the terms of their engagements with one another and with the lower classes.

Sovereignty and the Peril of Interest

The substitution of propriety for interests is an important, but often-overlooked objective of Hobbes's political thought. It is in some ways more troubling, and troubled, than his better-known reformation of opinions. Some readers see in Hobbes's recognition of the importance of opinion a small but critical opening for civic if not democratic virtue; others point out how Hobbes's own reformation (if not manipulation) of opinion is critical to his project.[24] The similar and perhaps greater problem presented by interests for sovereignty therefore raises the question about whether—and how—they may represent a tenacious democratic force.

Opinions, which for Hobbes are the "break[ing] off the chain of a man's discourse . . . in the Enquiry of the truth of *Past*, and *Future*" (47), arise when people ground their discourse in poorly joined definitions or no definitions at all (48). The former is a symptom of madness (51); Hobbes describes the latter, that is, beginning without definitions, as someone's beginning a discourse rather with some "contemplation of his own" (48). Opinion presents a complex problem for which Hobbes offers a threefold solution. In part, the problem with opinion is that inquiry is not allowed to run its full course toward the truth—a difficulty Hobbes addresses by means of *Leviathan* and his other works. But opinion also reflects the difficulty of knowing the future, which Hobbes addresses in parts 3 and 4 of *Leviathan* by turning to scripture.[25] Last, Hobbes's redefinition of one's own as a matter of propriety rather than of interests is a further—and critically overlooked—basis for reforming opinion.

---

24. Dietz, "Hobbes's Subject as Citizen"; Lloyd, *Ideals as Interests in Hobbes's Leviathan*.

25. Hobbes does note opinion and belief as causes of disorder, but Lloyd goes on to treat these as synonymous, so Hobbes's worries about opinions become worries about beliefs; see Lloyd, *Ideals as Interests in Hobbes's Leviathan*, 39–41. But Hobbes distinguishes opinion and belief: opinion regards one's *own*, and belief (or faith) regards the stock one puts in not doubting the ability of another to know the truth. While Lloyd is convincing that engaging beliefs is a critical part of Hobbes's work in parts 2 and 3 of *Leviathan*, its grounding in Hobbes's concerns about opinion may be overdrawn, particularly in light of the importance given to scriptural examples in part 3.

By this latter effort in particular Hobbes shows how reason and sovereignty combat people's ill-defined notions of their "own" and hence bring their contemplations in line with the truth. Hobbes thereby suggests that if opinion cannot be eradicated, it at least can be reformed to support sovereignty—a task all the more important for Hobbes, given that in *Behemoth* he famously concedes the importance of opinion as a practical foundation of order. This point is often raised by readers seeking the slightest glint of democratic hope in Hobbes's work: "The power of the mighty hath no foundation," writes Hobbes, "but in the opinion and belief of the people."[26]

But interest threatens to disrupt powers that are constituted by reason or can otherwise be given practical foundations in the reformation of opinion. In other words, though opinion can be reformed in part by the sovereign's specification of one's own, interest remains especially intractable. Although interest is closely related to belief, faith, and opinion for Hobbes—many of his references to interests share passages with these other terms—interest itself cannot be reformed like opinions or regulated like propriety to serve as a basis for sovereignty and therefore of peace. Instead, sovereignty is best organized to account for and quarantine interest's destructive potential in other ways, which themselves illustrate how "interest" entails a plurality that is beyond reduction or reform. This irreducible plurality underwrites Hobbes's fear that interest will continue to be a source of potential trouble even under conditions of sovereignty, a difficulty that is most fully revealed when Hobbes confronts two problems within the commonwealth: the interests of counselors, and the inefficacy of sovereign assemblies.

COUNSEL. Counsel, according to Hobbes, is a teaching relationship aimed at changing and shaping experiences and desires; as such, it is critical to Hobbes's humanism. More particularly, counsel is a form of language comprising imperatives regarding desire and aversion,[27] in the shape of conveying counselors' and other's experience of their actions' consequences (*Leviathan*, 179). Whereas the imperative language of command instructs a person to act for the good of the one who commands, when providing counsel "a man saith, *Doe*, or *Doe not this*, and deduceth his reasons from the benefit that arriveth by it to him to whom he saith it. And from this it is evident," Hobbes continues, "that he that giveth Counsell, pretendeth onely (whatsoever he intendeth) the good

---

26. Thomas Hobbes, *Behemoth; or, the Long Parliament*, ed. Ferdinand Tönnies (Chicago: University of Chicago Press, 1990), 16.
27. Hobbes, *Leviathan*, 45.

of him, to whom he giveth it" (176). Counselors will always appear to serve the good of those they counsel, so Hobbes instructs the reader to ascertain the difference between good and poor counsel by means of examining interests. "The first condition of a good Counsellour," Hobbes writes, is "that his Ends, and Interest, be *not inconsistent* with the Ends and Interest of him he Counselleth" (179, emphasis added). Although Hobbes does not fantasize that the interests of a counselor and his ken will coincide, much less be the same (so intrinsically plural they are), he does aim to preclude conflict.

Being both an imperative language of desire on the one hand, and aimed at the benefit of its audience on the other, counsel educates people to the proper desires of their persons. But being a *form* of language, counsel is therefore prone to the *problems* of language. Exploring at length in illustrating how the sovereign (and other persons) may receive counsel, Hobbes examines these problems in turn: metaphors, as we have seen before, must be excluded from counsel because "they openly profess deceipt" (52). But just as in speech more generally, the inconstant signification that comes from interest does not openly profess its deceit, but rather obscures it. Hobbes's discussion of counsel therefore recalls his earliest association of "interest" with "inconstant names." He writes that the "Vertues, and Defects of Counsell, are the same with the Vertues, and Defects Intellectuall. . . . They that give Counsell to the Representative person of a Common-wealth, may have, and have often their particular ends, and passions, that render their Counsells always suspected, and many times unfaithful" (179). Hobbes is concerned about how interests corrupt counsel because there too signification is inconstant owing to diversity in what counts as one's own. Counsel is corrupt precisely to the extent that counselors—like judges in assembly—are "bribed by their own interest" (178).

Among multitudes, counsel degenerates to exhortation, doing little more than stoking opinions with rhetoric and deceit. Here the corrupting influence of a counselor's interest remains hidden owing to the lack of dialogue (178). Striking an almost Socratic note, Hobbes appears somewhat more sanguine about the prospect that dialogue and cross-examination can reveal the corrupting influence of interests when one individual counsels another (178), though the need for dialogue itself shows the impossibility of excluding interests entirely. Part of the sovereign's work of purging inconstant signification is exercised, importantly if not primarily, in his ongoing and direct relationship with counselors and other teachers. And the work to be done is not the reformation of their interests, but rather ascertaining the difference between their interests and his own. Short of dialogue, however, poor counsel is worse than none at all; direct experience is less likely to be tainted, because "the naturall objects of sense . . . work upon [the Representative person of the Commonwealth] without passion, or interest of their own" (179). These objects lack passion, because they lack internal motion; they lack interest, because they neither speak nor have the worldly attachments of a counselor.

Given Hobbes's own efforts to be a good counselor, his worry that any plural and deliberative relationship or body will encounter the difficulties of inconstant signification reaches to concern about the reception of *Leviathan* itself. Before propounding ten basic tenets of civil law (each corresponding to one of the Ten Commandments), Hobbes the latter-day Moses records his worry that his work will not be read, carefully studied, and truly understood. Whether *kings* see sovereignty clearly "concerneth my particular interest, at this day, very little" (232–33), he writes. If it should "fall into the hands of a Soveraign, who will consider it himselfe," it must be received "without the help of any interested, or envious Interpreter," for bad counsel could twist Hobbes's work to uselessness. The subjects are his greater concern. "All men know," he writes, "that the obstructions to this kind of doctrine, proceed not so much from the difficulty of the matter, as from the interest of them that are to learn" (233)— indicating the great obstacles to be overcome by the multitude to receive his teaching. But he pushes forward nonetheless, continually cautioning his readers to scrutinize what among their attachments to defense of differences and particularity may impede their understanding of his text, and therefore, their proper subordination to sovereign power.

SOVEREIGNTY AND ASSEMBLY. The view that Hobbes sees interests as forces that powerfully and tenaciously disrupt sovereignty withstands even his most apparently sanguine remarks about the possibility of a "public interest" and the fitness of sovereignty to serve it. These remarks have given many readers some comfort that Hobbes is concerned about public welfare and even a common good. And they have been ignored by others who (like Skinner) simply note Hobbes's opposition to interests. Yet even Hobbes's remarks in regarding the possibility of a "public interest" suggest that appeals to interest reflect contestation around contracts that Hobbes is at pains to preclude. The possibility for a public interest, it turns out, depends on this interest not being itself a contractual matter. And a sovereign, as we know, is not a party to the contract that authorizes his person. Therefore, the public interest represents the monarch's particular interest, which a true commonwealth in turn identifies with the "public." But in order to arrive at a public interest so constituted, Hobbes must make the case for monarchy—and in elaborating this case, the disruptive power of interest plays a crucial supporting role.

The interest of the monarch is the exception that both proves the rule of interests as disruptive and subversive and spares subjects from how destructive plural interests are in politics more generally. "A Monarch cannot disagree with himselfe, out of envy, or interest," Hobbes notes, "but an Assembly may; and that to such a height, as may produce a Civil Warre" (132). Where the sovereign is an assembly of natural persons, as in the case of democracy and aristocracy, these persons may share prosperity and fortune but not interests (131), let alone *an* interest. What unity there is in any assemblage—or multitude—is necessarily contingent, and a sovereign assembly is therefore threatened by the same instability as a multitude. "Because by the diversity of Opinions, and Interests of men," a representative assembly "becomes oftentimes, and in cases of the greatest consequence, a mute Person, and unapt, as for many things else, so for the government of a Multitude, especially in times of Warre" (115). Even if a common enemy unites the multitude, when foreign war comes to an end, the multitude "must needs by the difference of their interests dissolve, and fall again into a Warre amongst themselves" (119).

Only when the person of the sovereign is one individual human being is "the private interest . . . the same as the publique" (131). Elaborating this claim, Hobbes writes:

> Whosoever beareth the Person of the people, or is one of that Assembly that bears it, beareth also his own naturall Person. And though he be carefull in his politique Person to procure the common interest; yet he is more, or no lesse carefull to procure the private good of himself, his family, kindred and friends; and for the most part, if the publique interest chance to cross the private, he preferrs the private: for the Passions of men, are commonly more potent than their Reason. From whence it follows, that where the publique and the private interest are most closely united, there is the publique most advanced. (131)

Echoes of the political pamphlets through which "interest" became a vogue word are unmistakable here.[28] Yet Hobbes's remark suggests that even those tracts which claim that the monarch is in a special position to know or safeguard

---

28. Gunn, "'Interest Will Not Lie.'"

"the Interest of England" miss the essentially particular and conflicting nature of interests. They err in offering a legal term regarding competing claims as the model for government, rather than seeing that the "public interest" is the one interest that can follow from the institution of sovereign power. The interest of the natural person identified with sovereignty does not threaten sovereignty *per se* because the sovereign does not contract with the subjects. Therefore, interest as a matter of contesting the performance and contingency of contracts does not threaten sovereign monarchy the way it erodes an assembly (132). The public can only have an interest when it is represented in the person of a monarch; otherwise it has many interests, dissension, and strife (115).

Instead of reading Hobbes's endorsement of monarchy as an assurance that the sovereign will serve the interests of his subjects, we must read it as a response to his contemporaries' invocations of a public interest that guards against the corrosive effects of plural claims upon the fitness of people for government. So although Hobbes acknowledged (and in some respects repeated) his contemporaries' discussions of how the ruler could be made to serve the public good, he sees interest as too unreliable to solve the problem of good government, and indeed as a constantly threatening impediment to the contractual relationships he posits as the right solution. Just as acceptance of the sovereign's actions as one's own is fundamental to the contract, so too commonwealth entails accepting the particular interest of the monarch's natural person as the only possible semblance of a common one.

Difference, the multitude, domestic affairs, riches, and the corrosion of reason: Hobbes's theory is not based on interests, it is a plea to leave interests behind, precisely because the fluctuation and insecurity of these attachments show up in public discourse as a heuristic flexibility that foils the apprehension of truth. Contrary to reason, interests threaten continual interference in sovereign power, by rendering inconstant language, counsel, and recourse to reason. No account of Hobbes's view of interests can be complete without accounting for this picture of interests. Why, then, have modern readers been so keen to find Hobbes's philosophy as based upon, rather than inimical to, interests—and what about the politics of interests do these accounts obscure?

Hobbes as Social Scientist

It's a familiar point that most interpretations of Hobbes's work in the past century fall into two camps: those which emphasize subjection, obligation, and fear; and those which emphasize interests.[29] But just as Hobbes's own references to "interest" are overlooked when interpreting Hobbes as a theorist of interest, also rarely noted is that this division in interpretations has a historical dimension of its own. The interest-based interpretations emerged only in the middle of the twentieth century, and the readings based on subjection, obligation, and fear reemerged relatively recently. *This* history adds another layer to the problem of interest in Hobbes, namely, what modern readers' mistaken attribution of "interest" to Hobbes reveals about the twentieth-century vogue of "interest" in political studies. This more recent fashion may reflect political science's following the currents of modern philosophy in at least one respect: just as modernity figures reason as the bridge between objectivity and subjectivity, political studies figure interest as the bridge between the transcendent and the psychological. Yet the ill fit of Hobbes's view of interests with the views attributed to him throughout the latter half of the twentieth century suggests the shortcomings of turning to "interest" to bridge these pairs.

Readings of Hobbes as a theorist of interest first emerged in the 1930s, as A. E. Taylor defended his Kantian, deontological reconstruction of Hobbes *against* a view that Hobbes's thought is founded in people's desires.[30] Reflecting a tenet of Kantian philosophy, Taylor held that desires and duty are distinct.[31]

---

29. See, for examples of the Hobbes literatures categorized in this way, Samantha Frost, "Faking It: Hobbes's Thinking-Bodies and the Ethics of Dissimulation," *Political Theory* 29, no. 1 (2001), and Dietz, "Hobbes's Subject as Citizen."

30. The most immediate and critically negative reception of Hobbes in the 1660s and 1670s did rephrase some of his points in the newly fashionable and disapproving term "self-interest," particularly as popularly depicted by "Hobbish" characters appearing in Restoration drama. See James Black, "The Influence of Hobbes on Nahum Tate's King Lear," *Studies in English Literature* 7, no. 3 (1967). These characterizations of Hobbes's theory are historically telling, but are nonetheless inapposite to my purposes in this chapter.

31. Taylor argued that seeing Hobbes's theory as based in desires confuses two questions: "Why I *ought* to behave as a good citizen?" and "What inducement can be given to me to do so if my knowledge of the obligation to do so is not in itself sufficiently effective?" The answer to the first question, for Taylor, lies in God's pronouncement of natural law; the second question is distinct and philosophically irrelevant. "Even if we reject [Hobbes's egoistic moral] psychology *in toto*," he writes, "so long as we grant the premise that civil society rests upon a 'covenant' to obey whatever shall be enacted . . . I am only free to be guided by my personal opinion as to what is equity when the civil law has seen fit to leave me free." See A. E. Taylor, "The Ethical Doctrine of Hobbes," *Philosophy* 13, no. 52 (1938): 36, 45. Howard Warrender carried this debate into the 1960s. Following Leo Strauss and A. E. Taylor, Warrender continued to argue—most prominently against John Plamenatz—that Hobbes's theory is based primarily in moral obligation rather than self-interest. See Warrender, *Political Philosophy of Hobbes;* Plamenatz, "Mr. Warrender's Hobbes"; and Howard Warrender, "The Place of God in Hobbes's Philosophy: A Reply to Mr. Plamenatz," *Political Studies* 8, no. 1 (1960). But unlike Strauss, Warrender finds coherence in Hobbes's thought by arguing that obligation remains steadfastly if covertly connected to the commands of God. Warrender discusses the idea that Hobbes's subject is obligated through self-interest, though Warrender explicitly

Seeming not to notice that it cannot but be in a person's interest to perform his obligations under the Hobbesian covenant, Taylor described as "interests" the inclinations he argued could not be at the foundations of Hobbes's philosophy. Although Taylor was right to note that interests cannot serve as proper foundations of sovereignty, his identification of "interest" and desire made him right for a fatefully wrong reason. Not only does Hobbes treat interests and desires differently, "interest" is poorly suited for Taylor's defense: one cannot wholly exclude interest from duty, because there is always an element of "one's interest" in the performance of one's duty and an element of duty in acting upon one's interest. Whatever the merits of the Kantian interpretation of Hobbes, lost in this discussion is the aspect of Hobbes's view of interests that cannot be squared with a modern debate in these terms, namely, Hobbes's rejection of interests as a model for the institution of commonwealth because they reflect a plurality of contested claims to one's own. The difficulty (if not impossibility) of excluding the plural side of interests altogether motivated Hobbes himself to reject interest as a vehicle for securing sovereignty, even if opinions and propriety could be reformed and interests quarantined so that each person might conform him- or herself to the others.

Political science through the middle of the twentieth century was evidently inapt to draw on Hobbes's own view of interests as contestation, but well suited to promote the debate around Hobbes as a theorist of interest in the terms that confused the Kantian debates. Perhaps because of the ability of Taylor's ill-chosen term to slide between subjective and objective, between the psychological and transcendent, the place of interests swiftly became a new center of a debate over Hobbes's thought. In short order it displaced the Kantian terms "immediate inclination" and "duty," then it replaced a wider range of Hobbesian ideas, spreading through the literature like an invasive weed. The vexing tension between Hobbesian depictions of psychology and obligation become instead a question of what interests Hobbes "really thinks" are at the basis of

---

argues that viewing the subject's obedience as a product of self-interest is already precluded by an understanding of *Leviathan* as a theory of obligation. See Warrender, *Political Philosophy of Hobbes*, 204 and 209. That is, the deontological aspects of Hobbes's thought make speculation as to the interests of Hobbesian subjects irrelevant to an understanding of Hobbes's philosophy. Warrender further argues that Hobbes holds a distinction between good and evil on the one hand, and pleasure and pain on the other—and that the egoistic psychology that motivates self-interested behavior is addressed to the latter. Citing Hobbes's *De Corpore Politico*, Warrender argues that self-interest is a Benthamic psychological hedonism that Hobbes explicitly rejects; see Warrender, *Political Philosophy of Hobbes*, 210. Strauss, by contrast, rejects the notion that Hobbes stood against political hedonism. See Leo Strauss, "On the Spirit of Hobbes's Political Philosophy," in *Hobbes Studies*, ed. K. C. Brown (Oxford: Basil Blackwell, 1965), 3.

political order.³² Given midcentury behavioralist attachment to interests as such a basis, it's no surprise that the question of interests in Hobbes's theory attracted the attention of various interpreters who examined Hobbes's *scientia civilis* as a precursor to modern political science. Sheldon Wolin provides a prominent and influential example—particularly in that Wolin criticized, rather than celebrated, the behavioralist interest-based science of politics he saw Hobbes as inaugurating. In *Politics and Vision* Wolin describes Hobbes as centering a philosophy of politics upon interest as that which "unites the members of any political association."³³ For Wolin, Hobbes is the consummate theorist of interest and the forebear to the ascendancy of liberalism and social science.³⁴

Hobbes's placement of interest at the center of political association is all the more formidable an achievement, according to Wolin, because of three essential features, still familiar to twentieth-century social science, that Wolin attributes to the concept of interest. First, Wolin intimates that Hobbes insists "on the 'rationality' of individual interests," rationality that threatens to destroy the public character of reason. Second, interests are "radically individual, unceasingly dynamic, and fundamentally unsharable" by nature. And third, they are essentially competitive, because "the doctrine of interests presupposes . . . a condition of relative scarcity" (*Politics and Vision*, 277). Hobbes's success in basing sovereignty on these interests is worrisome, according to Wolin, because in its wake, "to the extent that politics did not appear vitally linked to interests, it held no compelling attraction" (280). Hobbes transforms the

32. Even though many modern interpreters still seek coherence in Hobbes's philosophy, deontological reconstructions of Hobbes's philosophy mostly subsided after the 1960s. Though reasons for this change are complex, the basic contours are relatively evident. Strauss's view that Hobbes was a nonbeliever who prudently couched his secular arguments in appeals to Christianity and God gradually attained the status of a received truth; see Leo Strauss, *The Political Philosophy of Hobbes, Its Basis and Genesis* (Oxford: Oxford University Press, 1936), 74–75. Meanwhile, Oakeshott persuasively dissolved the search for a single coherent reconstruction of Hobbes's political thought, acknowledging that Hobbes's doctrine is sensibly if not seamlessly fashioned from several perspectives, including Hobbes's egoistic psychology. See Oakeshott, "Introduction," li. So Oakeshott assembles Hobbes's deontology from (at least) two different kinds of obligation: self-interest on the one hand, and moral on the other (lx). The mix of these, found in *Leviathan*, Oakeshott calls "political obligation" (lxi). Later, both Wolin and Macpherson dismantled the barrier separating the philosophical interpretation of Hobbes's thought from its place in history, opening new lines of inquiry to replace timeworn debates over the nature of obligation in Hobbes. See Macpherson, *Possessive Individualism*, 1–8, and Wolin, *Politics and Vision*, chap. 8 and 478–79 n. 124.

33. Wolin, *Politics and Vision*, 277.

34. Wolin's later reading of Hobbes is perhaps more familiar, and it points in fundamentally different directions from his study of Hobbes in *Politics and Vision*. While my critique of *Politics and Vision* supports Wolin's later argument regarding the shaping of subjects by sovereignty, I bring this insight to bear on the problem of interests which Wolin's later work mostly neglects. See Wolin, *Hobbes and the Epic Tradition of Political Theory*.

radically individual quality into a single interest that, while transcendent, does not unify the members of society but rather preserves their atomization, precluding the in-between plurality of a public sphere. Wolin's ultimate concern about Hobbes's innovation is therefore straightforward: "To elevate interest" as Hobbes did "was to single out what was essentially private and least capable of representation at a public level" (277)—"public," for Wolin, meaning not governmental but rather deliberative and plural. Modern, Hobbesian political science has lost its public face, a fact revealed in its inability to conceive of politics as an activity with fundamentally transformative power (285).

Wolin's reading of Hobbes in *Politics and Vision* was widely influential in the literature on "interest," even if it was superseded (by Wolin himself, and others) in the literature on Hobbes.[35] It's ironic that Wolin's reading of "interests" as central to Hobbes's theory, to social science, and to liberalism stands behind the many and various celebratory historical discussions of political interests that I have revisited and contested in the previous two chapters—Wolin's own critical despair notwithstanding.[36] And although he wishes to loosen the grip of social science on the minds of those who study politics, the modern, social-scientific view of "interest" he finds in Hobbes's texts has a firmer hold, and has proven potent as a rubric for reading Hobbes even among newer (but no less powerful) schools of political thought.

The ascendance of behavioralism in political science when Wolin published *Politics and Vision* has its analogue in the recent fortunes of rational choice theory in political science and political theorizing. Therefore, it's perhaps inevitable that rational choice theorists would also turn to Hobbes to find a forebear of their new *scientia civilis*. The three aspects of "interest" that Wolin identified as endemic to liberalism and social science in the era of behavioralism have counterparts in the three "dogmas" of moral philosophy David Gauthier adopts from economics and finds in Hobbes's work.[37] Lending to "Hobbes's

---

35. See Wolin, *Hobbes and the Epic Tradition of Political Theory*.
36. Citing Wolin (not Hobbes) as an authority, J. A. W. Gunn writes that "there seems to be no basis for denying that Hobbes places unusual emphasis on self-interest." By way of Gunn's book, Wolin's reading of Hobbes made its way into Albert O. Hirschman's account. Citing this passage of Gunn's work, Hirschman too treats Hobbes as the foremost early modern theorist of "interest." Subsequent writings that have taken Hirschman's essay as their point of departure similarly offhandedly impute to Hobbes the view of persons that modern liberalism and social science present. See Gunn, *Politics and the Public Interest*, 59, and Hirschman, *The Passions and the Interests*, 42.
37. David Gauthier, *Moral Dealing: Contracts, Ethics, and Reason* (Ithaca: Cornell University Press, 1990). Gauthier's first and second dogmas echo respectively Wolin's second and first elements. See also Gauthier, "Hobbes's Social Contract." For a somewhat different rational-choice reading of Hobbes, see Hampton, *Hobbes and the Social Contract Tradition*.

conceptions ... the precision of contemporary formulations," Gauthier's first dogma rewrites Hobbes's statement that "private Appetite is the measure of Good, and Evill" (*Leviathan*, 111) as saying that Hobbes "treat[s] value as dependent on choice or appetite" as expressions of "utility and preference."[38] These utilities and preferences are the object of the second dogma, "that rationality is maximization: the rational individual 'will maximize the extent to which his objective is achieved.'"[39] This objective, so pursued, is by Gauthier's third dogma nontuistic, and expressed in terms of interest, presumably as a synonym for preferences and utilities: "Persons are conceived to take no interest in one another's interests ... in Hobbes's account. [Man] may have to accommodate [his fellows'] interests to attain his own, but in themselves their interests are not his concern" (*Moral Dealing*, 13). Taken together, these dogmas assert that private appetites are what the person is said to maximize by means of reason understood as individual, private deliberation (13). Gauthier argues that sovereignty—in the institution of the contract—restructures the regularities in the behavior of persons, constituting a moral order as "a uniquely dominant set of conventions ... for men who, seeking their own preservation, must seek peace" (16). In other words sovereignty takes individuals as they are and substitutes right reason for natural reason (20–22)—an argument similar to the one Wolin offers, albeit in a different idiom, about the "sovereign definer."[40]

Both of these social-scientific accounts of Hobbes treat interest as a faculty or appetite that each individual holds or enjoys privately. Identifying an interest in self-preservation as fundamental to the enjoyment or security of that private faculty or appetite, they see Hobbes as creating political order that fundamentally reinforces or respects the individualism, or nontuism, of each individual by doing away with conflict but not with egoism. Yet by rendering interests private, unsharable, and nontuistic, and the enjoyment of these interests as predicated on securing the egoistic self that is said to "have" these interests in the state of nature, Wolin's and Gauthier's readings of Hobbes miss what's most distinctive in Hobbes's view of interests. They miss how interests always threaten to disrupt reason, covenants, and order more generally. They miss Hobbes's assertion that interests are never a foundation of sovereignty, though in the unique guise of the "public interest" they can be its effect. Hobbes seeks to eliminate the open contestation and shaping of personality

---

38. Gauthier, *Moral Dealing*, 12.
39. Gauthier, *Moral Dealing*, 11. Gauthier is quoting D. M. Winch, *Analytical Welfare Economics* (New York: Penguin, 1971), 16.
40. Wolin, *Politics and Vision*, 266.

that appeals to interest bring to politics, preserving this shaping instead for sovereign power. Therefore, these readings of Hobbes, and the social-scientific paradigm they represent, miss how the institution of the contract and powers of sovereignty reconfigure the person and its desires, and exclude the attachments of the multitude and even civil society that prompt contested appeals to interest in the first place. The problem for Hobbes is not that interests are individual or unsharable, but rather that they are inconstant and contested.

Given how uneasily the three "essential elements" or "dogmas" of interest fit with Hobbes's own preoccupations about interests, Hobbes's theory suggests ways to rethink interest as a basis for the social science that Wolin, Gauthier, and many others hold Hobbes to have in part prefigured. Suspending the equation of "appetite" and "self-preservation" that underwrites seeing interests at the foundation of sovereignty—in Wolin's, Gauthier's, and many others' views—opens Hobbesian interest theory to the possibility that morality and rationality are not the only changes effected by Hobbes's contract. Rather, it highlights how the object of desire and of the law of nature, namely, the "self" to be preserved and its appetites, are subject to correction and amendment. In accepting the temptation of the modern language of interest to equate appetite and self-preservation, we assume and indeed naturalize the kind of subject that Hobbes, who sees a side of interest distinct from these, has in mind to create. We do so without seeing the possibilities of subjectivity otherwise—possibilities of which Hobbes was himself acutely aware—but more important, our way of assuming and naturalizing these proper subjects obscures not only subjectivity as an effect of power, but also the power of appeals to interest to disrupt proper subjectivity. Hobbes's theory turns out to be a way of seeing the present-day language of interest as a resource for the political transformation of persons and communities today, in light of our widespread theoretical convictions that sovereignty cannot offer a compelling account of subjectivity.

Self-Preservation as an Interest

As a most fundamental and indeed incontrovertible interest, self-preservation is a linchpin of present-day political thinking among citizens, pundits, and professional students of politics. Hence the fascination—and horror—at suicide bombing in present-day political culture, according to which the very idea that another human would willingly die in the service of an alternative to (the present) order is a source of terror for most. Hence we arrive at the present-day appeal—perhaps even the modern inevitability—of seeing an interest in self-preservation as the natural law of political order, and Hobbes as its Moses.[41]

Hobbes does link peace to a desire for preservation, the opposite of which is death, by means of reason. "The Passions that encline men to Peace," he writes, "are Feare of Death; Desire of such things as are necessary to commodious living; and Hope by their Industry to obtain them. . . . And Reason suggesteth convenient Articles of Peace, upon which men may be drawn to agreement" (*Leviathan*, 90). But describing this trio of reason, peace, and the self to be preserved as an interest is troubled by Hobbes's need to wrestle determinations of one's own from the domain of interests and secure them as propriety. And so although Hobbes does remark, after surveying the laws of nature, that "all men agree on this, that Peace is Good" (111), the "for whom?" is less obvious than it may appear to present-day readers whose commonsense notions of person are defined by the only apparently straightforward appeals to embodiment and individuality. Therefore, Hobbes's frequent qualification of the object of self-preservation as one's "own" must be treated in light of the propriety, which, as we have seen, is the rules defining one's "own" enabled by sovereignty. This qualification is frequent in Hobbes. His definition of the "First Right of Nature" provides only the most prominent example. "The Liberty each man hath," writes Hobbes, "to use his own power, as he will himselfe, for the preservation of his own Nature; that is to say, of his own Life; and consequently, of doing any thing, which in his own Judgement, and Reason, hee shall conceive to be the aptest means thereto" (91). Hobbes's emphasis on the preservation of one's own in this passage recalls his remark that one's "own" is a matter of propriety and therefore is determined in the civil state (101); similarly, Hobbes elsewhere emphasizes the person—as opposed to the physical individual—as what is to be preserved in a commonwealth, and therefore as the proper object of the will (94). Hobbes writes that "the motive, and end for which this [i.e., pertaining to the covenant] renouncing and transferring of Right is introduced, is nothing else but the security of a man's person, in his life, and in the means of so preserving life, as not to be weary of it" (93). Even if the law of nature were to secure one's natural person (which to a present-day reader might signify

---

41. Warrender may have been the last major scholar of Hobbes to argue for a distinction between self-interest and self-preservation. See Warrender, *Political Philosophy of Hobbes*. Jean Hampton reads Hobbes as a psychological monist on the argument that although people have many desires, the desire for self-preservation is predominant. See Hampton, *Hobbes and the Social Contract Tradition*, 17. Therefore the contract serves to subordinate other desires to the interest in self-preservation. S. A. Lloyd describes self-preservation as a "transcendent interest" in Hobbes's work; see Lloyd, *Ideals as Interests in Hobbes's Leviathan*.

consciousness and embodiment), determination of this natural person is indistinct from Hobbes's concern to capture one's "own" for sovereignty; Hobbes defines the natural person as "he ... whose words or actions ... are considered as his owne" (111). The passive voice raises the question "by whom?" and the answer, of course, is "by others." Within a commonwealth, these others are those who have contracted with their peers to obey the sovereign's command.

Hobbes gives us other reasons to resist locating the self to be preserved in the body as a stable and self-evident object for the subjects' deliberation, maximization, or concern, despite his well-known remarks about "Wounds, and Chayns, and Imprisonment" and the like (93, 98). In the first instance we must remember that chains and imprisonment are not merely confinements of the body, but are also powerful limitations on communication and the scope and nature of relationships with others. Consider also Hobbes's comment in *De Cive*, that "it is ... neither absurd nor reprehensible, neither against the dictates of true reason, for a man to use all his endeavors to preserve and defend his body and the members thereof from death and sorrows."[42] Hobbes's distinct references to the body and members, and the language of the sorrows and death of "members thereof," rather than sorrows for the death or injury of the body, suggests that people's bodies extend beyond what Hobbes elsewhere called "the Body naturall" (115)—at least, when it comes to the defense that self-preservation is meant to entail. The early modern notion of marriage as a covenant in which man and woman are united into one body aptly exemplifies this way of thinking about the body. In marriage, a man's body includes the members of his household, not to mention its goods—the body corresponds to dominion, and even may be contested and inconstant as the interests pertaining to that dominion.[43] Otherwise, what might it mean for a member of the corporeal body (e.g., a hand) to experience sorrows, in light of Hobbes's attack on metaphor?[44]

Hobbes's discussion of injury supports the view that even what counts as the body, let alone the more complex and extensive self to be preserved, is first

42. Hobbes, *De Cive*, 1.7. For rational-choice discussions of this passage, see Gauthier, *Moral Dealing*, 14, and Hampton, *Hobbes and the Social Contract Tradition*, 23–24.
43. See, for examples of this discourse, John Winthrop, "Christian Charitie: A Model Hereof," in *The New England Puritans*, ed. Sydney V. James (New York: Harper & Row, 1968), 84, 89, 91–92. Early modern historians have further cautioned against taking early modern invocations of "the body" as referring to modern notions of the corporeal body. See, for example, Stephen Greenblatt, "Psychoanalysis and Renaissance Culture," in *Literary Theory/Renaissance Texts*, ed. Patricia Parker and David Quint (Baltimore: Johns Hopkins University Press, 1986).
44. The *OED* lists a sense of "sorrow" meaning bodily injury or physical pain as obsolete in English by the fifteenth century.

determined by sovereign power, and then becomes a matter to be meditated upon by the subject. He writes: "Because every Subject is by this Institution Author of all the Actions, and Judgements of the Soveraigne Instituted; it followes, that whatsoever he doth, it can be no injury to any of his Subjects; nor ought he be by any of them accused of Injustice" (*Leviathan*, 124). Because the sovereign is not a party to the covenant, and because his every action is a sovereign action authorized by those who have covenanted, subjects have no grounds for complaint against the sovereign. "Consequently," he continues, "he that complaineth of injury from his Sovereign, complaineth of that whereof he is the Author, and therefore ought not to accuse any man but himselfe; nor himselfe of injury; because to do injury to ones selfe, is impossible. It is true that they that have Sovereign power, may commit Iniquity; but not Injustice, or Injury in the proper signification" (124). It is impossible for the sovereign to commit injustice, just as it is impossible to do injury to oneself. Nevertheless, Hobbes does *not* say that it is impossible to complain of injury to oneself—but as Hobbes sees it, one ought not. But how can a subject accuse him- or herself of injury, if doing injury to oneself is impossible? The contradiction disappears if this complaint is a moment of discovery of one's own, that is, of propriety. A complaint of injury directed at the sovereign is properly directed to oneself: it is a moment in which one discovers his or her proper person, including the desires proper to this person.

This propriety must also include the appetites and passions that Hobbes's psychological account in the opening of *Leviathan* figures as themselves embodied. Passions *per se* do not confront human society with the specter of disorder; rather, society's problems are caused by a few passions in particular, which must be reformed, namely, envy, pride, and other ways people encounter their differences (119). Thus a covenant reconstructs reason and language and by doing so, the appetites and the body as well. Therefore, the "own" that is the object of the right of nature, that furthermore outlines the boundaries of the natural person, including his holdings, relationships, and desires, is in the first instance determined by sovereign power.[45] Interests stand in permanent opposition to the proper performance of the covenant in that they

---

45. This observation also fits with Tom Sorrell's reading that Hobbes situates felicity, "the smooth and orderly achievement of the many distinct desires one has in a lifetime," as the individual's predominant aim (without identifying felicity as self-interest). Nowhere does Sorrell claim that the order of these desires is set in advance of the contract, so Sorrell's reading accommodates the view that contracting can change and reorganize the desires one has. See Tom Sorrell, *Hobbes* (New York: Routledge, 1986), 100–101. Sorrell does mention interest very offhandedly, as though it is a synonym of desire, but does not rely on the word to do work in his reading of Hobbes.

represent the distortions of human discourse caused by goods and actions that are improper from the point of view of commonwealth. And so describing, as present-day readers do, both appetite and self-preservation as interests as a basis of Hobbesian science and a means of Hobbesian politics obscures how thoroughgoing is the subjection effected by Hobbes's reorientation of one's "own" from interests to propriety.

Hobbes is clear that sovereign power conforms subjects in their persons: the Sovereign "hath the use of so much Power and Strength conferred on him, that by terror thereof, he is inabled to conforme the wills of them all" (120). And not only their wills are conformed; Hobbes invokes the image of society as like a wall whose builder casts aside stones that cannot be easily cut to fit the others (106). This conformity is not absolute, but it nonetheless carries into the various enjoyments that commonwealth makes possible, which Hobbes says are primarily justified by their promotion of security (231). Even though Hobbes famously recognizes the commercial society of a commonwealth as open to various freedoms, subjects enjoy these freedoms as subjects so long as they remain in continual conformity with the person they have authorized whose desires are turned from vainglorious pursuits to the humble business of propriety and commodious living. Sovereignty does not respect identity; it generates it against the counter-generative power of appeals to interest.

As for peace or self-preservation as an "interest"—a staple of liberal, modern, and Western self-imagination—we must see how Hobbesian sovereignty seeks to stabilize and conform a self that is then apt to be preserved, and how appeals to interest, with their contestability, ever threaten the ability of sovereignty to achieve this aim. Because Hobbes appropriates the determination of one's own from the contested attachments that characterize interest, locating it instead in propriety consistent with sovereignty, self-preservation cannot be said to be an interest in Hobbes. Or at the very least, describing self-preservation as an interest must be seen as introducing contestation and changeability into the goods and actions that are considered one's own. By the same token, neither appetites nor egoism can rightly be said to be interests for Hobbes: appetites and egoism can be turned toward self-preservation once the proper person is defined by sovereign power, particularly given their basis in memory and the power of recent memory to trump the more distant (16). But interests, has we have seen, cannot be so reformed: they can only be quarantined by rigorous and dialogic examination of subjects' attachments, and by identification of the public interest with the private interest of the monarch, whose sovereign person is party to no covenants whose performance appeals to interest are designed to contest.

Wolin is concerned to diagnose the shortcomings of Hobbes's view of interest as carrying over to behavioralist social science; Gauthier rectifies the shortcomings of Hobbes's theoretical imprecision by reconstructing the contract in the social scientist's formal vocabulary of rational choice. Each misses elements of Hobbes's theory that could complicate social scientists' reliance on interests as a regular and knowable foundation of politics. Gauthier, for his part, obscures how deeply "right reason" reaches into subjectivity, in light of Hobbes's theory that both appetites and the self that one seeks to serve or preserve are to be crafted in awe of sovereign power. As for Wolin, we are left with the irony that he does to Hobbes's theory of interest what he claims social science does to politics, namely, obscure what's political about it in the sense of pertaining to plurality and contestation. Indeed, more so than opinion, Hobbes's picture of interests as prone to plurality and contestation and resistant to a monistic and transcendent mode of reason is a picture of publicity itself—a democratic prospect that Hobbes's exclusion of interest is meant to deny.

Contested Interest and Modernity

For all its brilliance, Hobbes's mistake is to have based a science of the commonwealth in the prospects of fitting natural language to geometry. As much twentieth- and twenty-first philosophy has shown (not to mention Locke and others among Hobbes's nearer successors), language cannot perform the function that Hobbes assigns to it in *Leviathan*. The inconstancy that interests contribute to language turns out to carry the day, rather than being a special if troublesome case. Therefore, the sovereign's task of serving as the great definer is impossible. But we still have much to learn from Hobbes: he perceptively highlights the threat to notions of sovereignty presented by appeals to interest and the myriad subjectivities they justify and provoke. Moreover, the agents shaped and activated by appeals to interest in politics enjoy their power independently of both the natural boundaries of right and law on the one hand and sovereignty or political order on the other. Being in language, "interest" is in-between.

Hobbes's concern about interests as disrupting signification and impeding sovereignty is a cautionary tale for all those who would look to interests as a stable foundation for political order and political inquiry. Appeals to interest disrupt the regularities that Hobbes's sovereign on the one hand, and the text of *Leviathan* on the other, must impose to subject people and to secure their persons. If we apply a modern notion of interest as calculating self-regard in lieu of Hobbes's own ways of creating order from people's myriad differences, we are liable to miss how Hobbes marshals reason to suppress desires and how subjects' encounter with the sovereign power they have authorized changes the "selves" that they may desire to preserve in the first place.

Hobbes's hope is that the plurality of the multitude can be contained and suppressed by this transformation, but this is where Hobbes goes wrong, owing perhaps to his mistaken view that the inconstancy of signification he associates with interest can be overcome. Political theorists and social scientists would do well to heed the lesson of Hobbes's failure in this regard. Rather than seek in interests a stable foundation for political order or the sovereign agency of individuals, they should instead remain, like Hobbes, attentive to the ways in which competing appeals to interest have the power to invoke and contest political identity. Then Hobbes's view of interests becomes a resource for Wolin's hope that politics is and remains a fertile site for the local and ever incomplete transformation of persons and communities.

5 A HISTORIOGRAPHY OF LIBERAL INTEREST AND THE NEOLIBERAL SELF

Neoliberalism: Writing the Juridical Out of Political Thought

In the foregoing chapters, I have characterized as "liberal" and "social-scientific" a view of interest, as a psychological faculty of rational, calculating self-regard, that has been routinely but wrongly attributed to episodes in the conceptual history of interest—its relation to financial practices, its vogue in seventeenth-century England, and the philosophy of Thomas Hobbes. In this chapter, I contend that the liberalism behind this conceptual prolepsis is of a relatively recent kind—that it is of neoliberal, rather than of classical liberal, vintage. Preliberal thinkers and classical liberals, I shall argue, recognized the plural and contested nature of interests and reluctantly conceded the need for juridical institutions to govern these contests. They were, of course, more sanguine than Hobbes about the prospect that plural and contested interests could be a part of, rather than inimical to, the orderly conduct of political life. But they grappled, in various ways, with the problem of specifying the meaning and limits of individual autonomy in light of the need for institutions—juridical and otherwise—to manage plural and contested interest.

A somewhat different picture of what it means to be a person is central to more recent liberal political discourse.[1] This is a picture of persons as individual actors whose intrinsic autonomy and rationality, coming together in their

---

1. By "political discourse," I mean the terms by which persons understand the order and disorder in their society, the ways in which the norms and putative facts of this society are represented to and by them.

self-interest, is the basis for their liberty.[2] When these actors encounter others, their liberty is preserved as long as self-interest is allowed to govern their actions. The most variant of liberal political discourse, neoliberalism, promotes an appreciably different view of the role of interest in the modern polity from the one that animated classical liberal thinkers. What is new to this political discourse is that the choices being made and the exchanges taking place in the market become the model for all human relationships and activities. Everything, in this view, is at bottom an act of exchange. In this picture, legal structures intervene primarily to promote the breadth of choices and the reliability and fairness of exchanges; they do not play an avowed role in structuring the actors' self-understandings. Actors' interests are prior to, rather than inflected by, legal order. And such a legal order is a just one less because it shapes a person's autonomy than because it promotes the widest latitude of its exercise. As a distinctive form of political rationality, this newer liberal notion of interest broadly informs contemporary liberal political theorizing. It undergirds in myriad ways the substantive positions that make up the debates in this arena of political philosophy. In this light, we may see how various contributions to liberal political thought in the last three decades similarly situate interest as a backdrop to justice and the exercise of autonomy.[3]

To characterize neoliberalism as "more sanguine" about the role of interests in political order than even the early and classical liberals would be an understatement. Doubtless, recent promulgators of liberal social policy and political theory are keen to see their view of interest as consistent with the one that emerged in the seventeenth century, was realized in the Enlightenment, and was consolidated in the founding of the American republic. But I argue that the language of interest that recent scholars and commentators claim to bring forward from the seventeenth century and classical liberalism, in order to justify neoliberalism, is in fact a quite different animal. It is a stark reduction of the

---

2. In such a picture, passions support autonomy owing to their not being imposed upon subjects from the outside; reason supports autonomy by enabling subjects to channel passions into the single end of self-preservation. See Hirschman, *The Passions and the Interests,* and Mansfield, "Self-Interest Rightly Understood."

3. Raymond Geuss, "Liberalism and Its Discontents," *Political Theory* 30, no. 3 (2002). To mention the most prominent example, John Rawls packaged interests neatly at the foundation of liberal theory. Interests, he writes, are shared to the extent that individuals "live better" with others than they would in isolation, and in conflict to the extent that each person wants a greater rather than a lesser share of the goods to be distributed in society. See Rawls, *Theory of Justice,* 4 and 11. While Rawls and his interlocutors have refined various parts of his theory over the subsequent decades, this view of interest remains at the foundation of the revised theories. Rawls's "original position" is one of many examples of how the liberal "self" and its interests presuppose reasoned exchange about political alternatives.

early modern language of interest, with its nuanced recognition of liberty as pertaining to bearers of legal status. Indeed, from the point of view of these earlier conceptions of interest and of liberties, the present-day reduction in the language of interest threatens to erode the very autonomy and liberty that earlier writers supposed that the juridical determination of interest could ensure. This threat comes from subjecting people to the relatively invisible governance and control by markets, rather than to democratically accountable political institutions and the law.[4] This newer form of government and control by markets may be seen as "neoliberal government"—with the important caveat that the term "government" here encompasses forms of governance and control not limited to the public legal and administrative institutions usually captured in the sense of "government," as the word is more narrowly, and more commonly, defined.[5]

Much political theory written in the last thirty years or so has uncritically, if unwittingly, adopted neoliberalism's view of interests. This can be seen in the paucity of attention given by cultural and critical theorists to the concept when compared to their many engagements with other "modern" political concepts like sovereignty and representation.[6] The narrow picture of interest in liberal political discourse also has prompted calls from contemporary political theorists for political and ethical theory, not to mention empirical study, to go "beyond self-interest" in order to incorporate motivations that are pluralistic, nontuistic, and noncalculating.[7] But Stephen Holmes distinguishes himself from these sayers of nay to "interest" by arguing, in *Passions and Constraint*, that interest is not only essential to modern politics, but good for it.[8] He thereby shores up the presumption of self-interest that lies at the foundations of liberal theorizing. Following Hirschman's invitation to consider the connection between the seventeenth-century language of interest

---

4. David Harvey, *A Brief History of Neoliberalism* (Oxford: Oxford University Press, 2005); Engelmann, *Imagining Interest*, 8–9; Aihwa Ong, *Neoliberalism as Exception* (Durham: Duke University Press, 2006); Brown, *Edgework*, chap. 3.

5. Many, though not all, writers choose the term "governmentality" to clarify the distinction, though I think that most if not all of the neologism's attributes can be captured in the older and broader usage of the term "government." See Tully, "Governing Conduct," and Foucault, "Governmentality." When I examine the work of Arthur Bentley in the next chapter, we shall see that his use of the term "government" includes much of what recent scholars wish to signal by the term "governmentality."

6. In *Hegemony and Socialist Strategy*, Ernesto Laclau and Chantal Mouffe include Interest with Representation and Sovereignty as the three elements of classical political theory most in need of late-modern critique and reconfiguration. See Ernesto Laclau and Chantal Mouffe, *Hegemony and Socialist Strategy* (New York: Verso, 2001).

7. Mansbridge, "Self-Interest in Political Life."

8. Holmes, *Passions and Constraint*.

and modern subjectivity, Holmes has argued that self-interest uniquely brings inherently and radically egalitarian elements to liberalism, republicanism, and democracy—that is to say, to every political philosophy with widespread support among political theorists today.

Holmes would appear to have remained more classically minded than the neoliberal thinkers, some of whom include his onetime University of Chicago colleagues, in that he is concerned more with politics than with economics and dissatisfied with market models of "consumer satisfaction and economic exchange" as models for government decision making.[9] Yet true to his liberal temperament, he remains wary of the potential for government involvement in social life to threaten autonomy.[10] Indeed Holmes brings to this liberal temperament the same convictions regarding self-interest as the basis of liberal theorizing that we have seen in Hirschman's, Wolin's, and Gauthier's accounts of politics. And while his substantive contributions to contemporary liberal theorizing do not lie at the center of present-day debates, his study of the historical emergence of the notion of self-interest is nonetheless important to contemporary liberal theorizing in its provision of a narrative for the historical conditions that undergird liberalism's contemporary promise. Herein lies Holmes's importance to my account: he is both a liberal theorist and a writer of interest's conceptual history.

In the foregoing chapters, I have scrutinized several conceptual histories of interest, and I have found the standard interpretive tradition that they embody to be hobbled by the presumption that interest is in essence calculating self-regard. In those chapters, my aim was to right and rewrite the record, recovering a proper place for the juridical in those historical episodes and reflecting on their theoretical significance. In this chapter, I proceed somewhat differently, closely examining Holmes's prominent historiography of interest in particular. I attend to how he constructs his arguments, how he handles evidence, and the points at which he conceals juridical and plural interest. And, I reflect on the theoretical importance of that concealment or denial. In short, I scrutinize and theorize the politics of writing conceptual history. I examine how recent liberal theorizing has tucked the identity-provoking side of interest away at its historical and theoretical foundations, so that it can go on to elaborate other conceptions, like liberty or rights, untroubled by the lessons that appeals to "interest" may hold for political liberalism.

9. Ibid., 179.
10. Ibid., 36.

Holmes's historical study of the discovery of self-interest as a motivation, and its emergence as a dominant style of reasoning, would appear to be as classically minded as his liberal theorizing. His attention to preliberal and early liberal thinkers like John Locke and J. S. Mill in particular may be taken to signal a classical liberal mindset. But Holmes's defense of present-day liberal arrangements on the basis of conceptual history, as I read it, is a textbook example of the perils of supposing that a concept as heterogeneous as interest can be viewed through the lens of any single, straightforward sense, especially its sense of "calculating self-regard." By means of adding the prefix "self-" to invocations of interest in the historical record that, on their own terms, approach this self as a question, Holmes smuggles into the foundations of his argument persons already conscious of themselves primarily as uniformly discrete, and hence capable of straightforwardly calculating self-regard. A closer look at some of the texts cited by Holmes reveals juridical sites of self-formation where Holmes supposes the self to be a basis for, rather than an outcome of, appeals to interest.

With this in mind, I turn to writings of J. S. Mill to examine how a classical liberal grappled with the language of interest. However famously Mill extolled a "marketplace of ideas" as adjudicating individuality, it is well known that he presumed, quite uneasily given his concern for autonomy, extra-economic social institutions (e.g., education, the law) as sites of self-formation. I show how Mill's recognition of the need for sites of self-formation can be read through the ways that the language of interest opens, rather than finalizes, self-identity. Holmes, in presuming the identity of the self and its interests as a backdrop to citizens' engagement with each other in society and its institutions, renders self-formation invisible to political theory. And while other contemporary liberal theorists have examined at length the various sites of character formation essential to engendering a just liberal order, they too suppose these sites to be subsequent to, rather than caught up in, the articulation of a person's interests.

My critique of Holmes's historiography may appear to be itself historicist and perhaps even polemical, because I would venture that uses of "interest" that accord with faculty psychology—including monistic benefit, desire, and reason—are of secondary importance in the seventeenth-century idiom Holmes explores as fundamental to liberalism. But my argument is really a theoretical one that takes this historical disjuncture as a point of departure toward achieving two aims. First is to explore the politics of method in conceptual history. Positing a conceptual center to the exclusion of heterogeneity in the uses of the word "interest," I argue, is a practice of neoliberal government, in that it forecloses alternatives to interest as calculating self-regard, making this self appear as a natural basis and indeed origin, of interest. Second, and more important, recovering what Holmes's proleptic "self" obscures in early modern invocations of interest returns us to the power of the language of interest in politics. In light of Holmes's (and other neoliberals') intellectual and policy projects, this recovery suggests the power of appeals to interest to evade and erode discourses of neoliberal government where its critics have seen the language of interest as hopelessly complicit. Plural and contested interest, as we find it in the early modern period and in the present-day language of interest, exceeds the calculating self-regard lamented by neoliberalism's critics and celebrated by champions of neoliberal reforms.

Interest, Neoliberal and Otherwise

Economic liberalism sees a spontaneous and harmonious order generated from price-taking transactions among autonomous, individual agents; neoliberalism is a political movement that espouses this order as a means not only toward economic development, but as the sole means to political liberty as well. In practical terms, neoliberal policies bring ever greater facets of life under the purview of market-like structures in which choices are organized by prices. Choosers are motivated by an inherent ability to maximize on the basis of the ordering of their preferences. These choices are to be made in markets for goods of every kind—not only consumer products, but also health care, education, and so on—even law enforcement in its most straightforward form. So, for example, during holiday travel periods, California drivers are greeted on the highway with large lighted signs bearing the message "Click It or Ticket." While the law links an infraction to a punishment, the sign registers the situation more coyly. With its economy of lighted bulbs, it frames wearing a seatbelt as a choice in which the value of gratifying one's desire to ride without wearing restraints must be valued and "traded" against the cost of violating the vehicle code.[11] And this cost itself, as any risk-taker knows, is to be calculated in terms of the fine multiplied by the probability of getting caught.

Framing compliance with the vehicle code in terms of such a trade-off illustrates how the logic of the market becomes a "commonsense" (not to mention catchy) means of governing legal subjects. Neoliberalism becomes a kind of

---

11. A sign affixed to a trailer that is parked in various spots at the University of California in Santa Cruz brings the message to motorists leaving the campus a step further, reading "Click it or Ticket: You Decide."

government when we extend this logic of trade-offs and maximization to most areas of life: not only law and policy, but to any area of life where we begin to think of responsibility mainly in terms of facing the consequences of our choices.[12] In the case of neoliberalism, deliberation regarding this regulation is moved from public spheres to private ones, turning citizens not into legislators but instead into choosers whose maximizing actions are choreographed by the punishments and rewards of a fused economic and juridical order that is approached as a market.[13] Seeing neoliberalism this way highlights how, the asseverations of Milton Friedman, Robert Nozick, and other self-styled libertarian thinkers notwithstanding, markets nonetheless structure, regulate, and therefore govern conduct, even if they govern not by means of public institutions, but rather by collapsing the distinction between public and private.[14]

The connection between neoliberalism and "interest" can be succinctly stated by noting that neoliberalism figures interest both as a psychology that drives rational choices and as the good that is achieved by these choices.[15] Subjective and objective interests are thus rendered neatly compatible: questions of false consciousness on the one hand, or of a "real interest" that exceeds what people can realize by means of price-taking choices on the other, are not so much answered as they are rendered unintelligible. Also foreclosed is the messiness and contestation that the language of interest presents in politics—contests that are not so much resolved as they are disciplined or denied.

Holmes and the Liberal Norm

Holmes defines liberalism broadly as "a set of principles and institutional choices" embedded in history, noting that its earliest defenders (he names Locke, Hume, Montesquieu, Madison, and Mill, among others) "were deeply immersed in contemporary controversies . . . responding to local challenges,

---

12. Engelmann, *Imagining Interest*, 2.
13. Ibid., 1.
14. Tully, "Governing Conduct"; see also Engelmann, *Imagining Interest*, 1.
15. Engelmann, *Imagining Interest*, 3–4. The view that individuals can achieve their interests by means of exchange alone presumes commensurability among each individual's plural attachments—and here is where faculty psychology comes in. The connection of interest to such a faculty has a history subsequent to the seventeenth century but roughly coincident with classical liberalism, in the work of Jeremy Bentham. Bentham's articulation of interest as a "spring of action" offers a conceptual mechanism by which agents' plural ends are not only rendered commensurable, but are moreover coordinated by means of choosing among options. See Engelmann, *Imagining Interest*, chap. 4.

defending specific reforms, struggling with circumscribed problems."¹⁶ His historical approach outlines liberalism's advantages over its autocratic, aristocratic, and theocratic foes; he also argues for its superiority to collective ownership (*Passions and Constraint*, 16–17). Given Holmes's certainty that liberalism is still a linchpin of the political good, it is perhaps surprising that he does not defend liberalism against what he identifies as the modern "illiberal arrangements" of identity politics and theocracy. And nowhere does Holmes even note the epistemological challenges of twentieth-century philosophical developments often cited by contemporary critics of liberalism, or address the ill-health of modern-day liberalism's secular assumptions. Though in Holmes's view liberalism was formed in its confrontations with historical challengers, today it appears to stand on its own.

But Holmes's defense of liberalism is nonetheless novel and important. One of his aims in *Passions and Constraint* is to illuminate the complex landscape of moral discourse in which liberalism took root and flourished. Critics who find reductive liberalism's view of all human motivation as self-interested, he argues, and who therefore see the assumption of self-interest as an empirical or ethical liability, have lost sight of the fact that egalitarianism in the modern liberal and democratic polity rests on this assumption. Restoring the moral side of self-interest by locating this morality in history, Holmes seeks to buttress interest as a moral foundation for present-day liberal political theory.

The history that Holmes invokes is familiar to us by now. His account may be unusual for the emphasis it places on interest, but in truth it illuminates an axiom of liberal theorizing, namely, the presumption of self-interest that resides at its foundations. From Albert Hirschman, Holmes adopts the thesis that shortly after "interest" was introduced into English political discourse, as a rational and therefore model and indeed positive motivation, individual self-regard (or self-love) was rehabilitated and the modern "interested" individual was born.¹⁷ But Holmes criticizes Hirschman for focusing mainly on what Holmes calls the rhetorical "narrowing strategy" pursued by early modern writers, who (according to Hirschman) reduced the language of interest toward uses closely related to economy. Holmes does see the problem that this rhetoric of interests presents: seeing its outcome in both Marxism and liberal economics, Holmes concedes that the use of "interest" to designate the many motivations

---

16. Holmes, *Passions and Constraint*, 13. For the prospects and pitfalls of casting seventeenth- and eighteenth-century materials as protoliberal, see Geuss, "Liberalism and Its Discontents."
17. Hirschman, *The Passions and the Interests*; see also Hirschman, "Concept of Interest."

once characterized as a variety of passions is indeed an "impoverishment of our language of moral psychology" (*Passions and Constraint*, 43–44).[18] This foreclosure of an older, broader humanistic notion of interest (as the "totality of human aspirations") is what lends an ambivalent if not pessimistic tone to Hirschman's examination of the rise of interests in the early modern period.[19]

Holmes counteracts this loss by arguing that a *secret* history of self-interest lies in what he calls a *two*-sidedness of the term's semantic development. This other side supports the political liberalism that Holmes seeks to distinguish from its economic variant. And at first, Holmes's attention to another side of interests appears to be just what is needed to resurrect the plural side of the term. But instead, Holmes sees that the term "narrowed" in meaning toward the calculability that appertains to economic life, while it simultaneously "expanded" regarding the realms of human life that could be described as calculable (*Passions and Constraint*, 62–63).[20] "On the one hand," he writes, "the concept [of self-interest] became . . . progressively more narrow and specialized: having first meant any rational style of behavior, it came to refer exclusively to moneymaking. On the other hand, during the same period, the concept broadened to the point of becoming a tautology," which is to say, any action could be attributed to the self-interest of the actor (*Passions and Constraint*, 63). Holmes describes this development as "paradoxical," but how these two changes are contradictory he does not say.

Disputing the view that tautology is a liability for interest arguments (a view I also disputed, to different ends, in Chapter 3), Holmes argues that tautological interest is a "profoundly egalitarian and democratic idea" (63). In other words, Holmes makes the very emptiness of tautological interest that so bothered Hirschman and other liberals into the source of its appeal. Holmes's claim is this: seeing a broader range of actions as interested means seeing a broader range of persons as sharing this motive; the possibility that every person can be seen as self-interested means that no one's actions are morally or politically superior to those of anyone else. "Self-interest," says Holmes, "is an intrinsically egalitarian and universalist principle" (xii). Therefore, the focus of Enlightenment writers on self-interest "emphasize[s] a motivation that all human beings equally share" (4). From this point of view, the rehabilitation of

---

18. See also Holmes, "Secret History of Self-Interest," 268.
19. Hirschman, *The Passions and the Interests*, 32.
20. As support for this claim, Holmes cites Hirschman's own unsupported argument regarding a "semantic" drift in the language of interest; see Hirschman, *The Passions and the Interests*, 38.

original sin as self-interest replicates the egalitarian implications of original sin in politics as well, but with a uniquely modern, positive twist. And not only is interest profound in its support of equality: the discovery of interests is essential to democratic politics. "The question answered by modern democratic procedures," he asserts, "cannot even be formulated until the universality of self-interest is assumed" (66). Holmes's argument to this effect is therefore of fundamental importance to the principle of equality that animates much of liberal theory, as well as democratic theory, in the present day.[21] And even when liberals derive principles of equality by other than historical means, interest remains the spring of choices that are made (in, say, an original position) that animate this principle.[22] Seen in this light, even the extinction of a subtler seventeenth- and eighteenth-century moral vocabulary has, according to Holmes, a typically overlooked but monumentally important political payoff whose gains are reaped in liberal political orders to this very day.

Having made interest into the basis for liberal and democratic egalitarianism, Holmes distinguishes the reductive view of interests in liberal economics and Marxism from the democratic view of interests at the basis of liberal politics. The former, he writes, relies on self-interest as a *description* of behavior, but the latter makes self-interest into a *norm* (*Passions and Constraint,* 27). Therefore, critics who have accused liberals of psychological reductionism may have a target in liberal (and Marxian) economics, but liberal politics is not so reductive (24). He therefore recounts the complex moral vocabulary from which liberalism has sprung to demonstrate how "self-interest" is a normative prescription for politics rather than an all-encompassing description of people's motivations. And to describe interest as a normative principle of liberalism does not stop at disabling the charge that interest falls short ethically and empirically as a principle of human action: by drawing interest to the side of a moral good, Holmes flies in the face of centuries of moralists' denunciations of Machiavelli, Hobbes, utilitarianism, and the like.

Holmes's claim that the egalitarianism of interest is effective not as description, but instead as a norm, is striking. Although it may depart from liberal economics, the politics of such a claim are neoliberal nonetheless; neoliberal

---

21. For another example of liberal argument that derives principles of equality from Enlightenment thought, see Brian Barry, *Culture and Equality* (Cambridge: Polity, 2001), 12.
22. As I remarked in note 2, Rawls provides perhaps the most eminent and influential example. On the liberal assumption of interests as prior to politics more generally, see Mary G. Dietz, *Turning Operations* (New York: Routledge, 2002), 23.

government, after all, makes a virtue of interest.²³ What's more, the rhetoric that Holmes argues supported self-interest as a normative principle was itself descriptive: "To say that all individuals *are* motivated by self-interest," he writes, "is to assert that, from a political perspective, all human beings are fundamentally the same. There are no higher types" among motivations that justify some persons' power over others (*Passions and Constraint*, 26, emphasis added). The true paradox of interest lies in what it means for the supposedly normative force of politics based on self-interest to reside in its ostensibly descriptive power: self-interest is appealing as a norm *only* if it is supported by the conviction that self-interest is a description. Otherwise, where compelling normative exhortations toward political action are concerned, could we not do better? Urging people to act in a public-spirited manner falls into the trap of idealism that Holmes derides (32), so the normative element of self-interest lies instead in the exhortation that we be suspicious of others, expecting them to calculate to their own advantage—an expectation that even present-day psychology recognizes as self-fulfilling.²⁴ While it is by now a routine gesture in political thought to note that the distinction between description and norms is treacherous, the difficulty it presents here is of a special kind. Holmes's seeing descriptive claims and normative ones as exclusive prevents him from grappling with the political implications of his very own argument that these norms get their power from their descriptive conceit. In other words, Holmes's distinction between the normative and the descriptive hides how the norm structures that which it claims merely to describe, by virtue of its claim to be merely descriptive.

The appeals to interest proffered by the writers whom Holmes sees as formulating early liberal ideas were neither descriptive nor normative, but were instead prescriptive. And they prescribed not a one-dimensional style of behavior, but rather a proper basis for action secured by law. But whereas early liberal thinkers grappled explicitly with securing this proper basis, Holmes misses the truly intriguing paradox in the concept of interest—the normative power of descriptive interest—because he substitutes a quite modern preconception

---

23. Classical liberalism, by contrast, makes interest that which promotes social order where virtue is unnecessary or ineffectual. Although examples from Adam Smith precede classical liberalism, they are so often cited that it is worth noting them here. One is his remark about the self-interest of the baker providing the bread. See Adam Smith, *An Inquiry into the Nature and Causes of the Wealth of Nations* (New York: Oxford University Press, 1993), bk.1, chap. 2. Often conflated with this passage is his famous reference to the invisible hand; see Adam Smith, *The Theory of Moral Sentiments* (Indianapolis: Liberty Fund, 1984), pt. 5, chap. 1.

24. Miller, "Norm of Self-Interest."

of interest. This modern preconception is of the "individual" as coterminous with the self-evident identity of the natural person. The rich ways that the term was deployed in response to local challenges, in defense of specific reforms, and in struggles with circumscribed problems—examples of which have been my focus in previous chapters—are obscured. Thus, the power of appealing to interest is foreclosed in the historical record and covertly transposed to the writer of conceptual history. Holmes's historiography is therefore a practice of discourse that simultaneously facilitates neoliberal political-economic aims yet obscures itself as a form of governmentality.

Neoliberalizing the "Concept of Interest"

Holmes replaces Hirschman's mild unease about the binding of liberal democracy to the language of market capitalism with optimism about their mutually reinforcing and essentially positive relationship around self-interest. Holmes writes of people motivated by self-interests or every person as "having interest." He takes it for granted that these interests are intrinsically personal or individual, neatly corresponding to the "self" that is said to have an "interest" and who, on that basis, can engage in the rational, calculating style of behavior appropriate to liberal autonomy and equality. This behavior includes participation in democratic institutions, where these prepolitical selves can engage in "institutionally anchored procedures *both* for aggregating pregiven interests *and* for rationally evaluating and redefining interests in the course of public discussion" (*Passions and Constraint,* 179).

Yet this view of interest, with all its commonsense appeal, reflects two conceptual moves that are needed in order to structure self-interest as a liberal norm. While these conceptual moves are problematic in light of the features of language and concepts I outlined in Chapter 1, the problem with Holmes's conceptual approach goes beyond the needlessly blinkered view of interests that it fosters. His way of writing conceptual history also has a politics, one that fits neatly with neoliberal government. Holmes's conceptual moves allow him to identify what he variously calls the "idea," "notion," or "concept" of interest on the basis of a decision—*his* decision—regarding what is intrinsic or essential to interest. Holmes (and his readers) can then find this idea "represented" not only by uses of the word "interest" in the historical record, but in writers' and actors' other words and phrases. Other possibilities in this historical record, ones in which the language of interest does not support what Holmes sees as the core liberal idea, get lost.

Holmes's first conceptual move is to equate interest and self-interest. Holmes's avowed focus is on the self-regard denoted by the term "self-interest," but throughout his examination of the arguments advanced by the earliest defenders of liberal ideas, Holmes assumes that all interest—whether invoked directly by an author, or imputed by the author's apparent reference to a calculating motivation—is self-interest. Not only do explicit references to interest that are in any way collective or transitive go ignored, but any possible ambiguity regarding the individualism of interest is set aside. He goes so far as to make the plainly anachronistic assertion that various uses of interest have self-interest at their origin.[25] The practical equation of self-interest and interest allows Holmes to make claims about the desirability of liberalism based in significant part on interest; he needs to presume the "self-" of self-interest to make his conclusions about liberal individuals—their equality, their autonomy—plausible.

Holmes's second move is to define interest as intrinsically rational. "To dispel the clouds" that have obscured the historical morality of interests and encouraged critics of liberalism, Holmes says that "we must focus sharply on the all-important contrast between calculating interest and noncalculating passion" (*Passions and Constraint*, 42, 46). Holmes acknowledges in a footnote that he has chosen to focus only on this contrast to the exclusion of noncalculating "interest" or "calculating passion," whatever these might be (278 n. 13). Interest and calculability are so closely tied in his view that he can paraphrase Hume's idea that "the very idea of interest-driven behavior is meaningless . . . unless we can identify some behavior that is *not* interest-driven" by declaring, in the next sentence, "the idea of calculating action loses all content if it can no longer be opposed to action that is *not* calculating" (46).[26] Holmes footnotes the alternative to calculating interest as an "interest" that denotes a "pleasure principle, . . . a form of self-interested motivation that is almost wholly free of rational forethought or the comparison of alternatives" (*Passions and Constraint*, 278 n. 13). Consigning the exterior of calculating self-interest to the "pleasure principle" suggests that all interests are foremost psychological—a conclusion that follows easily from the presumption that interest is self-interest. The remaining differences then are whether the interests in question are rational or not, and this is where the "narrowing strategy" comes in. Holmes's focus primarily on the calculating "essence" of interest, and his insistence that anything else that

25. For example, Holmes writes: "As it gradually spread into common usage, the concept of self-interest accustomed people to discovering *conflicts of interest* in every sector of social life." See Holmes, *Passions and Constraint*, 64. According to the *OED*, "self-interest" appears only in the mid-seventeenth century, after well over half of all the senses the dictionary records had appeared.
26. Holmes quotes Hume, but does not cite a text.

parades under the name "interest" is something like a passion, blinds him to the uses of "interest" that lie outside both the faculty of calculation and rational psychological states, drives, or motivations.

Holmes has bounded "interest" on two sides: it is originally and essentially self-interest, and it is now rational in the sense of calculating. All interest already has a self behind it, so an exhortation to act on the basis of interest is merely to import a rational style—and therefore, moral equivalence—to actions serving that self. Thus can Holmes turn Hirschman's claim about the "semantic drift" of "interest," into a pillar of egalitarianism: "interest," originally self- and now rational and everywhere, lays the foundation for democracy.[27] Surely not all appeals to interest in political language imply only or merely calculation, nor do they refer exclusively to psychological states—but what these uses have to tell us about liberalism have now been excluded from its history and its foundations.

When it comes to interest at least, a conceptual center and neoliberalism make a happy couple. Like neoliberal government, conceptual historiographies that posit a conceptual center crowd heterogeneity and plurality toward commensurability and singularity. Having defined "interest" as calculating self-regard, and thereby having made calculating self-regard essential to interest, we can find interest hiding any variety of words and phrases, while becoming oblivious to the diversity of ways that "interest" is used. Holmes may therefore be seen as doing to "interest" what Hobbes saw fit to do with words like "just" and "free"—rendering their meanings univocal and frozen and thereby denying their politics. Following Holmes's definition of interest, we become fixated on "interest" as a sign of people's calculability, and on the opposite of "interest" as their passionate or irrational nature. And so Holmes's liberalism mirrors the problem with Hobbes's writing more generally. The student newly encountering Hobbes discovers to her astonishment that his apparent absolutism is "common sense," not realizing that this commonsense appeal stems from her having accepted Hobbes's innocuous-seeming definitions uncritically. So too the reader of Holmes is struck with the "common sense" of his argument from interest, having accepted these definitions as, in their own way, unremarkable.

Faced with the commonsense appeal of such a definition, displacing a conceptual center with a word-focused approach becomes a form of critique, one that may generate a critical theory of interest. In its sensitivity to how a word

27. Hirschman, *The Passions and the Interests*, 35–55; cited in Holmes, *Passions and Constraint*, 62. Like Hirschman, Holmes offers no evidence of such a narrowing in the language of interest, despite his acceptance of Hirschman's calling the change a "semantic" one.

brings multiple valences together, a practice of looking more closely at the work of a word like "interest" in political argument not only breaks a term's uses back into heterogeneous parts, but it also renders decisions about how to fit the parts together, and the contingencies of these decisions, visible. Such decisions can thus be rendered conscious, if consciously provisional.

Up till now, I have examined Holmes's conceptual methodology. My principal aim in what follows is to disclose, in Holmes's presentation of "liberal" textual artifacts, the effects of a modern preconception of the relation of identity and its entailments. I am concerned less to offer a "better" reading of the artifacts Holmes provides—though I think there is room for a better reading—than I am to interpret the significance of his prolepsis for theoretical understanding of the language of "interest." Engaging "interest" in the works that Holmes sees as foundational to liberal ideas—that is, *prior* to the influential monistic and nontuistic formulations that emerged in eighteenth- and nineteenth-century social theory—can reorient a political theory of interest toward aspects of its contemporary usage that work against the grain of neoliberal political discourses.

A Critical Historiography of "Interest"

If Holmes's assumptions about interest—that it is always already self-interest, and that it is rational—are suspended, the evidence he himself provides for the "secret history" of self-interest tells a different story. This story reveals thinkers grappling to square liberal ideas with a juridical, rather than rational and individual, vocabulary. These writers faced the problems of the political recognition and aggregation of interests—a problem of democracy that is not resolved simply by recognizing that all persons are interested, but instead struggles with understanding how they are so interested—and, therewith, faced the extent to which interests are significantly configured within political settings. Examining how Holmes obscures classical liberalism's grappling with juridical interest illustrates not only that and how the self is a production of appeals to interest rather than their origin, but how the neoliberal presumption that interest is always already self-interest obscures how the language of interest both provokes the self and renders this provocation incomplete. That every person may be said to be self-interested does not necessarily make self-interest itself egalitarian or democratic; instead, "that every person may be self-interested" is a liberal program entrusted to political institutions, some of which, like the law, are representative, and some of which, like education, are not. The side of "interest" that has gone unnoticed in most histories of political thought since the middle of the twentieth century holds promise for the possibilities of interest in our politics that are not tethered to Holmes's neoliberal historiography of interest. It reveals the "self-" that Holmes adds to "interest" to be a neoliberal supplement, one that quarantines the otherwise contested provocations of identity that the language of interest facilitates for political inquiry and argument.

The trouble begins when Holmes paraphrases Richard Hooker's sixteenth-century claim that "common people are motivated by self-interest, while religious and political elites are motivated by virtue and devotion to the common good"[28] as the context in which claims of universal self-interest, in which every person is seen as "having interests" have a radically egalitarian potential (*Passions and Constraint,* 63). But the passage Holmes cites shows the situation to be far less clear, at least as far as interests are concerned. "The greatest part of men," writes Hooker, "are such as prefer their own private good in all things, even that good which is sensual before whatsoever is divine."[29] Nothing in the passage (or the surrounding paragraphs) refers even obliquely to elites' virtue or devotion to the common good. In fact Hooker suggests quite the opposite, writing just before this passage that "no man in reason might take upon him to determine his own right, and according to his own determination proceed in maintenance thereof, inasmuch as every man is toward himself and them whom he greatly affecteth partial" (*Ecclesiastical Polity,* 190). Why might Holmes assign "self-interest" to the former passage of Hooker's writing but not to the latter? Could there be a difference between "self-interest" and a person's preference for his or her own private good? After all, one might "have" a preference for a private good in the same way that one "has" an interest, but again it would be odd to say that one "has a *self*-interest" here. Whereas one can "be self-interested," the phrase "to be preferential of one's private good" is not idiomatic, suggesting a difference that exceeds Holmes's logical "conceptual" equation of preference, benefit, one's own, and good with interest.

Hooker's phrase, "preference for a private good," is more amenable to the term "interest" (unadorned with "self"), with its openness to subsequent determinations of the relevant interest through political give-and-take, than to "self-interest," in which the person is presumed. In the latter passage (whose potential translation to "interest" Holmes does not consider), one's partiality

28. Richard Hooker, *Of the Laws of Ecclesiastical Polity* (New York: Dutton, 1954), 193; cited in Holmes, *Passions and Constraint,* 284.
29. Hooker, *Ecclesiastical Polity,* 192.

extends not only "toward himself," but extends as well to "them whom he greatly affecteth"—subtle but complex acknowledgment that this kind of preference always extends beyond the "self" upon which "self-interest" is ostensibly centered. Hooker's claim is consistent with the extensive notions of the self that early modern juridical practices reflected and supported—including coverture and estate. Defining the boundaries of these selves by means of appeals to interest was, as we have seen, a trope of major political importance from the seventeenth century through the nineteenth.[30]

Continuing with his argument about the egalitarian features of individual interest, Holmes cites *Cato's Letters,* by John Trenchard and Thomas Gordon, to the effect that "Tyranny being nothing else but the Government of one Man, or of a few Men, over many, against their Inclination and Interest."[31] Here, "Interest" is singular, while "the many" is a plurality, which suggests that Holmes himself has shifted to a notion of "interest" that is no longer as easily individual as "self-interest." Instead, the interest of the many may be captured by the notion of a public interest or even a common good such as Holmes claims Hooker thought motivated religious and political elites. And of course, the passage between individual self-interest and broader, transitive, and even common interest is a rocky one; simple aggregation will not pave the way, let alone an equation of "interest" and "self-interest" by fiat. Holmes unwittingly demonstrates this complication at the very moment that he presumes that the egalitarianism of self-interest secures the foundations of democracy. Quoting Mill, Holmes avers that democratic procedures "were said to provide 'the means by which identity of interest may be insured between the representatives and the community at large.'"[32] But by Mill's formulation, democratic procedures merely ensure that the representatives articulate and thereby create the "interest" of the community, in ways that inform and constitute, rather than represent, the self-interest of each citizen.[33]

This subtle gap between the way we use "self-interest" and the way we use "interest" is a less secret part of these terms' history than the one Holmes claims to tell, and suggests a distinction that Holmes has obscured. Reflection on the

---

30. Coverture also remained such a trope into the nineteenth century, though it became more contested. See Mary Poovey, "Covered but Not Bound: Caroline Norton and the 1857 Matrimonial Causes Act," *Feminist Studies* 14, no. 3 (1988).

31. John Trenchard and Thomas Gordon, *Cato's Letters, or Essays on Liberty, Civil and Religious, and Other Important Subjects,* vol. 1 (Indianapolis: Liberty Fund, 1995); cited in Holmes, "Secret History of Self-Interest," 284, 345 n. 104.

32. Holmes, "Secret History of Self-Interest," 285.

33. This is a crucial feature of Mill's articulation of interest in terms of liberty. I will illustrate this claim when I examine Mill's *On Liberty.*

gap in Holmes's argument also suggests the incompleteness of neoliberalism's capture of the language of interest. On the one hand, a person can be said to "have an interest," but not a "self-interest." On the other hand, a person can be said to "be interested" or to "be self-interested." A critical difference in the use of these phrases may suggest one way to interpret the difficulty of moving from self-interest to the general political "interests" that populate Holmes's secret history. The latter phrases are more indicative of a person's motivations or state of mind, but less indicative of the broader connection of benefit or involvement expressed by the former. It seems odd to call self-interested a person who does not *know* his or her interest. Moreover, self-interests do not aggregate the way interests are presumed to do; groups (e.g., nations or clubs) do not have self-interest and are not self-interested, even if the members of these groups are said to be self-interested, and even if these groups are said to promote their members' self-interest. In sum, the term "interest" admits of contest, especially over the makeup of the self that is said to be self-interested. It cannot be said, therefore, that interests correspond in any logical way to the individual self. Moreover, to the extent that politics inheres in the question of membership, the individual self upon which Holmes's liberalism depends must be less distinct from political power than Holmes avers precisely to the extent that its political means and ends are expressed in the language of interest.

Classical Liberalism: J. S. Mill

J. S. Mill is unique among the authorities Holmes cites for having presented liberal political principles under the name of liberalism. Looking at Mill's political thought is an opportunity to compare Holmes's twenty-first-century liberal perspective with a classical counterpart. Whatever differences we find here will signal in turn the departures of Holmes's historicized liberalism from its classical historical object and may in turn signal elements of the "neo" in neoliberalism. As it turns out, Mill's thought exhibits the problem of interests and the boundaries of identity, and also shows the role played by juridical and plural interests in mediating this problem—and returns us to the troublesome relation of the individual to the community that is obscured by Holmes's focus on interest as calculating self-regard. My aim, in turning to Mill, is not to elaborate the problems of liberal individualism in general, but rather to show how a classical liberal, when confronting these problems with the language of interest, confronts and draws upon the juridical aspects of that language.

Expounding his case for individual liberty, Mill attempts to distinguish between self-regarding actions, which do not affect others' interests, and other-regarding actions, which do. Making this distinction is crucial for Mill's argument about the proper role for limited government, a favorite liberal priority. Mill contends that "to individuality should belong the part of life in which it is chiefly the individual that is interested; to society, the part which chiefly interests society."[34] That is, society can legitimately limit a person's actions only when the actions have significant negative consequences for other persons— this is the famous principle of noninterference, or the "Harm Principle." The boundary between these kinds of actions determines the limit of the authority of society over the individual and, in Mill's theory at least, reflects the boundary of the "self."

Most readers of Mill have found it necessary to look far beyond his elaboration of the Harm Principle—often considered a case study in atomistic individualism—to appreciate (and to criticize) the means and ends of self-formation that Mill's work, on the whole, is seen to advocate.[35] Perhaps this is because present-day political theorists usually frame their engagement with Mill in terms of the role that rights claims play in contemporary liberal societies. While Mill does attend to the question of rights in many of his writings, *On Liberty* is cast largely in the language of interests, a first indication that juridical notions inform his view of self-formation. Our inclination to translate this idiom from interests to rights may itself reveal the degree to which the juridical side of interest has become unfamiliar or alien to us: we read Mill's discussion of interests, and discuss rights instead. Of course, if we allow ourselves

---

34. John Stuart Mill, *On Liberty and Other Essays* (New York: Oxford University Press, 1991), 83.

35. For a critique of the Harm Principle as atomistic, see Charles Taylor, "Atomism," in *Power, Possessions, and Freedom: Essays in Honour of C. B. Macpherson* (Toronto: University of Toronto Press, 1979). More recent readers have examined the various ways, from educational "tracking" to character development, that Mill embeds not only exclusion and discipline, but also an "ethos of critical judgment [in] . . . a practice of political claim-making through which character and community may be cultivated and contested." See Karen Zivi, "Cultivating Character: John Stuart Mill and the Subject of Rights," *American Journal of Political Science* 50, no. 1 (2006): 51. For other contributions to this literature, see Paul Passavant, *No Escape: Freedom of Speech and the Paradox of Rights* (New York: New York University Press, 2002); Nadia Urbinati, *Mill on Democracy: From Athenian Polis to Representative Government* (Chicago: University of Chicago Press, 2002); and Linda Zerilli, *Signifying Woman: Culture and Chaos in Rousseau, Burke, and Mill* (Ithaca: Cornell University Press, 1994). My own reading of Mill finds support for Zivi's argument, particularly with respect to the positive, agonistic, democratic possibilities contained in Mill's other writings, within the Harm Principle itself. Another way to consider the complexity of Mill's thought regarding the relationship of the individual to society is to consider his political-economic writings; see William Stafford, "How Can a Paradigmatic Liberal Call Himself a Socialist? The Case of John Stuart Mill," *Journal of Political Ideologies* 3, no. 3 (1998).

to hear the juridical language of interest at work in Mill's account, we come close to rights: juridical interest is, after all, a contested claim. The difference is that what counts as an interest is significantly more open than what counts as a right; declarations and enumerations of rights abound in political philosophy and public policy, while interests slip and slide their way through public discourse. And so Mill's reliance on the language of interest in *On Liberty* is a distinctive terrain on which to explore how juridical interest contributes to democratic participation and freedom.

By providing the caveat "chiefly," Mill has suggested up front—in his own elaboration of the Harm Principle—that the all-important interests are not easily determined. But he goes on to argue that the line must nonetheless be drawn. In what follows, I argue that the language of interest through which Mill articulates the Harm Principle contains the kernel of self-formative practices, and links these practices directly to agonistic, democratic possibilities that students of Mill's work have found in his other writings.

To see the language of interest this way in Mill's elaboration of the Harm Principle, we must attend to the movement of this term through the text and remain attentive to its juridical resonances. These resonances appear in his other works as well, even when he seems to follow the Benthamite tradition of seeing interest as a matter of psychology. For example, in *Utilitarianism* he writes that "laws and social arrangements should place the happiness or (as practically speaking, it may be called) the interest, of every individual, as nearly as possible to the interest of the whole."[36] Seeing "interest" here as the (no more easily defined) "happiness" is to miss that "interest" is, for Mill in this passage, the translation of individual happiness into a properly legal object. It is with a hint such as this in mind that we may attend to interest as a juridical matter, even when not resolved in judicial institutions, narrowly conceived.

The juridical nature of interest is a continuous trope throughout *On Liberty*, wherein interest is invoked to sketch the boundary between self-regarding and other-regarding action. Mill's appeals to interest are saturated not only with references to judgment, but also with law and jurisdiction. And the emphasis on harm as the context in which judgments regarding interest can be rendered draws us very close to the language of interest as it originated in juridical claims regarding damage or loss. "As soon as any part of a person's conduct affects prejudicially the interests of others," Mill argues, "society has jurisdiction

---

36. John Stuart Mill, *Utilitarianism, Liberty, and Representative Government*, Everyman's Library (New York: E. P. Dutton, 1947), 16.

over it."[37] Here, where jurisdiction is involved, "chiefly" is not of much help to Mill—a line must be drawn. But because judgment, regarding particular cases, is involved, Mill himself cannot say where this line is to be drawn. Even so, he is direct about who ought to decide whether an action by the possible offender has in fact impinged on the interests of another person. "On such questions," he writes, "[the public] are only required to judge of their own interests" (*On Liberty*, 92). They do so through legislation, which Mill says can be trusted to provide a "distinct and assignable obligation" to the "sympathies and interests" of "those nearly connected with [the offender]" (90). So the public, not the self, determines the relevant interest and names the offense caused by infringement of that interest.

Mill is talking about legislation enacted by "society" or by "a public" acting through "an overruling majority," yet also he writes of "the public" in the plural, and "their" interest*s* in the plural as well (92). And so how and by whom the deciding public is composed are correspondingly complex matters. How is a member of this public to think of her own interest, that is, to think of the "self" that her own decision affects? Is that self material and tangible? Is it composed of relationships, uncertain futures, and attachments to the past? Do her interests compete with those of others, or do they instead rise and fall by her participation in various relationships and even Mill's broader notion of the community? How an overruling majority of members conceives of its interests is of the utmost importance to Mill's argument, because it determines the boundary between self-regarding and other-regarding actions that is the lynchpin of at least the action side of *On Liberty*.

The answers to these questions are unsettled, and remain so, by the language of interest. But for us, Mill's statement that these matters are to be decided by a public is crucial. It recognizes a plurality of points of view—after all, he implies that there will be a minority, rather than unanimity—about what any member of this public believes her own interests, and those of others, to be. And more important, it suggests a political site, as jurors and as participants in legislation (e.g., as voters), for how the boundaries are to be drawn for oneself and for others.[38] Individual interests, it turns out, are more an outcome of political,

---

37. Mill, *On Liberty*, 83.

38. In this regard, Mill's discussion of interest in *On Liberty* adds a site of "artificial discipline" or character cultivation to those explored by Zivi. See Zivi's "Cultivating Character," 54. While the negative emphasis of Nadia Urbinati's reading of Mill as proposing "freedom from subjection" does not adequately capture the language of interest in Mill's account, her attention to the importance of citizen engagement supports well Mill's remarks here regarding the way interests are determined in practice. See Urbinati, *Mill on Democracy*, 155–66.

that is to say, collective and institutional decision, than a foundation of it, and we do not need to look beyond Mill's elaboration of the Harm Principle to catch a glimpse of it. However a member of this public thinks about her interests when casting a vote, the practices that precede voting and the institutions that count votes have an overriding, if provisional, say.

In *On Liberty* Mill offers some suggestions on how to proceed, but arrives again at juridical notions of right and injury. He explicitly includes as infractions of society's interests "infliction ... of any loss or damage not justified by [the offender's] own rights" and "even selfish abstinence from defending [his fellows] against injury" (87). Supposing injuries to be to the natural body and rights to be coextensive with this body, then perhaps we see these interests in a relatively narrow sense. But Mill also includes "envy, ... abasement of others, ... [and] egotism ... when they involve a breach of duty to others" (87) as injuries, suggesting that a broader conception of interests is also at play. The majority is to be trusted in this determination because "though often wrong, it is likely to be still oftener right [judging] of the manner in which some mode of conduct, if allowed to be practiced, would affect themselves" (92–93). Mill's view of education also suggests that the interests that persons are to judge as their own when legislating, and discover as their own in following law, are broader than individual rights and bodies. "I am the last person to undervalue the self-regarding virtues," he writes; "they are only second in importance, if even second, to the social. It is equally the business of education to cultivate both" (84). That Mill even makes the distinction suggests that there are objectively self-regarding virtues and actions, even if majority rule is the way to identify and effect them in practice.

Mill has proposed mediating community interest and self-interest by means of a boundary, but the location of the boundary is impossible to ascertain as long as we view "interest" as a psychological state or faculty like happiness. When we see its juridical side, we confront the political institutions (ideally representative, for Mill) that in fact decide, right in the very heart of what has been taken to be unleavened individualism in Mill's work. "Interest" as a motivation, by contrast, does not provide a way to determine the boundary between community and individual interest. And as for deriving community interest from individual interests, the effective causation appears most likely to go the other way. Self-interest does not *lead to* republican or even liberal democratic government for Mill. People may be seen as having interests, and government may be required to act upon the common or public interest, but Mill leaves the connection between these to be established by means other than autonomy.

There is no simple passage from parochial, narrow, or "self-" interests to comprehensive, group, collective, or otherwise political ones.

One must avoid the temptation to say that Mill could have solved these problems, had he seen them clearly, by being more specific about what an interest *is*. For if Mill had sought to make a principled or analytic argument to clarify the meaning of "interest," he would have denied the role each person—or each citizen, at any rate—has in elaborating, as a member of the public, what her interests, and those of others, rightly are. It is the autonomy of this role that present-day liberals, from Rawls and Dworkin to Holmes, so dearly wish to defend.

If interest is related to the boundaries of the "self" in the way Mill's elaboration of the Harm Principle suggests, our search for a stable and identifiable interest that corresponds to a stable and identifiable political "self" both *obscures* and *belies* an important problem in political theory. Persons are situated historically and socially, and these situations yield complexities and contradictions within persons. Our engagement with this problem may be frustrated when we turn to the language of rights, with its presumed universality. Interests, by contrast, admit of a plurality that can help us to grapple with these issues. Ascertaining the boundary Mill proposes only appears impossible as long as we cling to the idea that the person in question has a single, essential, and prepolitical "self" whose interests can be straightforwardly ascertained. Mill does not want any single institution, be it the state or the market, to arbitrate the boundaries of the self. Instead he turns to the practices of citizenship, to law, and perhaps most important, to education. This is the classical liberal in Mill.

Classical liberal political thought reflects and sustains an older notion of interest that is missing in contemporary neoliberal politics—but which is still intelligible in a present-day idiom. Mill is at least partly mindful of what Roman jurists, seventeenth-century radicals, reason-of-state authors, and Hobbes recognized: juridical forms of government do not take subjects "as they are." Rather, the person is an outcome, however provisional, of the decisions regarding its interest. Reflecting this aspect of the juridical, appeals to interest are a means toward elaborating the persons of states and citizens. So too classical liberalism elaborates persons and their properties under the pretense of protecting them; to the extent that liberalism is government by rule of law, it nonetheless organizes "the person" of subjects by means of decisions that bring particular cases under the norm.[39] These decisions, moreover, imply a "who

---

39. John Locke, *Second Treatise of Government* (Indianapolis: Hackett, 1980), §§27, 44, 95; Knox, *Hegel's Philosophy of Right*, §§219–22; Schmitt, *Political Theology*, 30–31, 59.

decides." In short, the political institutions of classical liberalism are rooted in the legal protection of interest understood as an amalgam of autonomy and property. The difference of this approach from neoliberalism lies in the former's recognition that interest is a matter of government. Neoliberalism, by contrast, views interest as a natural attribute of men and women.

Recovering these juridical elements within classical liberalism, and noting the means by which they have been obscured, highlights resources in the language of interest that are not captured by neoliberal government's apparent eradication of plurality and contestation. "Interest," then, may not be neoliberalism's principal tool so much as its enemy to be captured and indefinitely detained. To the extent that the very language of interest in politics reflects and sustains complexities in subjectivity that exceed the conceits and projects of neoliberalism, appeals to interest in politics can also be a site for its disruption.

Interest, Legal Autonomy, and Equality

Holmes identifies historical invocations of interest with the republican political discourse of early modern England. To what degree, then, does Holmes see what we might call a republican remainder in "interest," a space in which agents can be formed and reformed by virtue of their participation in the polity? Holmes would seem to concede such a possibility, given his view that passionate and destructive behavior can be replaced with self-interest. He acknowledges that self-interest must be *made* the foundation for the liberal political order with its "separation of powers, judicial independence, religious toleration, freedom of public discussion, and legal controls on the police" (*Passions and Constraint*, 3), and that this making involves remaking persons. Therefore, he can hold that "self-interest might emerge as a common, if not preponderant, human style, but only after massive and long-term reform of social manners" (26).

Yet Holmes's acknowledgment of political means by which persons can be made interested such that their interests are directed toward the public good is hardly republican: it comes in his discussion of Locke, who describes the way interests are sorted by law. But now the egalitarian elements of self-interest that Holmes has championed begin to look thin: "Law, in its true Notion," according to Locke "is not so much the Limitation as the direction of a free and intelligent agent to his *proper Interest*."[40] One cannot help but notice that

40. John Locke, *Two Treatises of Government*, ed. Peter Laslett (New York: Mentor, 1965), 347–48 (II, vi, 56); cited in Holmes, *Passions and Constraint*, 66; Holmes's emphasis.

here the community *determines* the "interest" of the citizen through law. One might then ask in what sense this is still *self*-interest, though Holmes does not approach this complication. In the face of the law's sanction, it is the individual's self-interest because it is made to be so. But, at the same time, the profound egalitarianism of "self-interest" is eviscerated if the law affects some persons' interests differently than others'—or if indeed (as in the case of coverture) some people *are* the interests of other persons. Even Locke recognizes the extent to which interests are not prior to, but also products of, political institutions, a complication that Holmes's focus on interest as the self-regarding faculty of calculation suppresses.

The origins of self-interest as calculating self-regard in English political discourse are better sought among more uniformly utilitarian thinkers.[41] Holmes does not draw these thinkers' contributions into his history of liberal thought, even though they connect selves to interests in ways that appear to privilege each person's self-regarding calculation equally. Jeremy Bentham's political-economic writings, often cited as origins of a psychological conception of interest, offer apt examples. Here too, however, we confront a degree to which interest is a motivation that connects stakes and shares—which are themselves inherently social—to knowledge. In the introduction to the *Manual of Political Economy*, for example, Bentham writes that "generally speaking, there is no one who knows what is for your interest, so well as yourself—no one who is disposed with so much ardour and constancy to pursue it."[42] Here interest is a spring not only to action, but also to knowledge. Bentham's larger aim in this discussion is to humble the legislator's claim to a superior position from which to know the outcomes of his legislative action. This is particularly the case, Bentham avers, in matters of political economy, where passions are far less likely to impede the ability of ordinary individuals to reason for themselves. A few chapters on, Bentham elaborates his view of interests and knowledge, writing that "knowledge itself depends in a great measure upon the degree of interest which the individual has in obtaining it: he who possesses the greatest interest will apply himself with the greatest attention and constancy to obtain it."[43] Here we have interest as a kind of possession, one which varies by degrees. Yet we must not take this interest to be mere curiosity,

---

41. Engelmann, *Imagining Interest*, especially chap. 4.
42. Jeremy Bentham, "A Manual of Political Economy: Now First Edited from the Manuscripts of Jeremy Bentham," in *The Works of Jeremy Bentham*, ed. John Bowring (Edinburgh: William Tait, 1843), vol. 3, chap. 1.
43. Ibid., chap. 3.

purely subjective interest; in its relation to knowledge, Bentham views interest as closely tied to matters of social recognition and property. The theme of relating interest to knowledge recurs in Bentham's *Defence of Usury*. "Nor let it be forgotten, that, on the side of the individual in this strange competition [between the legislator and the individual], there is the most perfect and minute knowledge and information which interest—the whole interest of a man's reputation and fortune—can insure: on the side of the legislator, the most perfect ignorance."[44] Here an individual's stake in reputation and fortune is what generates the best possible knowledge of interest; the individual's proximity to these matters is what privileges his or her knowledge over that of the distant legislator. Differences among persons, when it comes to reputation and fortune, rather than their inherent equality, are what make this form of knowledge relevant to Bentham's political discussion. And the substance of this interest involves inherently social matters of reputation and property. Interest, then, is less a style of reasoning than a proximate knowledge of stakes and shares, matters that always are liable to change, and to local dispute and adjudication. Bentham merely reminds us that it's implausible that a legislator at a distance can judge these matters well.

In sum, Holmes sees *making* people self-interested enough for liberalism as a prelude to a political project, rather than as the object of one. It's as though we are obliged to treat self-interest as an anthropological fact, rather than as a political effect, if we are to enjoy the benefits of liberal government. The republican possibility of interest is foreclosed even as the egalitarianism of self-interest is realized. Following a thought that resonates with what we have seen in Bentham, but one he does not draw into his liberal historiography of interest, Holmes cites a line of reasoning from Montesquieu: namely, that interested persons are made in the marketplace (*Passions and Constraint*, 25).[45] For this process to be egalitarian, all persons must be brought into the marketplace in order to be transformed into interested "selves." Herein lies the essentially positive bind of capitalism and democracy (both in the sense of "being in a bind" and in the sense of "a link between"): the market for labor makes people exchange; exchange makes them calculate; calculation makes them rational, and reason makes them equal. From this point of view, the secretly liberating

---

44. Jeremy Bentham, *Defence of Usury*, in *The Works of Jeremy Bentham*, ed. John Bowring (Edinburgh: William Tait, 1843), letter 13.

45. Holmes refers to Montesquieu's *Persian Letters*, but does not provide a specific citation. See Montesquieu, *Persian Letters*, ed. John Davidson (London: Gibbings, 1899), and Hirschman, *The Passions and the Interests*, 70–80.

and egalitarian political potential in calculating self-interest is tied to the commodification of labor. Any liberalism whose basis in self-interest is, at bottom, based in the market is inapt to bear the recognition that interest is genuinely political in its own right, both engendered in participatory institutions and yet retained as a claim of identity. Holmes's move to make self-interest a normative basis of liberalism is therefore ultimately dissatisfying. His implicit equation of self-interest and interest cannot support the liberal values of autonomy and suspicion of power upon which most accounts of liberalism depend.

"Interest" Against Neoliberalism

As Holmes sees it, whatever damage the ascendance of liberal economics has done to political-theoretical inquiry may be reversed by tilling up the richer moral vocabulary of classical liberalism. He argues that the often touted affinity between liberalism and the market, viewed through the historical secret "paradox" in the meaning of interest—that it came to refer exclusively to money-making, but broadened to the point of tautology—supports a fundamentally egalitarian principle of liberal democracy, perhaps against the moral vacuum of late modernity. Seen in this light, "interest" has a doubly emancipatory quality: it freed people both from the tyranny of their passions and from the tyranny of their leaders, fortunately unleashing capitalism along the way.

Though attributing so much to a change in a word's uses is problematic, this is the familiar Enlightenment story of the changes in the past five hundred years. Yet such an argument—and its self-assurance that it is a liberal, rather than a neoliberal one—is persuasive only if one accepts a series of analytical premises to promote a concept of interest as *always already* calculating self-regard. One must accept a distinction between "calculating" and "noncalculating" senses of "interest"; one must ignore the problem of relating self-interests to community interests (or mediating their conflict); and one must see the extension of a "narrow" sense of "interest" to a broad range of behaviors as not only paradoxical, but as exhausting the "semantic" range of the term. Holmes draws on the language of interest to remake subjects—its normative power—while hiding behind this language's descriptive and explanatory conceits and denying complexities in the language that can figure political agency otherwise. He thereby bridges the gap between the neoliberalism that he appears to disavow when he rejects consumer satisfaction and economic exchange as models for public choice (179), and the neoliberal government that proactively organizes persons' self-understanding toward the naïve individualism of the natural person.

In Holmes's neoliberalism, the normative side of interest is created by the foreclosure of the alternatives presented by appeals to interest in political discourse. It is created by hiding the regimes that structure the self, hence making interests appear as a realm of freedom and autonomy, rather than as a site for the provocation and realization of identity. The pursuit of interests (e.g., by choosing among "options") is an injunction of neoliberal politics that rests on the conceit that persons already have interests that stand apart from the political regimes that structure these choices and limits the recognition of interest to the outcomes of these choices. These conceits and effects are at home in political talk and policy, but they have been sealed from critical analysis in part by a practice of conceptual history—one that is ostensibly *of* liberalism and its components—that is neoliberal in its reduction of a contested word to a univocal concept. Articulations of "interest" become powerful resources for the formation and transformation of political identity that issue from political discourses but are never fully exhausted. "Interest" provides interlocutors with a word that is neither normative nor descriptive, but instead engenders action by shifting actors' *self*-understandings, meanwhile leaving in their hands a resource (namely, the word "interest") through which further to articulate their political identities.

This observation carries an important insight for the regimes of neoliberal government—discursive and economic—that would point to "interest" as their natural law. The language of interest in politics, which always bears traces both of its roots in contestation and its affinity to juridical modes of shaping political agency, persistently undermines the dream of interests as a marker of freely exercised calculating rationality on the part of actors whose identities are given in advance. This language resists the picture of politics as a market where these interests are exchanged in a free and orderly manner. To find in interest a language for eroding discourses of neoliberal governmentality we need only turn to myriad examples—including those of classical liberalism—of how this language may be contested at the very moment it is applied to limn and enforce the boundaries of agency. Still, neoliberalism can hardly do without interest; can it be reconstructed to incorporate the implications that the many uses of the term "interest" bring to politics? I suspect that it cannot. Intrinsic to neoliberalism is a suspicion of ascribing or acknowledging any role for politics that cannot produce or does not respect the inviolability of liberal "individuals" and their interests. The priority of "individual self-interest" to political involvement of any kind is indispensable to the neoliberal way of imagining personal autonomy.

Holmes's neoliberal historiography of interest reflects a more general drift in liberal thought across the twentieth century. And although the ascendance of the neoliberal program is most visible in the economics of the Chicago school, it can also be seen in political inquiry, and not only in political science's adaptation of the methods and models developed by economists in the latter years of the twentieth century. The presumption of interest as an individual and psychological phenomenon has deeper roots, in political science's earlier, behavioralist homage to psychology. And so even those who are keen for tomorrow's political inquiry to abandon the formalist and quantitative methods of economics are prone to falling back upon deeply entrenched notions of interests that political science has inherited from an earlier time. But although a critical theory of interest can begin by scrutinizing the kinds of regulatory power that lurk behind notions of self-interest in political studies, the question remains of how the study of politics may go forward, heeding the power of appeals to interest while seeking political knowledge.

6 INTEREST IN POLITICAL STUDIES

Action, Grouping, and Government

Behavioralism's Stubborn Legacy

"Interests in politics"—"special interests"—"interest groups." For the citizen-observer, these phrases conjure pictures of unduly influential associations bent on hijacking policy to their own narrow advantage. They are, in a broad vernacular, what is meant by "political interests." One politician may be brought low for taking bribes or for infractions of "family values," but as a class, politicians are despised for putting "political interests" above those of their constituents or the nation. And above all, for the citizen observer "political interests" threaten to remake the state or nation for the worse. They represent, to the everyday citizen, the essence of corruption.

This narrative may seem to be at a great remove from the notion of interest whose politics I have been exploring throughout the foregoing chapters. But in truth, the sense of "interest" that is at work in the notion of "political interests" in everyday language draws on that sense. Of course, the name that political scientists give to the study of political interest groups, "pluralism," reveals something of that connection. But it runs more deeply. The close relationship of interests and groups—or, as we shall see, groupings—offers insights regarding the place of juridical interests not only as manifested in political life, but for political studies as well. In this chapter, I show how the language of interest countermands some of the strategies that modern students of politics have used to get around the ways that interests sometimes puzzle political observers. I illustrated these puzzles at the opening of this book by noting Thomas Frank's account of American politics and Alan Greenspan's astonishment at the financial crisis in the fall of 2008. When I discussed these unsettling "failures" of interests, I gestured also to the strategies for containing them: the rubric of parsing interest into objective and subjective senses, and the liberal and critical-theoretical approaches to mediating the divide between these senses. I noted that these strategies turned on a picture of interest as essentially psychological, and as a reflection of autonomy. In the intervening chapters, we've seen how these presumptions have obscured the workings of the language of interest at myriad junctures of political life and literature. Having recovered a more encompassing picture of the language of interest and its theoretical entailments from these encounters with its history in political argument, we are ready to return to the question of its place in social science. Setting aside the misleading sense that the language of interest refers to a thing in the world, and bracketing a commitment to sovereign agency and methodological individualism, we can see that appeals to interest are an activity that aims at the constitution of political subjects.

Given that I have emphasized a plural dimension of interest throughout this book, pluralist thought in social science is a fitting place to begin this exploration. I start by turning to the work of pluralist social theory that gave birth to the term "interest group," *The Process of Government,* by Arthur Bentley.[1] The language of interest in these pages offers a point of departure for exploring the promise that juridical interest holds for a new pluralist and critical study of political life. As one might expect, a relatively small (though often ambitious) literature has sprung up around *The Process of Government* and Bentley's larger body of work, evaluating its strengths and weaknesses and mapping its forebears and progeny.[2] Some contributors to the Bentley literature have noted the importance of the natural languages of politics to his perspective on political study,[3] and I too begin down this path. But the importance of juridical and plural interest to that language has yet to be explored; undertaking this exploration and theorizing what it entails for political studies is the aim of this chapter.

---

1. Arthur Bentley, *The Process of Government* (Evanston, Ill.: Principia Press, 1908).
2. See, for example, Bernard R. Crick, *The American Science of Politics: Its Origins and Conditions* (Berkeley and Los Angeles: University of California Press, 1959); Paul F. Kress, *Social Science and the Idea of Process: The Ambiguous Legacy of Arthur F. Bentley* (Urbana: University of Illinois Press, 1970); Mika LaVaque-Manty, "Bentley, Truman, and the Study of Groups," *Annual Review of Political Science* 9 (2006); John H. Schaar and Sheldon S. Wolin, "Essays on the Scientific Study of Politics: A Critique," *American Political Science Review* 57, no. 1 (1963); James F. Ward, *Language, Form, and Inquiry: Arthur F. Bentley's Philosophy of Social Science* (Amherst: University of Massachusetts Press, 1984); Leo Weinstein, "The Group Approach: Arthur F. Bentley," in *Essays on the Scientific Study of Politics,* ed. Herbert J. Storing (New York: Holt, Reinhart & Winston, 1962); and Leo Weinstein, "Reply to Schaar and Wolin," *American Political Science Review* 57, no. 1 (1963).
3. Schaar and Wolin, "Essays"; Ward, *Language, Form, and Inquiry.*

I then examine the fate of juridical and plural interest, since it undergirds *The Process of Government*, in more recent developments. I examine the rise of behavioralism and the tactics of its critics, as exemplified in David Truman's *Governmental Process* and William Connolly's *Terms of Political Discourse*, noting how pluralism becomes a celebrated behavioralist research program just as the language of interest is emptied of its intrinsically plural content. Although Connolly himself is sensitive to the importance of political language for political analysis, his critique promoted rather than cleared away the behavioralist view of interests as individual and psychological. This discussion provides a window into the larger effort in positivist political science to treat interests as things available for empirical study. My aim, in examining these texts and these broader efforts, is to show how and why political studies have obscured the juridical dimensions of interest, and what recovering these dimensions means for students of politics.

Attending to this stubborn legacy of behavioralism is a fitting way to bring this book to a close, because behavioralism's displacement of an older pluralist vision of interest is, I believe, a crucial part of the intellectual climate that has help to expunge juridical and plural effects of interest from the dominant tradition of writing interest's history. The conceptual histories of interest that I have disputed and revised in the foregoing chapters—regarding the legality of usury, conflict in seventeenth-century England, the political philosophy of Thomas Hobbes, and liberalism—were themselves all written in roughly the third quarter of the twentieth century. This same period, from the 1950s through the 1970s, saw the rise and dominance of behavioralism in political science. For example, in Chapter 3 I remarked that Friedrich Meinecke, writing in the 1920s, had no difficulty seeing *interesse* as paralleling *stato* (status) rather than *ragione* (reason) in the writings of certain late sixteenth- and early seventeenth-century Italian scholars. Albert Hirschman's gloss of Meinecke's words, written in the 1970s, puts it the other way around. No one interpreted Hobbes's philosophy in terms of interests in the 1930s, but in the 1960s and 1970s, such interpretations were legion. And so on. I can no more than note that a preoccupation with behavioralism saturates, by dozens of small streams, the dominant tradition of writing the conceptual history of interest.[4]

---

4. To firmly establish a causal claim here would require dense exposition of scholarly personal connections and lines of citation that go beyond the scope of my study. But one such line is this: Sheldon Wolin's book *Politics and Vision* is, among other things, a critique of behavioralism carried out by means of textual analysis of canonical works. His critical claim that Hobbes's theory is founded on self-interest is cited by J. A. W. Gunn, in his study *Politics and the Public Interest in the Seventeenth Century*. Gunn's claim about Hobbes is cited in turn by Hirschman in *The Passions and the Interests*, as evidence that a notion of interest—as a faculty of calculating self-regard—was prevalent in the seventeenth century. And so on.

My exploration of mid-twentieth-century changes in pluralism in this chapter, however, does speak to the larger intellectual context that influenced this dominant tradition. This tradition and behavioralism alike are framed within the picture of interest as calculating self-regard that has overlain the juridical language of interest since the 1950s. This picture is of a piece with the one that has consistently and proleptically appeared in the dominant traditions of conceptual history and analysis, and it crucially buttresses neoliberal political initiatives today.

With these striking coincidences in mind, I examine directly some of the preoccupations that underlie the behavioralist conception of interests. Some of these preoccupations are liberal, like the commitment to autonomy or, to put it another way, sovereign agency. Others, like the distinction between object and subject, are more accurately characterized as modern. I argue that when we look to the language of interest to support these attachments, we miss the critical insights this language bears for the exercise of political agency, or a person's capacity to act with respect to others. In particular, we miss the ways that the very shape of agency is constituted and contested in political life, and by means of the language of interest itself. Bentley's text supports a recovery of these insights, because he was critical of these same preoccupations as they appeared in his time.

Though Bentley's work inspires revisiting these matters in the context of political studies, the language of interest itself provides the means to begin shedding these preoccupations. Given the importance of the juridical language of interest to political discourse—an importance revealed in various ways throughout my retelling of this concept's history—students of politics deny juridical and plural interest at the cost of severing their studies from political life. So doing, we lose touch with the insights that the language of interest, as it informs this life, offers for our understanding of agency and identity. These observations draw us back to the concerns regarding political study that framed a good portion of my introduction to this book and speak to the thesis of this work, that an appeal to interest must be understood as a provocation of identity, and that provocations of this kind are integral to political agency.

I close this chapter by returning to *The Process of Government*. I draw lines of analysis from this text that enable us to interpret the prevalent references to interest that I have so far been discounting—like individual, psychological interest or a national or common interest—from within a juridical and plural frame. And I explore the ways that the identity-provoking power of the language of interest reflects back on what modern students of politics often assume are the origin of interests themselves, namely, individuals. Taken together, these insights call for a fundamentally different approach to the study of interests in politics—not as powers of subjects or as objects of study, but as activities of constitution and government.

Interest in *The Process of Government*

Arthur Bentley famously (and epigraphically) offered *The Process of Government* as "an attempt to fashion a tool" for modern political science. The book is a generous offering indeed, given that its author never held a permanent academic position.[5] This work's influence on the field has been complex, in part because it has enjoyed several periods of renewed interest in the century since its publication in 1908. The linguistic turn and enduring interest in questions of social ontology have continue to bring readers to this text, readers who have examined its contributions to the social theorizing of order, of language, and of process.[6] Most awareness of Bentley's work among practitioners of social science, however, stems from the widespread view that *The Process of Government* was integral to the development of pluralist thought in political science. The text is also cited as a forebear to the pragmatist "group interpretation" of politics that some have recently suggested may play a vital role in the renaissance of nonformal and nonpositivist studies of politics.[7] Although the mainstream of pluralism itself was mostly introduced (later) by Harold Laski,[8] and Bentley's work on groups is therefore less seminal than is usually implied,[9] *The Process of Government* nonetheless revolutionized the field. It did so by centering the emerging science of politics on the category of interests, as seen in the collective and active political phenomenon Bentley called the "interest group."[10] In other words, not only did Bentley consider politics to be the phenomenon of groups and government to be a process, his writing suggests that

---

5. Ward, *Language, Form, and Inquiry*, 16–44.

6. Two book-length studies in particular are valuable to the student of Bentley's work. Paul Kress argues that Bentley's main concern, and contribution, was the idea of process. James Ward follows Bentley's contributions along the key concepts of order, government, and activity. See Kress, *Social Science and the Idea of Process*, and Ward, *Language, Form, and Inquiry*.

7. LaVaque-Manty, "Bentley, Truman, and the Study of Groups."

8. Harold J. Laski, *Studies in the Problem of Sovereignty* (New Haven: Yale University Press, 1917); Harold J. Laski, *Authority in the Modern State* (New Haven: Yale University Press, 1919).

9. John Gunnell, *Imagining the American Polity: Political Science and the Discourse of Democracy* (University Park: Pennsylvania State University Press, 2004), 21, 105.

10. Ward, *Language, Form, and Inquiry*, 44; Dorothy Ross, *The Origins of American Social Science* (New York: Cambridge University Press, 1991), 330–34.

group activities illuminate something critically important—if forgotten even in the renaissance of group theory—about interest. In light of this aspect of Bentley's contribution, I pursue a reading of his work that emphasizes interest, rather than order, or process, or groups, as his signal contribution.[11]

A theoretical enterprise as ambitious, and at times as difficult and equivocal, as Bentley's cannot be given its full due in the space of this chapter. The question here is less whether *The Process of Government* is a failsafe tool for studying politics—it is not—than how we may return to such an ambiguously influential text to achieve a more limited and immediate aim. In what follows, I examine some of the ways that the language of interest is a resource for critically addressing attachments to sovereign agency, and distinctions between "subjective" and "objective" interests, as they variously appear in political studies, like empirical research and critical theorizing. Bentley's work models a way to begin thinking about politics through the language of interest, without these presumptions and abstractions.

Political Language and Political Studies

The importance of interest to Bentley's account must be read through his exploration of the language of politics as critical to the endeavor of studying politics. This, in turn, requires attending to a distinction, commonly drawn by philosophers of science and important to Bentley also, between "natural" and "scientific" languages and understanding. The natural refers to commonplace or everyday ways of speaking and thinking about objects and events. Scientific language, by contrast, refers to a specialized idiom developed in the course of study that is hoped to improve upon or supplant natural languages altogether, by providing unambiguous, univocal, plainly observable (or "operationalizable") concepts in the place of natural language.

Most commentators have noted Bentley's commitment to seeing the contribution of natural language to political studies.[12] This commitment is evident in the absence of technical or philosophical jargon in *The Process of Government*,

---

11. Kress emphasizes process; see Kress, *Social Science and the Idea of Process*. Ward emphasizes activity, government, and order. Ward treats Bentley's inosculation of interest with his distinctive view of politics not as a theoretical contribution in its own right, but instead as a generic pattern that any political study will reproduce. "The best students of politics," Ward writes, "ancient and modern, had always recognized the connections between 'interests' and politics"—a claim all the more anachronistic for its placing "interest" in quotation marks. See Ward, *Language, Form, and Inquiry*, 78.

12. Bentley, *Process of Government*, 167; Ward, *Language, Form, and Inquiry*, 11; Schaar and Wolin, "Essays," 140.

an absence all the more notable when one considers that Bentley's scholarly training was rooted in nineteenth-century German sociology. However, even though natural language provided a crucial starting point for Bentley's inquiry, he was nonetheless keenly aware that, to paraphrase the later Wittgenstein, words are as likely to mislead as to lead us.[13] Bentley's discussion of "government" is a case in point. He surveys a range of meanings of this term, finding that the one most common in political discourses and studies alike, that is, activities confined to official public institutions, is misleadingly narrow (*Process of Government*, 260–63). He opts instead for a broader sense of "government," one that at first seems quite technical and unfamiliar to natural language: "the phenomena of groups pressing one another, forming one another, and pushing out new groups" (269). But this can still be seen to be a naturalistic sense, when we step back from his definition and consider it in light of the everyday occurrences of government as those which activate people both inside and outside public institutions (162–64). Bentley's use of the term draws on a sense employed more frequently by early moderns, as relating to the authoritative disposition of things and persons in society.[14]

Although Bentley's commitment to and engagement with natural language is widely recognized, the place of the language of interest presents an intriguingly complex case that has not received the attention it deserves. And here too we see Bentley substituting a more encompassing notion from natural language for narrower and more salient ones. So we see both Bentley's attempt to depart from natural language, with its specious claims of causation, and his effort to capture the promise of natural language for political study, and even perhaps to inform natural language for political life.

From the very beginning of this work, Bentley crusades against some of the most familiar ways of talking about politics, ways that are encompassed by the language of interest. Bentley denounces "the common way of explaining what goes on in society, including of course the processes of government . . . in terms of the feelings and ideas of the men who make up the society" (*Process of Government*, 3). He is uncompromising in his view that "motives, feelings, desires, emotions, instincts, impulses, or similar mental states, elements, or qualities" are not properly the "raw materials" of politics to be studied by political science (4). He derided explanations in these terms as "animistic" (19). Bentley was well aware that the language of interest comprises such feelings, impulses,

---

13. Wittgenstein, *Philosophical Investigations*, §187.
14. Tully, "Governing Conduct."

ideals, and the like. His critique of Albion Small, on the basis of Small's explanatory reliance on "soul stuff" (19), attends closely to Small's own references to interest. Bentley similarly derided notions of a "social will" or transcendent ideals—among which we may include "common" or "national interests"—as nothing more than "spooks" (19). "These ideals," he wrote, "whatever else they may be, are, as independent or semi-independent factors in explaining the social life and social progress, just nothing at all. . . . On the surface, taken at their own valuation, they are but illusion" (117). Bentley's categorical dismissal of feelings, of social will, and of ideals, which include just about every explanation for political phenomena we give in terms of interest, rides on Bentley's larger philosophical rejection of the competing psychological and idealistic paradigms of inquiry in his day. Therefore, Bentley's reliance upon, and valorization of, the role of natural language is situated within his larger philosophical orientation and, more specifically, within the alternative ontology he presents for the "raw materials" of political life.

But first, it is worth noting that Bentley's targets, namely, interpretations of political life that turn on psychological and ideal interests, have their counterparts today. And so aspects of Bentley's alternative ontology—or at least, the conception of interest that he promotes in *The Process of Government*—speak to ways that students of politics treat interests even now, more than a hundred years after its publication. On the one hand, they too are prone to treat interest as essentially psychological; in so doing, they draw on the ways that, in natural language, the word "interest" seems to refer neatly to desires and wants that we are apt to call subjective. Key to this sense of subjectivity are the inherently relative matters of conscious awareness and perception. On the other hand, they also posit "real" interests in the face of persistent irrationalities and perverse self-perceptions, drawing on a sense of interest that seems to refer to "what's objectively good" for the body said to have an interest. This idea, in turn, relies on an ontological sense of what that body truly is. The apparent ability of "interest" to refer to these two different kinds of thing has led generations of conceptual analysts to parse uses of "interest" as either "subjective" or "objective."[15]

When it comes to conceptual analysis, the terms "subjective" and "objective" have their own rather weighty philosophical baggage. For example, the

---

15. This rubric is a basic feature of many studies of interests; see, for example, Schubert, *The Public Interest: A Critique of the Theory of a Political Concept*; Sorauf, "Conceptual Muddle"; Downs, "The Public Interest: Its Meaning in a Democracy"; Held, *The Public Interest and Individual Interests*; Balbus, "Concept of Interest"; and Flathman, *The Public Interest: An Essay Concerning the Normative Discourse of Politics*.

term "objective" has both epistemological and ontological senses, but their difference is not generally examined in this context. Of course, relating various senses by means of this pair may have the virtue of acknowledging that the term relates otherwise diverse ideas. But in practice, the emphasis is on division in the language of interest, which other theoretical and technical conceptions—like sovereign agency or false consciousness—are brought on board to mediate. And so the realization that the two different things to which "interest" refers must be in some way related offers little over the cruder psychologism or idealism that Bentley denounced. Yet despite all of these complexities, or perhaps because they obscure complexities in the language of interest and in the world, the rubric of "subjective versus objective" remains the beginning point for most conceptual analyses of interest. Since Bentley himself railed against this abstract dualism as a way of grappling with political phenomena (*Process of Government*, 171), how he figures the language of interest in *The Process of Government* offers insights for how students of politics can think beyond and without these abstractions today.

Bentley's argument that both the ideal and psychological approaches to understanding interests are not merely inadequate, but thoroughly misguided, suggests that the very schema of "subjective" and "objective" excludes or obscures something about interests that must be central to an adequate description of politics. What is excluded here, and what Bentley's distinctive treatment of interests restores to studies of politics, is the side of interest that I have been calling juridical and plural. When this side is given its due in political studies, it reveals the lacunae in analyses that are misled by natural language's apparent ability to refer to things in the world, and which therefore proceed to parse the language of interest into "subjective" and "objective" senses. Bentley's analysis will suggest how this side of the language of interest crucially supports the larger intellectual enterprise of pluralist studies of politics, especially in its demand that we attend to the activities through which political agents achieve and contest their own identities.

Action, Groups, and the Natural Language of Interest

Bentley's dedication to the group interpretation of politics is among the most striking aspects of *The Process of Government*. The casual reader is therefore to be pardoned for seeing Bentley's contribution mainly in this light. But the idea of action or activity is really at the heart of this text, and it is this notion that informs Bentley's way of appropriating the language of interest for political studies.

Bentley held that his contemporaries were a long way off from an empirical science of politics, let alone a genuine understanding of political life, because they lacked both a clear picture of what genuinely political phenomena are and, more to the point, a way to measure them. "Understanding any of these phenomena," he says, "means measuring the elements that have gone into them" (202). Bentley's aim in *The Process of Government* is "the exact interpretation of society" (16), though sometimes he instead claims that his aim is "explanation" (18). Whatever the difference, if any, to Bentley, this book offers a framework for interpretation, a way of seeing truly what the "raw material" of politics is. Among Bentley's many arguments and insights, we shall see "interest" as an integral term in the phenomena that make up, that identify, the basic unit of political analysis, which for Bentley is action. "If we can get our social life stated in terms of activity, and of nothing else," he writes, "we have not indeed succeeded in measuring it, but we have at least reached a foundation upon which a coherent system of measurements can be built up" (202).

Action, for Bentley, is intrinsically plural, both in its relevance to political life and in its suitability for an eventual science of measurement. Action is the only genuinely observable quality of human beings (186) to which any notion of causation may be attributed (460). Actions in concert are measurable. "Activity is always the activity of men," he writes, corollary to his assertion that "human society is always a mass of men, and nothing else. These men are all of them thinking-feeling men, acting. Political phenomena are all phenomena of these masses" (203). The pluralization of these masses themselves, at the moment they become political, also indicates something crucial about activity. Action pertains not to a mass on the scale of "human society," but on an intermediate level, that of the group.

Bentley's view of politics rests upon and intensifies his emphasis on the group. "When the groups are adequately stated," Bentley writes, "everything is stated. When I say everything I mean everything. The complete description will mean the complete science, in the study of social phenomena, as in any other field" (208–9). By focusing on the group, Bentley aimed to illuminate the structure of life that makes it intelligible to observers and actors alike. But having identified the group, by its activity, as the measurable social phenomenon *par excellence* and the "raw material" of our study, he refines his focus one step further; the phenomenon of active masses, he holds, becomes political by virtue of contestation. Political groups, he says, are the most manifest and palpable of groupings, because their activity is near the surface of life; what brings them to the surface is the pressure they bring to bear on other groups by virtue of their open competition in a public arena (209–10). At this point, they do not merely involve government: they become government, in the distinctive sense I mentioned earlier: "the phenomena of groups pressing one another, forming one another, and pushing out new groups" (269). Politics is contestation that renders masses into groups.

Only after having elaborated all of this at some length does Bentley mention "interests" in a sense other than the ones he has criticized, namely, as feelings or ideals. The ground thus prepared for treating interests in a new way, that is, having laid out contested group action as the "raw material" of political life and political study, Bentley goes on to fix the term "interest" to these phenomena. In so doing, he makes the juridical and plural side of interest a crucial linchpin of social-scientific analysis, placing a neglected side of the natural language of interest at the center of that study. After all, natural language also knows groups as "interests," even if this sense of the word appears marginal to or derivative of the natural language of interest as a whole, and is practically never discussed in the many conceptual analyses that begin by parsing the language of interest into subjective and objective senses.

Unlike his way of writing about, say, government, Bentley offers no justification for writing about interest in a way that, judging by his chosen interlocutors, had become somewhat unusual in political studies. While we may not be surprised to learn that "there is no group without its interest," Bentley pushes further against the prevailing winds of interest talk in political science with the assertion that "as the term will be used in this work . . . [interest] is the equivalent of the group" (211). Aiming to wrest the student of politics away from psychological causes, Bentley hews hyperbolically to this "other side" of the natural language of interest in politics, just as one might lean far off the windward side of a boat to keep it from capsizing while sailing across a strong wind. The language of interest in Bentley's account is fixed to the claim that only the group, and never the individual, is worthy as a political phenomenon. Bentley's assertions to this effect are legion, culminating in the claim that the "question as to whether the interest is responsible for the existence of the group, or the group responsible for the existence of the interest" is "beyond scientific" (211–12). In short, Bentley disables psychological explanations of politics, like the one offered by Small, by appropriating one of their key terms. With this move, he draws his reader to attend to a side of the language of interest that is generally ignored, and to bring it into full contact with the description of political phenomena. Because a science of politics must remain close to natural language, and because psychological or ideal causes are unscientific, science inheres in seeing the group sense of "interest" as the central contribution of the natural language of interest to political study.

Having already equated interest and groups, he returns to activity. "Group and group activity," he declares, "are equivalent terms" (217). Lest this pronouncement seem to render activity altogether superfluous, he insists that "if we have said activity, then we have said it all" (211)—implying that group and activity are coterminous, given his statement that to have stated the groups is to have stated everything (208–9). Interest is drawn transitively into this equivalence: because groups are known by their activity, not by ascription, interest is group activity. Last, interest is contestation: Bentley declares that interest becomes effective and visible "in its activity in the face of opposition from other groups" (216). Interest groups are oppositional doings and active contestations; interest is contested group action. Upon these declarations, Bentley builds a series of powerfully suggestive equivalences. Each of these seems to push Bentley decisively beyond natural understandings, even to the point of advocating a scientific language. However, forced as the equation of "activity" with "interest" may seem, the resonance of Bentley's many assertions with the juridical and plural language of interest is striking. Recognizing that sense, we can appreciate and extend Bentley's commitment to natural language. It is of critical importance to how political studies must grapple with interests in political life.

Juridical and Plural Interest in The Process of Government

It is apparent that Bentley is working within a pluralist tradition, but we can detect the importance of juridical interest as well in *The Process of Government*. Bentley's arguments regarding interest are clearly plural in nature, particularly his insistence that interests are always multiple, and that the members of any society will always be divided along many lines, the way that an unlimited number of planes may be passed through the center of a sphere (207). The sense of these interests as groups has a clear juridical history and bears those traces as well. While it may appear quite removed from the family of uses that I have drawn out in the foregoing chapters, the long history of using the word "interest" to identify a group bears out the connection. In the late eighteenth century, this sense is most often connected to industry—a mining or shipping interest, for example. These sorts of interests abound in Adam Smith's *Wealth of Nations* or Madison's writings in *The Federalist Papers*. Set in this context, the juridical cast of the term comes to the fore. It pertains to those who have a stake or a share, and who act on that basis. Up through the eighteenth century, the interest involved was indeed often literally a legal one, in the sense that a company was a corporation licensed in a particular trade. (Here it's also worth reminding ourselves that, in the debates at Putney, the "permanent interests" of the kingdom included "corporations, in whom all trading lies.") By the end of the nineteenth century, this sense of "interest" could refer to a cause around which a social movement had formed, as in the "temperance interest."

Bentley's way of making "interest" a signal term for the study of politics draws on these uses of the term, with their juridical and plural overtones. They animate the insistence, appropriate to a theorist who is now identified with the pluralist tradition, that political agency works, and political identity is revealed, at points of contestation and collective action. Bentley's signal contribution is to allow this sense of "interest," which is neither psychological nor transcendent, to inform social science, and to displace the ersatz notions of causation that lurk within a notion of interest as psychological or ideal. It sets a sense of "political interest" that is most commonly on the mind of present-day citizens at the center of political studies. (Indeed, when I have mentioned the topic of my research to dozens upon dozens of acquaintances, this is invariably the sense of political interest that they first have in mind.)

This importance of contestation to Bentley is not always recognized, and is seldom given its due. Some readers, undeterred (or unconvinced) by Bentley's disavowal of causation, seek explanations of what motivates or lies behind interest group activity that range from tendencies, to intentions, to "underlying interests" that, as we shall see, are characteristic of Truman's appropriation of Bentley.[16] But Bentley avers that what lies behind interest group activity is contestation itself. Groups in conflict are the basic, fundamental unit of political analysis and the meaningful site of political agency; these agents get their identity in the conflicting pressures put upon them, and by them on others, in political arenas. And consistent with the inflections of juridical interests in political language, these identities are provisional because they are caught up in activity and process. The way Bentley's picture of interest draws on the juridical senses I have been tracing throughout this book extends to the questions of agency and the determination of individual identity as well. I will return to these extensions of Bentley's perspective at the end of this chapter.

This brings me to a point that even Bentley's more recent and sympathetic interpreters have not sufficiently explored. Why invoke "interest" at all, when

---

16. Weinstein, "Group Approach," 174–76; LaVaque-Manty, "Bentley, Truman, and the Study of Groups," 8.

"contested group activity" might have sufficed, and precluded the individual and its psychology to boot? The answer to this question lies in recognizing that Bentley's picture of political interest along juridical and plural lines does important rhetorical, as well as analytic work. It shakes students of politics free from fast-held and presumed-scientific assumptions about interests that derive from a reliance on a partial selection of natural understandings. To Bentley's concerns regarding natural language's attributions of causation, I have added the assumption that appeals to interest refer to things in the world. Countering these assumptions, Bentley's equivalences—even, and especially, the equation of interest and action—are linguistic relations extracted from, and revealing of, the natural language of interest in politics. As my own linguistic observations later in this chapter will illustrate, this side of interest does indeed emphasize activities of constitution, rather than of reference or representation. It reveals interest as the manifestation of politics, not its foundation. While active, contested groups and interests are two sides of the same coin for Bentley, examining the "interest" side has the advantage of bringing attention back to how Bentley wanted political studies to remain connected to the natural understandings of politics that circulate in political language (such as referring to public matters in terms of "interests"). It offers a resource for staging a critical theory of interest that sees the political power of natural language, particularly when it comes to the language of interest.

How far should we go to discount the aspects of natural language that cast appeals to interest in terms of feelings or ideals and attribute causation to these feelings and ideals? After all, Bentley's exclusion of this language appears to jettison natural understanding in favor of a more specialized idiom; to say that "interest" refers to groups appears to reduce it to a technical term with a univocal meaning. His attack on these other notions of interests therefore complicates the view that Bentley is keen for political study to draw upon natural languages. In this matter, as in others, the rhetorical mood of Bentley's writing seems to contradict his most straightforward statements. He claims that he has chosen his approach, of treating contested group action as the "raw material" of political study, merely because it is most appropriate for the interpretation of social phenomena (*Process of Government*, 171). His goal, he says, is "the scientific investigation of society" (166), which seems rather specialized until we consider that he has actually provided a tool for the interpretation of social life, which may be a broader goal. He concedes that our usual language of feelings and ideas is "adequate for everyday life" (169)—much the way that animism might be adequate for everyday life in a "primitive" society

(19). Coming from Bentley, this is not much of an endorsement. Indeed, Bentley shows unrelenting disdain for anyone who gets by on this language, even to the point of referring to this way of talking in everyday life as "an addiction" (187). Meanwhile, he argues that developing a better way of interpreting social reality, such as the one he offers in *The Process of Government*, could justify jettisoning entirely the current "animistic" and "spooky" language of feelings and ideas. We can dethrone the Zeus of this language—in other words, his governance of all domains of our lives—if we can provide order another way (166–67).

It turns out that the juridical and plural side of interest that Bentley places at the center of his interpretation of politics can provide that order. We can account for psychological and ideal notions of interest without dismissing them as crudely as Bentley is apt to do, and without reaching for abstractions like "subjective" and "objective." *The Process of Government* offers resources for this accounting, ones that are worth our while to explore. In order to draw out the insights from Bentley's work that can speak to these concerns, we need a clearer view of the language of interest, particularly regarding how contestation is central to it. We need a view of how speakers of that language partake in its power to actively group, and thereby to constitute, political subjects, and the role played by apparent invocations of feelings and ideals in that language. To make this argument, I augment Bentley's way of attending to natural language with analyses of interest talk that support Bentley's perspective, but which also may carry us beyond some of his immediate concerns in *The Process of Government*. The picture of interests that emerges from these observations is particularly timely given recent calls for a revival of group theory in political studies, alongside the persistence of questions regarding autonomy and sovereign agency in political theorizing.

Before extending the promise of Bentley's beginning and of its unacknowledged tensions, however, I wish to examine the conditions under which it was lost, and the preoccupations—with the rubric of subject and object, with sovereign agency, with false consciousness—that contributed to its abandonment. Bentley continued to develop his own intellectual work, but it enjoyed only scattered influence in American sociology and political science. David Truman's appropriation of Bentley's notion of the interest group, however, brought one of Bentley's distinctive contributions forward into the mainstream of political studies. But not only did Truman reinscribe the "interest group" with the psychological sense that Bentley disavowed, he also imbued interest with these preoccupations.

Interest in *The Governmental Process*

Political science's loss of juridical interest, as it supported the pluralist vision of *The Process of Government,* is vividly illustrated by David Truman's appropriation of the "interest group" paradigm in *The Governmental Process.*[17] Although behavioralist psychological explanations had been gaining ground in political science since the 1920s, in *The Governmental Process,* David Truman follows Bentley in positing interest groups as the special object of social scientific analysis.[18] Only now, the meaning of "interest group" drifted quickly from Bentley's redundancy in the service of pure description to a more traditionally scientific pair: one cause and one effect.

Subsequent to the appropriation of *The Process of Government* by Truman and his disciples, Bentley was routinely invoked as the maverick intellectual ancestor of group theorists—an association, disputed even in its infancy, that has nonetheless stood the test of time.[19] He also, therefore, took much critical heat on their behalf.[20] Most readers of Bentley acknowledge that, for well or ill, Truman's adaptation of the interest group to the techniques of behavioralist analysis involved a transformation of Bentley's project. But its effects on Bentley's distinctive perspective on interest have not been explored. As we shall

---

17. David B. Truman, *The Governmental Process* (New York: Alfred A. Knopf, 1953).

18. Ward, *Language, Form, and Inquiry,* 73.

19. Jack Schaar and Sheldon Wolin wrote, partly in response to behavioralists' appropriations of Bentley, that "his work was guided by a thoroughly philosophical orientation and intention," which they doubted "even his acknowledged followers [had] begun to understand, let alone accept." See Schaar and Wolin, "Essays," 127. Many commentators see Truman as Bentley's natural successor on the view that Bentley mainly promotes a "group theory" of politics. See Weinstein, "Group Approach," 158–60; Ward, *Language, Form, and Inquiry,* 78; and LaVaque-Manty, "Bentley, Truman, and the Study of Groups," 11. See also Schaar and Wolin, "Essays," 137, and Ward, *Language, Form, and Inquiry,* 46, 78. The difference between Truman and Bentley then becomes what LaVaque-Manty calls the difference between the general theorist and the practical—Truman is Lenin to Bentley's Marx (11). While there is some merit to LaVaque-Manty's view that Bentley's work fits into a rubric of pragmatism, the pragmatism of Truman's enterprise is less clear. When it comes to interests, some readers see group activity in Bentley's account as representing "underlying" or "particular" interests. LaVaque-Manty, "Bentley, Truman, and the Study of Groups," 8; see also Weinstein, "Group Approach," 176. LaVaque-Manty sees this as a fundamental strength of Bentley's approach; Weinstein views it as a telling contradiction. On my view, Truman cannot be said to share Bentley's account of interests at all, and this needs to be included among the reasons that Truman ought not to be seen as a rightful successor to Bentley's theory of politics. Kress and Ward have examined the extent to which none of these uses and abuses of Bentley's work took sufficient stock of his larger philosophical enterprise. But even Kress, who is apt to draw weightier distinctions between Bentley and Truman, missed the degree to which Truman reintroduced the very psychological view of interest that Bentley rejected as a causal force. See Kress, *Social Science and the Idea of Process,* 85–87, and Ward, *Language, Form, and Inquiry.*

20. Crick, *American Science of Politics;* Weinstein, "Group Approach."

see, Truman decisively abandons the way that Bentley drew upon the juridical and plural aspects of the language of interest to articulate a pluralist theory of politics as he adapts midcentury findings and techniques in sociology and social psychology.[21] Truman promotes instead a picture of interest, amenable to behavioralism, as a psychological foundation that results in groups. This move had broad-ranging implications for social science, and for the study of interests by political theorists, who have adhered by and large to the picture of interests that Truman advocates even when they criticize or otherwise distance themselves from behavioralism.

Psychological Interest

Truman's individualism is covert; he opens *The Governmental Process* with a discussion of the relation between individual and society that appears to honor Bentley's disavowal of the distinction between the two. Truman deems the distinction "misleading" and "a fiction," particularly when one of its sides is taken as prior to the other.[22] He insists that "'the individual' and 'the group' are at most merely convenient ways of classifying behavior, two ways of approaching the same phenomena, not different things" (*Governmental Process*, 48). Apparently echoing Bentley, Truman writes that "a group is 'real' in the sense that the interactions that are the group can be observed, and these terms [group, institution, nation, and so on] are convenient ways of describing interactions. . . . Men exist only in society; society is the interaction of men" (29). But this passage also hints at a difference between Truman and Bentley that will decisively separate their treatments of interests. Recall that for Bentley, activity consonant with the group was the sign of membership in the group; group identity itself, at least in the case of politics, was formed at points of contestation. Bentley focused on contested group activity; Truman focuses instead, as the passage above shows, on *interaction among* members of a group. "A minimum frequency of interaction is necessary," he writes, "before a group . . . can be said to exist. It is the interaction [among group members] that is crucial, not [their] shared characteristic" (24). While Truman thus evades the dangers of ascription and dodges, for now, the question of the observer's role in scientific knowledge, this view contrasts sharply with Bentley's focus on external and especially conflicting relations, where group identities are formed

---

21. Kress describes the limited extent of Bentley's reception and influence in the years before Truman's *Governmental Process*. See Kress, *Social Science and the Idea of Process*, 81–15.
22. Truman, *Governmental Process*, 29, 49, 140.

in the context of differences and contestation. The change from Bentley may be slight, but it is greatly amplified when Truman's analysis turns from groups in general to *interest* groups. Then, even interaction falls away as Truman prioritizes the individual psychology of "attitude" over group activity, foreclosing the most useful theoretical insights of Bentley's position.

Whereas Truman defines groups generally in terms of their members' interaction, interest groups are defined instead by shared attitudes. Now practically refuting his earlier insistence that interaction and not shared characteristics make up the group, Truman insists that "interest" stands for the desires and wants that motivate group activity. In Truman's formulation, an "interest group" is constituted by the "shared attitudes" of its members, where "shared" corresponds with "group" and "attitudes" corresponds with "interest" (33–34). Truman's disavowal of the distinction between individual and society notwithstanding, attitudes are fundamentally individualistic. He describes their differences as coming down to variations in embodiment, mentality, and experience (22)—a trinity that secures individualism, and the individualism of differences, in Truman's account of politics. This trinity, which Truman calls the "hard facts of personality differences" (49), are all-important. Now, even interaction has disappeared.

Truman neither acknowledges nor explains this shift; perhaps it is meant to preempt an important criticism, namely, that pluralists' focus on politically active groups blinds them to how institutionalized politics systematically prevent some groups from engaging in institutional politics, or from forming (and therefore interacting) at all.[23] Such a conclusion would be consistent with Truman's sensitivity to the challenges that inequality posed for the survival of democracy.[24] Having turned to attitudes, Truman amends his predecessors' views of interest groups by establishing that interest groups "make certain claims upon other groups in society for the establishment, maintenance, or enhancement of forms of behavior that are implied by the shared attitudes"— whether or not all the members of the group work in concert at all.[25] The kind of "sharing" that is at work in Truman's account is not of the sort that we saw in the "stake or share" that generates an interest. Truman's picture of "sharing" is, instead, a matter of coincidence. The differences in question are prior

23. David Nicholls, *Three Varieties of Pluralism* (New York: St. Martin's Press, 1974), 26 and 32. Regarding how Bentley may have fallen into the trap of reproducing the structural exclusion of groups from political analysis, see Kress, *Social Science and the Idea of Process*, 61.

24. Ira Katznelson, *Desolation and Enlightenment* (New York: Columbia University Press, 2003), 113.

25. Truman, *Governmental Process*, 33.

to politics. A group's claims over others, on the basis of coincident attitudes, when pursued in public institutions, render them political (*Governmental Process,* 37). In contrast to Bentley, interests are now prior to politics, rather than caught up in the political process. Pluralism is now apt to identify the not-yet political groups, if it can find a means by which interests, defined as shared prepolitical psychological attitudes, can be represented in political analysis even when they are not yet represented in political movements or institutions.

Sovereign Agency as an Interest

Quietism and a status-quo bias are real concerns for social science, especially when one considers the patterns of disenfranchisement and widespread apathy in many modern societies. Of equal and related concern is the prospect that the researcher will end up ascribing particular interests or characteristics to persons. Truman's way of addressing these problems, however, overdetermines political studies' attention to interest with a commitment to sovereign agency. His way of seeing interest as essentially psychological channels attention to epistemological questions regarding who knows what an interest is, and how they know. The relatively recent neoliberal prejudice that I examined in the previous chapter, that the individual is in a privileged position to know, fits nicely into this rubric and forecloses many of its dilemmas. And in it we can hear resonances with the view, which I examined in Chapter 3, that interest is a kind of humanistic knowledge.

This notion of interest is lodged in the individual, subjective determination of attitudes and aims. These attitudes and aims become objects suitable for research by means of psychometric techniques of measurement. Truman notes that attempts "to examine interests that are not at a particular point in time the basis of interactions among individuals, but may become such ... would indeed be risky ... without the modern techniques for the measurement of attitude and opinion" (34). These modern techniques empower pollsters and psychometricians to "discover" latent groups in attitudes that are shared but not (yet) the basis for collective action. Jettisoning Bentley's insistence that a categorically unique framework be elaborated to study politics, and his placement of interest at the center of this frame, Truman refigures interests as psychological phenomena that are represented to political science by means that are not themselves proper to politics, but rather are scientific on extrapolitical terms.

Survey research techniques ostensibly enable researchers to recognize actual and incipient groups without ascribing characteristics (or interests) to persons.

Thus subjected to the techniques of psychology, administered through survey research, the individual who "has interests" becomes the object of political science. Of course, a kind of ascription is at work here all the same, however unremarkable it may seem. By channeling our attention to epistemological questions, the view of interest as psychological tacitly forecloses the ontological questions that the language of interest opened in Bentley's account, and the ontological contests that appeals to interest sustain. In other words, implicitly holding that a person's "real interest" lies in sovereign agency forecloses some alternative ways of conceiving of persons. A social ontology of individuals is presumed. We thereby miss how ontological questions—regarding "what counts" as the interested body in question—are themselves at play in the language of interest. And this move locates political agency squarely where Bentley himself, as we shall see, hesitated to confine it: within the psychological dot of the grammatical subject's "I."

Consider the scene of survey research, which is an idealization of sovereign agency in practice. The research subject works alone to complete a questionnaire that has been adjusted to eliminate researchers' biases. The survey responses "represent" the subject's interests in the sense that they are made into objects for study; and the survey "respects" the subject's interest in the sense that it does not violate the objectively human interest to direct one's own affairs. While empiricist studies are meant to merely observe peoples' interests (through their actions, such as voting or filling out a survey), a normative and even ascriptive side in its commitment to respecting an individual person's determinations of her own interests is generally presumed. Subsequent to Truman's behavioralist revolution, studying interests in the course of studying politics has meant in practice studying the behaviors of individual persons whose agency is presumed to be individual, and whose autonomy is presumed to be the objective interest. Subjective interests are aligned with objective ones by the techniques of modern survey research.

When Bentley's contemporaries turned to psychology, their science was largely stipulative, in the sense that theoreticians posited drives, motivations, or instincts as a means of explaining political action or social behaviors. Bentley meant to replace this with something observable—something that could be described, rather than presumed. Truman's behavioralism, empowered by psychometric techniques, follows this spirit in Bentley. But seeing individual attitudes and preferences as the basis or precondition for action, Truman, like Holmes, misses the insights about interest that we saw at work, for example, in Mill: that the determination of interests lies in the participatory and provisional give-and-take of politics. It cannot reside in some "subjective" interest that corresponds to the rational process inside the mind of the natural person (as "individual"), because when it comes to interests in politics, more than one person is always at stake. Nor can it reside in some neutral, "objective" attribute of persons (as known by science or philosophy). Nor can it reside in the notion of autonomy that is supposed to link these (such as the notion that allowing a person to have a privileged say corresponds to an objective attribute, a "human interest"). All of these insights from the history and the language of interest are replaced by the same notion of interest that I earlier identified as neoliberal. The question, therefore, is not whether promoting sovereign agency is a worthy goal. Instead, the question is what insights regarding agency are lost when the language of interest is pressed into the service of this goal.

Viewed through the lens of the language of interest, the incongruence of Truman's group interpretation of politics with Bentley's descriptive theory of politics stems not, as one critic has it, from Truman's good-faith attempt to use *The Process of Government* as a tool for political science.[26] Nor can Truman's break from Bentley be fully explained by his devaluation of Bentley's notion of process.[27] It also, and importantly, reflects Truman's abandonment of Bentley's insights regarding what in the natural language of interest is most compellingly political. Identifying preferences and attitudes as the basis and essence of interest, as Truman does, forecloses the group-action side of interest, and the broader juridical side of the language of interest that supports it, from political studies. Individuals *have* interests, but are not seen as *interested* by means of politics and action, as Bentley's perspective—and the juridical and plural language of interest that support it—insists.

Truman was by no means alone in his view; one need only consider the influence of Mancur Olson's *Logic of Collective Action* to see how a view of interest akin to Truman's rippled throughout political science.[28] Yet even Truman's fiercest critics followed him in focusing on "interest" as individual, to the exclusion of its other uses.[29] While Bentley prioritized the juridical and plural group-action side of interest over its sense of individual psychology, Truman and others not only reversed the priority but obliterated the former by reducing it to the latter. Throughout political science, the psychological basis of interest, and therefore

26. Weinstein, "Group Approach," 179.
27. Cf. Kress, *Social Science and the Idea of Process*, 74–75.
28. Olson, *Logic of Collective Action*, 1–3.
29. See, for example, Michael Rogin's critique of Truman. See Michael Rogin, *Ronald Reagan, the Movie, and Other Episodes in Political Demonology* (Berkeley and Los Angeles: University of California Press, 1987).

the individual's privileged knowledge of his or her own interest, continues to be invoked to denounce any articulation of common or general interests as an ideological sham.[30] Meanwhile, the effective power of common or general interest claims in political discourse has not yielded to the positivist, individualist doctrine: politicians and activists still find it productive to invoke "the national interest" or more parochial (but no more reliably attitudinal) interests like "a black interest" or "women's interest." In light of the evident power of these uses of "interest," Bentley's suspicion that interest cannot be equated with attitude or desire, his finding "interest" in the formation and activity of groups, and his effort to keep the juridical, plural, and group-action side of interest available to political study turn us back to the language of interest.

Objectivity and the Contestability of Interests

Truman's turn to psychology and psychometrics as a means of observing interests responds not only to concerns that group theory is quietist, but also to epistemological and ontological problems that the grammar of "interest" poses for positivist inquiry. Since it is critical for the idea of a positivist science of politics that political phenomena be things available for study, positivist studies of politics want to focus on what interests "really are."[31] In other words, they want to know what the word "interest" in natural language refers to. This approach has a counterpart in other philosophies of social science: adherents of pragmatic scientific realism and critical theory alike, for example, argue that theories give meaning to the patterns people see in facts; the interest that some body is said to have is taken to be a fact of some kind.[32] Given that an appeal to interest seems to refer to a thing, this would seem to be a straightforward move on the part of positivist, pragmatic, and critical approaches to studying politics. After all, we often say that one "has an interest" just as we say that one "has furniture." By analogy, the objective and

---

30. See, for example, volume 5 of Friedrich, *Nomos V: The Public Interest*; Schubert, *The Public Interest: A Critique of the Theory of a Political Concept*; and Held, *The Public Interest and Individual Interests*.

31. Wootton, *Interest-Groups*, 6.

32. On critical-theoretical versions of this view, see Fred Rush, "Conceptual Foundations in Early Critical Theory," and Stephen K. White, "The Very Idea of a Critical Social Science: A Pragmatist Turn." Both of these articles may be found in *The Cambridge Companion to Critical Theory*, ed. Fred Rush (Cambridge: Cambridge University Press, 2004). For an elaboration of this position in philosophy of social science, see Keith Topper, *The Disorder of Political Inquiry* (Cambridge: Harvard University Press, 2005).

factual quality of interest seems as self-evident as that of furniture, or any other property that some body is said to have. These approaches set the terms for studies of political interest that preclude the identity-provoking power of interests, which as we have seen throughout the foregoing chapters, animated political debates and analyses from seventeenth-century political pamphlets, to the philosophy of Thomas Hobbes, to the writings of J. S. Mill—and the social theory of Arthur Bentley. But in searching for a factual object in interest, these researchers tune in only to the conceit of an appeal to interest to be a fact about persons to be represented in political practices or institutions, even if the institutional logic of representation affects how persons (or states) calculate in pursuit of the interest.

Given this approach to interests as facts, when observers of politics are confronted with the many ways that collective interests are invoked in political discourses—"special interests," "women's interests," "national interest"—they are apt to approach these articulations with an air of suspicion. Sometimes this suspicion is rendered as a question of representation. After all, who is to say what women's interests are? But the factuality of these interests is rendered conspicuously doubtful once it is noted that the invocation of collective interests at hand could hardly be compatible with everything that could be said about the interests of the collectivity in question, let alone every person said to be a member of the collectivity.[33] Indeed, for any statement of the interests of a nation, a group, or a consumer, there is a competing perspective; contest and disagreement is where interest is both most problematic for social science and, paradoxically, so useful in political discourse. So, for example, some say the national interest is peace; others, the national interest is preemptive war. Some say the African American interest is in self-determination, others find it in full integration. Is the workers' interest in the availability of jobs, or in higher wages? We see that the consumers' interest is low prices; yet the consumers' interest is safer products. In light of such easy disagreement about women's interests, the national interest, and so on, one may be tempted to say that, strictly speaking, there is no such thing as "women's interest" or "the national interest," but instead that this phrase more properly signals a particular, or "special" interest (generally the speaker's) masquerading under the affirming banner of a broader one. Since the "thing" to which these invocations of "interest" refer must be a fact about some body, that body must be an individual.

---

33. Jane Mansbridge describes how this analytic feature of interest is translated across different political and methodological spectra. See Mansbridge, "Self-Interest in Political Life," 137.

After all, the very identity of the group in question, what we might call the shape of its body, is in doubt.

But the problem of conflicting invocations of interest appears in microcosm within the person. Indeed the commonplace notion of a person having conflicting interests itself contradicts at least one notion of what an interest *is*—what is good for some body—and is therefore a problem for the factuality of interests. Take, for example, the statement "Marcia is not interested in her health, even though being healthy is in her interest." The sentence is not contradictory, but it nonetheless presents a difficulty for theorists or scientists who want to know her interest the way they know a thing. They are apt to get around this problem by noting that Marcia's lack of interest in health refers to her attitudes or her ideas, and so it is neatly distinct from questions of her bodily health. Now Marcia's love for French fries, on the one hand, and her benefit from low LDL-cholesterol levels and complex carbohydrates, on the other, are equally real and are equally interests that Marcia "has," but they are compartmentalized, as though they referred to two different things.

Following this pattern in resolving incongruities in how the word "interest" is used, social scientists and political theorists routinely invoke a distinction that I have already begun to examine in relation to Bentley—namely, between "subjective" interests on the one hand, and "objective" interests on the other.[34] With such a dichotomy in hand, philosophers, politicians, pundits, and activists everywhere can be found advancing the view that persons do not always well or rightly know their own interests—and therefore begin to speak of persons' best interests, real interests, or objective interests instead.[35] But referring conflicting statements regarding a person's interest to a dichotomy of objective and subjective preserves rather than deflects the presumption that interests are individual and psychological. It therefore abets the foreclosure of political studies from the plural, group-active side of the language of interest. Political

---

34. Flathman, *The Public Interest: An Essay Concerning the Normative Discourse of Politics*, 14–31; Balbus, "Concept of Interest," 152; Wendt, *Social Theory of International Politics*, 224–33; Raymond Geuss, *The Idea of a Critical Theory: Habermas and the Frankfurt School* (New York: Cambridge University Press, 1981), 45–54.

35. Geuss, *Idea of a Critical Theory*; Karl Marx, "On the Jewish Question," in *The Marx-Engels Reader*, ed. Robert C. Tucker (New York: W. W. Norton, 1978). Particularly promising for its potential to disrupt the "objective-subjective" binary rubric for analyzing interests is Richard Flathman's attempt to situate any invocation of "interest" on a continuum from objective to subjective. Before realizing the critical promise of this continuum, however, Flathman turns to a linguistic examination of the term "public." See Flathman, *The Public Interest: An Essay Concerning the Normative Discourse of Politics*.

scientists can reassure themselves that proper research techniques render even the most apparently subjective interests into objective material for political analysis, thereby respecting the real interest of the subject in the autonomy of her attitudes, reasons, and desires. Liberals and theorists can seek the coincidence between objective and subjective interests by holding that once the objective interests of autonomy, dignity, or ideal speech situations are met, subjectively felt interests are to be privileged as determining substantive objective interests.[36] The trajectory of critical theory over the past forty years illustrates to what extent it has converged with liberalism on a notion of autonomy and communicative competence as the standpoint from which to judge the justice of contemporary political conditions.[37]

Marxist resisters to the assimilation of critical theory to liberalism have leaned more heavily on the distinction between subjective and objective interests, in order to preserve the space for radical critique of prevailing social conditions.[38] But the presumption of interest as psychological lives on. "An objective interest means," Terry Eagleton, who is one such theorist, explains, "a course of action which is in fact my interest but which I do not currently recognize as such. If this notion is unintelligible, then it would seem to follow that I am always in perfect and absolute possession of my interests, which is clearly nonsense."[39] Even here, interest remains a matter of individual consciousness; objective interest is what a person could recognize as her interests but for the injustices of the prevailing social order. Where contestation and plurality are recognized at all, they are a matter not among persons, let alone groups, but between present self-consciousness and a single superior alternative of which the individual is presumed, at present, to be unaware. All of these attempts suspend the possibility that this conflict and contestation are intrinsic to the language of interest—as reflected both in its grammar and its deployment in political argument. Instead they seek to overcome the conflict by techniques of attitude measurement or an ideal social order. Common to these efforts is an attempt to secure the objectivity of interests and the sovereign agency of the person said to "have" these interests—objectivity and sovereign agency that the language of interest does not respect. Indeed, as we shall see, the language of interest is among the forces that shape that agency.

36. Geuss, "Liberalism and Its Discontents."
37. White, "Critical Social Science."
38. Geuss, *Idea of a Critical Theory;* Terry Eagleton, *Ideology, an Introduction* (New York: Verso, 1991); Hoy, *Critical Resistance.*
39. Eagleton, *Ideology,* 217.

Interest in *The Terms of Political Discourse*

Conflicting and contradictory uses of terms like "interest" are the beginning point for William Connolly's analyses of political concepts in his early and influential work, *The Terms of Political Discourse*.[40] This book begins to address the difficulties that the grammar of interest poses for empiricist political science, but it nonetheless shares postwar political science's concern to respect—and to buttress—the link between interest and sovereign agency. Therefore, it could not recover the connection between interests, constitution, and contestation that theorists like Bentley made central to their perspective on political studies, and which supported earlier skepticism regarding sovereign agency.

The Terms of Political Discourse seeks to "render political discourse more self-reflective by bringing out contestable moral and political perspectives lodged in the language of politics," thereby "dissolv[ing] the appearance of neutrality in conceptual analysis" as practiced by many political scientists (213). The student of politics must see the contested quality of political concepts and the commitments that underwrite her definition of concepts (20–21).[41] Connolly furthermore renders explicit the losses that result when political scientists mine the natural languages of politics for words that they then "harden" into technical terms with stipulated, univocal meanings (*Terms of Political Discourse*, 48–62). Connolly's emphasis on contestation therefore resuscitates a key part of Bentley's insight regarding the role that "interest" plays in the natural languages of politics, and works to extend this role to political studies.

But Connolly's embrace of contestation goes only so far. Following Truman in at least one respect, the psychological view of interest is Connolly's point of departure and individual autonomy is the point to which he returns. "The sorts of wants that enter into the meaning of interests," he writes, "are exactly those deemed somehow important, persistent, basic, or fundamental in politics" (46). Within the confines of interest as a fundamental desire, Connolly sees the contests over the term's uses in political discourse as an opportunity, if not

---

40. Connolly, *Terms of Political Discourse*. Connolly's subsequent work has criticized sovereign agency in various ways; in what follows, my object is not Connolly as a political thinker but rather *The Terms of Political Discourse* as an influential argument. The importance of this book, first published in 1974, is indicated by its having gone into three printings and having been awarded the Lippincott Prize in 1999 for its importance to the field more than twenty years after its publication.

41. Connolly sometimes writes as though contestability is a feature of *some* concepts and not others, or that terms become political to the extent that they are contestable. It is likely, of course, that contestability is not a feature of an exclusive set of concepts—the possibility of contestation may lie in all concepts. Whether this is a problem for Connolly's argument is not relevant here since I am concerned with "interest," which is contested.

an imperative, to be clear about the political stakes of defining "interest" for political studies, and then to choose a side. Connolly argues that what's at stake in defining "interest" for political studies is the preservation of autonomy, agency, and responsibility—congruent with a liberal conviction that each sane adult individual is the best judge of her own best interests. Even so, Connolly rejects the power of psychometrics to know individuals' interests by measuring their attitudes, offering instead what I am tempted to call a politically correct definition of "real interests." It is corrected politically in that Connolly justifies it not by engaging the language of interest, but by invoking a "democratic ethos" that is curiously close to neoliberalism. Here is the definition:

> Policy x is more in A's interest than policy y if A, were he to experience the *results* of both x and y, would *choose x* as the result he would rather have for himself. (64)

Conflict or contestation around interest has now been reduced from even the competing claims of groups to an individual's choice between two policies.[42] Moreover, the subjunctive in Connolly's definition points to an ideal situation for the articulation of interest that is always already hypothetical. Knowing what some body would choose if he *were* to experience the results of x and y, when he has not experienced x and y, is impossible—not even the "he" who would choose can know it. While the hypothetical has the advantage of stemming the hubris of social science, it tellingly reveals that real interest, and the sovereign agency Connolly means it to serve, is impossible.

While Connolly insists that we see how the terms employed by social science reflect and replay broader political contests, and argues that scientific language must remain in contact with the natural languages of politics, his own definition of "interest" stops short of reconnecting it with the ways "interest" is used in natural language. Connolly's insistence that interest be grounded in an individual agent of action and responsibility reproduces the social scientists' attachment to interest as a vehicle for sovereignty and misses how everyday uses of "interest" differently and contestably figure the identification of interested bodies that are a focus of political studies. His approach exemplifies this power of invoking interest insofar as he himself proposes that the term be used to restrict political identity to an individual notion of sovereign agency. To that

---

42. Robert Parks's approach exemplifies using choice as a rubric for analyzing interest; see Parks, "Interests and the Politics of Choice."

end, Connolly notes, "to be clear about interests we must specify the kinds of persons we are talking about" (45). Connolly senses that opening "interest" as a conduit for its political effects may proliferate sites of agency and complicate his ambition to secure individual sovereignty. If we hesitate to exclude invocations of interest that do not reflect atomism or individuality, do we open the door to kinds of persons who are not sovereign agents or even natural persons?

Contemporary usage of the term "interest" shows no particular tendency toward atomism, nor does it privilege the individual as a site of agency and responsibility. Talk of groups as "having an interest," of a group of people as "an interest," or of the "community interest" or the "national interest" or the "public interest" all connote interests that may incorporate or transcend the benefit of individuals or their needs, wants, preferences, and desires. Indeed, people speak of interest in ways that have little or nothing to do with people at all, whether individually or in groups. For example, we may hear a lawmaker justifying her vote "in the interest of patriotism," or a law justified before the Supreme Court as serving "a compelling state interest." Connolly avoids both the insights into the unsettled identities of interested bodies that an engagement with these nonindividual invocations of "interest" provides, and the role of contest in these invocations. He writes as though a person cannot be truly said to have conflicting interests. And he writes as though no person will ever find herself aligned with and avowing interests that extend nontransitively beyond or against her sovereign agency—as when people become married, or join a religious order, or take responsibility for raising a child, or martyr themselves to a cause. Each of these actions speaks to, and indeed shapes, a person's interest in ways that sovereign agency does not capture. In short, Connolly restricts consideration of "interest" to individual persons in atomized circumstances, thereby denying the flexibility of the grammar of "interest" even as he decries the atomism he says is endemic in social scientists' discussions of interest. Bentley's theory of interest suggests a way to tap into the broader, unsettled, and unsettling language of interest in politics as a means of theorizing nonindividual notions of interest and diagnosing this language's troubled relationship to sovereign agency.

Interest as Constitution

Setting aside the individual as a privileged site for the location of interest, and entertaining the possibility that collectivities can truly be said to "have interests" beyond the aggregation of the attitudes or choices of the persons they comprise, raises uneasy questions: What if there are no limits to what counts as an "interest"? Is "interest" just anything we say it is? If so, has it lost its meaning? These questions arise as long as we cling to the view that interest is a thing, forgetting that invoking interest is something that users of language—including political actors and students of politics—*do*. Let's examine a use of "interest" that is not about agents or even about people, in order to see what such a use achieves; the environment will work as an example. Speaking of an "environmental interest" suggests a group advocating some environmental policy or another, but it can also mean the environment more generally. The phrase "in the interest of the environment" (as we might describe legislation or using a canvas grocery sack) excludes the former possibility and hence draws us closer to our target. Under what circumstances would there be a point to using such a phrase? In the first instance, the phrase justifies or explains an action, like enacting or enforcing the law, or using the sack.[43] But the very need for justification or explanation suggests that its point is not self-evident or incontrovertible. Rather, there is some contest regarding the action's meaning or effects.

Suppose, as a matter of controversy, we are faced with two different policies, each of which can be plausibly argued to be "in the interest of the environment." Why, given the powers of science, are such policies still controvertible? (Let us assume that willful ignorance and grand deception are not to blame.) Such contestation is possible because the advocates differently view what *counts as* "the environment." Like any abstraction encompassing complex and multifarious phenomena, "the environment" itself has no set boundaries. Moreover, it changes over time, and in ways that are not preordained. If this were not the case, then an argument explaining or justifying action on its behalf, in terms of "interest," would be pointless, like speaking of the interest of a rock. To return to our controversy, each advocate includes some features and relationships among environmental phenomena and downplays, discounts, or excludes others. For some, the environment is a primordial configuration of ecosystems; for others, it is their current stability. For still others, it may be a resource for economic expansion; others still may understand it to be a nice spot for a picnic. Each of these perspectives yields distinct criteria for what counts as the interest of the environment, and each exhorts or explains a different kind of action. And each appeal to interest, when it comes to the environment, is a theory regarding what kinds of relationships to draw among all the elements that may count as "environmental," including relations of exclusion.

43. Ball, "Interest-Explanations."

These observations have implications for how present-day students of politics connect interest and identity.[44] To the extent that interest is a theory, it is also an action-oriented one. Identity must be understood not merely in its relation to contemporaneous difference—what makes something "the environment" as opposed to something else, say, Las Vegas—but also as tied up with processes and events that unfold over time.[45] The example of the environment illustrates how speakers use "interest" to ascribe a temporal identity, achievable in the future by action, to the environment. Even though appeals to interest appear merely to justify or to explain action on such a basis, they always are an activity of conjuring identity from complex and contested phenomena and a field of possibilities—even if these appeals cannot, in themselves, be said to "cause" the identity they promote. And since time does not reach an end, neither can this identity be achieved once and for all.

Juridical and Plural Interest in Political Inquiry

The observations of the previous two sections reflect a powerful, persistent, and important juridical and plural "family resemblance" among uses of the term "interest" in present-day English. These uses are consistent with Bentley's insistence that we see interests as groupings of multifarious phenomenal persons, active groupings that arise from contestation. The link he draws between "interest" and contestation reflects the heterogeneity that is intrinsic to the grammar of "interest" and alive in the natural language of interest in politics. In this light, Bentley's theory of interest explores conspicuous aspects of the language of interest that positivist social science and normative political theory mostly exclude.

But bringing these juridical and plural resonances back to the way that political studies handle the concept of interest is not a merely additive project. We should not see these as nothing more than an overlooked aspect of political language that is, at the end of the day, distinct from the ways that students of politics have become accustomed to dealing with interest, including the idea of interest as calculating self-regard, or parsing appeals to interest into "subjective" and "objective" senses. Therefore, it is instructive to follow Bentley's way of setting the juridical and plural side of the language of interest at the center

---

44. Rogers Smith, "Identities, Interests, and the Future of Political Science," *Perspectives on Politics* 2, no. 2 (2004).

45. Patchen Markell, *Bound by Recognition* (Princeton: Princeton University Press, 2003), 12–14.

of politics beyond some of his immediate concerns. *The Process of Government* suggests how we may see juridical interest as informing, inflecting, and even encompassing the invocations of interest throughout political studies.

In this penultimate section of this chapter, I read passages of *The Process of Government* for insight regarding the broad ways that the juridical and plural side of interest should inform political studies of interest. At times, these passages point in directions that are admittedly orthogonal to Bentley's larger intellectual project. Whatever methods of literary criticism may support reading passages such as these against the grain, Bentley himself modeled this practice in his own critical engagement with predecessors whom he admired, as a means of developing an alternative.[46] An occasionally unorthodox reading of Bentley, drawn from points where the juridical language of interest supports his theory of pluralism, cuts against the picture of sovereign agency that appeals to interest are most often supposed to respect. It also opens a window upon the encompassing perspective that seeing appeals to interest as intrinsically juridical and plural offers to political studies.

Interest as Government

As most readers of Bentley and I myself have remarked, Bentley was concerned to connect political studies to the natural languages that inform political life. But the language of interest, I noted, was a peculiar case. Bentley forcefully excluded from an explanation of political life most of what the language of interest seems to be for: referring to a psychological feeling or drive, or to transcendent or enduring benefits, goods, and ideals. I have also mentioned Bentley's palpable disdain for the ordinary causal explanations we give in these terms, even while he claims that his own perspective is merely one among many. The language of interest appears, therefore, to be a case where Bentley is extraordinarily discriminating about natural language, and even keen to avoid its entailments.

But the examples I have drawn upon in the foregoing sections, occasioned by my encounters with Truman, with Connolly, and with some other social-scientific perspectives on interests—not to mention all of those that I marshaled in the preceding chapters—show how saturated the language of interest is with juridical and plural inflections. Mindful of this saturation, we can approach the language of interest in political studies with a view to the myriad

---

46. Bentley deeply admired Small's work but used juxtapositions of Small's statements as a rhetorical technique to push beyond Small's perspective. See Bentley, *Process of Government*, 31–41.

roles that these inflections nearly always play. *The Process of Government* supports this endeavor.

Bentley gives the multifarious natural language of interest a role to play in political discourse and political studies—when set in a proper frame. It would be a mistake to read Bentley's statement that "it is not the set of reasonings put forth by men on either side" of an issue that matters "but the position that they assumed . . . that is the vital political fact" (*Process of Government,* 205), as saying that Bentley takes no heed of the power of speech, of "reasons given," in political life. Rather, "the language . . . in which ideas and feelings are presented," he writes, "is one form of activity" (180). Given the importance of activity to his account, we should not trivialize such a remark. He goes on to say that "this language . . . is prominent in government and politics" and that "we must not neglect it" (180). Recall that for Bentley, the prominence of this language in government means that it participates in the contests that form groups. It is only when we "follow every day theories and set the "feelings" and "ideas" *off by themselves* as the "causes" of activities" that we run into trouble and end up displacing a descriptive science of government with a dubious search for causation (180).[47] So even as Bentley cautions that a reason given by an actor is not the last word, he directs our attention to the activity of giving reasons.

When feelings, desires, and other motivations are expressed in appeals to interest, we must attend to *these* appeals as being themselves processes of government. When political actors appeal to their, or others', interests, they claim not so much that they have coincident feelings (although that may be the case), but more important that they stand to benefit by acting upon them. And when they invoke ideals like a common or national interest, they point to something achievable but not preordained. Although Bentley's disavowal of "the common interest" may dismay those who look forward to the resolution of enduring social conflicts, his rejection of transcendent interests is of a piece with his rejection of psychology. They both reflect his concern about the pretense of independence and power of causation that citizens and social scientists alike are just as apt to afford ideas (like nations) and ideals (like common interests) as they are to afford desires.

Ideals and ideas invoked in appeals to interest are also integral to the process of government. Here again we follow Bentley, viewing government not in a narrow sense of activities confined to official public institutions, but instead more broadly, as "the phenomena of groups pressing one another, forming

47. Italics added.

one another, and pushing out new groups" (*Process of Government,* 269). This definition draws the term "government" into a close relationship with Bentley's central equation of activity with group activity. And we recall that, when contested, this group activity becomes political, and is interest. To the extent that government differs from interest at all, then, it is in emphasizing moments when the political agency of group activity is itself prompted mainly by the pressures and forces of difference and contestation in human society. Groups being interested, and hence their constitution, is the essence of politics and is the process of government. From the complex and heterogeneous "mass of men" (203), government is a process of provoking political agency, as group activity, identified in contestation with other groups.

The governmental aspect of interest becomes more pronounced when Bentley describes interests as "settling or consolidating themselves upon masses of men" (206). When Bentley states that "what we actually find in this world, what we can observe and study, is interested men, nothing more and nothing less" (212) we are invited to read "interested" as a past participle, not an adjective. We are reminded that "interest" is a verb. The examples that Bentley gives of the ways people can be "interested" are staid (and at times unfortunate)—he cites ownership and occupation, gender, race, and blond hair—but the point of his examples is that the possibilities are ever changing, layered, cross-cutting, infinite, and that no one dimension is fundamental (208). These differences become a basis for "interestedness" at the point at which any such grouping makes a contested claim upon another. Indeed, these claims are themselves government; they call other interests, understood as active groupings, into becoming.

Bentley's reason for disavowing the reality of such interests as "off by themselves" or prior to the activities of government points beyond the usual cynicism that any invocation of a common interest is a partisan one in a savior's clothing. Rather, it draws our attention to the point of *invoking* a common interest, namely, its potential to prompt action that aims to forge unity from any complex heterogeneity—be it a phenomenal person, a group, a nation, or even humanity. And because the point of departure for an appeal to interest is a complex amalgam of heterogeneous parts, we may appreciate how this object's wholeness (as a nation, as a community) is contested and to be achieved by action, not given in advance. That is, work toward achieving wholeness will be contingent and itself contested with the language of interest. Once appeals to interest, whether as shared feelings or as ideals, are themselves understood as activities of government, the balance between their importance to the student of politics and their relevance to her science is restored. "If we try to take the group without the interest," Bentley writes, "we simply have nothing at all" (213). The language of interest is itself an integral part of the group process.

Sovereign Agency and Individuality

A return to Bentley's action-oriented theory of "interest" preserves aspects of the word that lend it power in politics, namely, the way it figures identity as contested and contestable *and* as a tool for laying claim to their fixity. Bentley invites us to see the language of interest as provoking and mobilizing agency and identity rather than as reflecting a political process by which individual interests are aggregated. But whereas much critical theory has left individuals intact while they see identity as formed by contingent affinities to collective identities, moments in *The Process of Government* press us to take the critical insights afforded by the language of interest inward as well, to the question of subjectivity itself.

Bentley writes that "human individuality" is a "prepossession ... appear[ing] to have extravagant importance," one which must be "stripped away" for a science of politics to emerge.[48] The pure description of interests as groups will allow the political scientist "to take the emphasis off the disreputable grammatical subject which makes all the trouble by its pretense of independence" (*Process of Government*, 190)—a patently Nietzschean observation that, for all its currency in present-day political theorizing, has nonetheless eluded theoretical reflection on interests. As Bentley banishes the psychology of the individual and the idealism of the whole, he severs interest from sovereignty by diverting attention from the bodies whose sovereignty it is too easy to presume. Indeed, the very idea of sovereignty falls with a thud in Bentley's own analysis: "As soon as [sovereignty] gets out of the pages of the lawbook or the political pamphlet," he writes, "it is a piteous, threadbare joke" (265). Taken alone, however, these attacks on individuals and on sovereignty may be nothing more than barbed asides. The question remains whether stripping away the prepossession of human individuality leads not only upward, in analysis, to the group, but inward as well, to questions of subjectivity itself. Can the picture of "interest" as a phenomenon of group activity in this text usefully—and grammatically—be extended back to persons?

A few notorious, if amusing, examples point the way toward an affirmative answer. "The 'President Roosevelt' of history," he writes, "is a very large

---

48. Bentley, *Process of Government*, 204.

amount of official activity, involving very many people. Any other 'President Roosevelt' of public life, physical, temperamental, moral, is but a limited characterization of certain phases of that activity" (176). He returns to this example later, writing that "'President Roosevelt' does not mean to us, when we hear it, so much bone and blood, but a certain number of millions of American citizens tending in certain directions" (322). While this colorful example speaks clearly to persons occupying conspicuous institutional offices, and therefore connects straightforwardly to patterns in appeals to interest exploited by Rohan and rejected by Hobbes, *The Process of Government* drives the same point home when speaking of individuals more generally.

Bentley gives us some reason to see individuality as itself a process of government, in the sense in which he uses this term. The government in question is one that shapes agency in fundamental ways. The picture of identity that comes out of *The Process of Government* stands in contrast to the view that preexisting individuals are passively imprinted with "intersectional" identities where multiple group affiliations cross. Bentley might seem to support mainly the latter view when he writes that "joint activities, of which governmental activities are one form, are the cloth, so to speak, out of which men in individual patterns are cut" (176). But we see him pushing in the direction of seeing individuality as government when he writes that "interest groups are of no different material than the 'individuals' of society. They are activity, so are the individuals. It is only a question of the standpoint from which we look at the activity to define it" (215). If interest groups are activity generated out of points of contestation among a larger, heterogeneous "mass" of differences, Bentley invites us to see individuality this way as well. Even the individual is an activity of grouping, an activity in which the agent has a share, though perhaps no greater a share than anyone else who appeals to his or her interest in the moment of contest.

Aspects of the language of interest that support Bentley's pluralist vision of politics also cuts deeply into the picture of individual subjectivity that underwrites present-day commitments to sovereign agency. Think back to Marcia, whose interests—in the pleasures of food, and in cardiac health—are apt to conflict. Marketers, public health workers, and Marcia alike will appeal to these interests, not so much in the name of imparting knowledge about them, but to provoke or justify her action in the face of competing claims about them. The kinds of action she takes in the face of these provocations will shape who Marcia becomes and what avenues of action are available to her in the future. It is no wonder, then, that "interest" is so poorly suited to a task that so many students of politics have assigned to it, namely, safeguarding the sovereign agency of the natural person. The language of interest is a practice of government by which that very agency is shaped and contested.

Conclusion: Appeals to Interest as Action, Grouping, and Government

Appeals to interest in politics are an integral part of the activities of grouping or of constituting political subjects—activities that, for Bentley, were the essence of government. The object of political study is this activity itself. Misled by natural language into thinking that appeals to interest refer to things that are independent of or prior to this activity of grouping and constituting, students of politics have obscured the activities that appeals to interest entail. Seeking to render interest commensurate with the modern picture of interest as a thing in the world, and as a kind of knowledge about that thing, they have burdened their analyses by importing the abstract and complex philosophical jargon of "object" and "subject." And these students have supposed that this language reflects their commitments to sovereign agency and to the individualism that this commitment presupposes.

The language of interest does not support any of these tactics of political analysis. Bentley's own rejection of natural language's specious claims of causation, and his emphasis on the juridical and plural aspects of the language of interest, model the steps that we must take beyond these commitments and this modern picture. In taking these steps, away from the notion that the language of interest refers to a thing, we have considered the ways that appeals to interest disrupt the sovereign agency of the individual subject. We have seen that these appeals are based in the irreducible heterogeneity of persons and masses, and are provocations toward the active realization of identity from this heterogeneity. We have seen how arguments from interest partake of the governmental power of appeals to interest to shape the political phenomena of groups and persons alike. The whole of this position cannot be attributed to Bentley alone. But it does reflect an extension of the very language of interest that supports the pluralist and action-oriented vision of *The Process of Government*, albeit into domains that are not its central focus. Political agents, we see, use the language of interest as a provocation to action. It is this provocation, and not the conceit that "interest" refers to a thing in the world or a kind of knowledge of that thing, that demands the attention of the student of politics.

EPILOGUE

The Language of Interest as a Critical Theory of Politics

In *Hegemony and Socialist Strategy,* Ernesto Laclau and Chantal Mouffe cite interest, alongside representation and sovereignty, as elements of classical political theory most in need of late modern critique and reconfiguration.[1] This book, first published in 1985, became a touchstone for many political and cultural theorists who sought to elaborate a critical democratic theory independent of the materialist presumptions of socialism and removed from the saturation of everyday life with liberalism and capitalism. Its call for a new way of conceptualizing interests is of especial importance to critical and cultural theory, and not only because the presumption of interest as calculating self-regard saturates justifications for liberal democracy in a world ever more structured by the market, but also because the political analysis of traditional Marxism, and of much of its critical progeny, is inflected with this picture as well. And philosophy has largely contained its analysis of interest within the modern rubric of distinguishing subject from object.

While representation and sovereignty have enjoyed a great deal of attention in the decades since *Hegemony and Socialist Strategy*—one need only consider, for examples, the explosion of postcolonial critiques of representation and the resurgence of interest in Carl Schmitt—the concept of interest has remained largely untouched by the intellectual developments of the intervening years. We have recently been better informed about the intellectual origins of monistic interest and its calculating rationality,[2] but the alternative to this picture

---

1. Ernesto Laclau and Chantal Mouffe, *Hegemony and Socialist Strategy* (New York: Verso, 2001)
2. Engelmann, *Imagining Interest*.

of interest, in its history and present-day vitality, had yet to be duly explored. While students of politics have time and again noted, along their way to other arguments, that interests appear to be "socially constructed" or that there is something amiss with seeing interests as prior to politics, these insights have never been systematically developed. A conceptualization of interest toward which these commentators gesture has never been rooted in history. Responding to these lacunae, *Appeals to Interest* grapples with interest outside the classical patterns, by which I mean those which arose late in the eighteenth century and have prevailed in the last hundred years.

In this book, I traced the language of interest to its source, namely, the word's origin as a technical term of Roman law regarding disputes over property. Its critical dimension resides, as I see it, not in the narrower picture of rights that we often associated with property, but instead from its relation to proper personality. When this relation migrated, along with the term "interest," into political language, the contests of the sort over personality that formerly engendered legal claims became open-ended. Hence the pluralism of appeals to interest has become one of its most striking features. Early modern political debates regarding the contours of political action, the philosophy of Thomas Hobbes, and classical liberal thought all bear the stamp of interest's juridical and plural inflections. So too, some of the political-theoretical questions we have inherited from that period can be better addressed once we allow the juridical and plural side of interests to come to the fore. These questions include how conceptions of sovereignty cover the way that state and citizen identity are shaped; the contours of democratic participation and collective action; and the problem of individual freedom in a market-oriented society. Along the way, I argued that our blindness to juridical interest is a relatively recent development, and I ended by noting how this blindness reflects the often-unnoticed imperatives of theorizing in an age marked by the ascendance of behavioralist research paradigms and neoliberal political discourses.

Throughout this discussion I have illustrated how the language of interest enlivens political discourse today in ways that we are likely to miss when we approach interest as a matter of calculating self-regard, and when we refer disagreements over interests to abstract philosophical dualisms like "objective and subjective." We have seen that appeals to interest are provocations to action on behalf of realizing an identity that is one among a field of possibilities. The conceit of such a claim, I have argued, is that the identity is given in advance, but the occasion and effect of the claim lies in the plurality of options for action and identity formation.

From this point of view, the language of interest itself models a critical theory, in a sense that Ernesto Laclau has articulated in the years since *Hegemony and Socialist Strategy*. A critical theory, he argues, will not propose an alternative social order on the basis of objective interests, in the way of an older tradition. Rather, it will attend to the patterns of agents' contingent participation in the constitution and dissolution of their own political identities.[3] The language of interest in politics, as I have sketched it in this book, vividly reflects the way that people participate in this constitution, by means of the proximity of interest claims and action. It also reflects the inherent contingency in their participation, owing to the unlikelihood, if not impossibility, of arriving at an uncontested and all-encompassing statement of an agent's interest. Agency, in such a picture, is not a matter of sovereignty but instead a matter of constitutional claim-making. Matters regarding interest, therefore, call for proximate action—and in these matters, there will be no last word.

This claim-making goes on every day in political life. In its pluralism, its contestation, and its potential to remake (and therefore to corrupt) the polity, it reflects a large portion of how ordinary citizens think about "political interests." And it has played a large role in the study of politics—a role that is to be recognized, and then played with the care and respect due to our subject matter. But given this power of appeals to interest to shape political agency, the social scientist or theorist might be even more inclined to eschew discussions of interest in her work. Perhaps she is deeply wary of the ways that social science research has been deployed in the more pernicious disciplinary efforts of a technocratic society. More likely, she feels she must honor the prime directive against activism masquerading as scholarship. For any variety of reasons, she may follow ascendant political science research paradigms in abandoning discussion of interest, opting to write in terms of preferences and utility instead of interests. And then, having jettisoned "interest"—whether because of the tangle of controversies this term has readily and persistently provided, or because of its intimacy with the political life of shaping agency and identity, or merely because it is considered too fuzzy, too resistant to operationalization, for political science—she may all the more easily retain the focus of positive inquiry or formal theory on a pregiven agent and the calculating form of its rationality. If she is of a particular critical bent, she may go on to criticize the notion of agency inherent in these approaches, but she will do so by means of exploring desire or affect. These forces may be very alive in political life, but they are at a remove from political language.

3. Laclau, "Identity and Hegemony," 48–49.

It is precisely because of the intimacy of interest and political language that political inquiry must continue to grapple with the language of interest. This language reveals agency as plural and incomplete; it pulls us up short when we try to rely on facile distinctions between individual and collective phenomena, or prioritize one or the other in our study of political life. This language demands that we face squarely the inadequacy of autonomy and sovereign agency as foundational conceptions for political thought and empirical inquiry. It does so not from the perspective of a free-standing social theory, but instead from encounters with everyday political argument. Political inquiry severs itself from that argument at the peril of its continued relevance, not only in the world of scholarship, but also to citizens working toward a democratic polity.

Selected Bibliography

Altieri, Charles. *Act and Quality: A Theory of Literary Meaning and Humanistic Understanding.* Amherst: University of Massachusetts Press, 1981.
Anderson, Benedict. *Imagined Communities.* New York: Verso, 1983.
Arendt, Hannah. *The Human Condition.* Chicago: University of Chicago Press, 1958.
Austin, J. L. *How to Do Things with Words.* New York: Oxford University Press, 1978.
Baeck, Louis. "Spanish Economic Thought: The School of Salamanca and the *Arbitristas*." *History of Political Economy* 20 (1988): 381–408.
Baker, G. P., and P. M. S. Hacker. *Wittgenstein: Rules, Grammar, and Necessity.* Oxford: Basil Blackwell, 1985.
Balbus, Isaac D. "The Concept of Interest in Pluralist and Marxian Analysis." *Politics and Society* 1, no. 2 (1971): 151–77.
Baldwin, John W. *The Medieval Theories of the Just Price: Romanists, Canonists, and the Theologians in the Twelfth and Thirteenth Centuries.* Philadelphia: The American Philosophical Society, 1959.
Ball, Terence. "Interest-Explanations." *Polity* 12, no. 2 (1979): 187–201.
———. *Transforming Political Discourse: Political Theory and Critical Conceptual History.* New York: Blackwell, 1988.
Ball, Terence, and J. G. A. Pocock. "Introduction." In *Conceptual Change and the Constitution,* edited by Terence Ball and J. G. A. Pocock. Lawrence: University Press of Kansas, 1988.
Barber, Benjamin. "The Politics of Political Science: 'Value-Free' Theory and the Wolin-Strauss Dust-Up of 1963." *American Political Science Review* 100, no. 4 (2006): 539–45.
Barry, Brian. *Culture and Equality.* Cambridge: Polity, 2001.
———. *Political Argument.* New York: Humanities Press, 1965.
Bartels, Larry M. "What's the Matter with *What's the Matter with Kansas?*" *Quarterly Journal of Political Science* 2006, no. 1 (2006): 201–26.
Benditt, Theodore M. "The Concept of Interest in Political Theory." *Political Theory* 3, no. 3 (1975): 245–57.
Benhabib, Seyla. *The Claims of Culture: Equality and Diversity in the Global Era.* Princeton: Princeton University Press, 2002.
Benn, S. I. "'Interests' in Politics." *Proceedings of the Aristotelian Society* 60 (1960): 123–40.
Bentham, Jeremy. *Defence of Usury.* London: Payne & Foss, Pall-Mall, 1816.

———. *A Fragment on Government and Principles of Morals and Legislation.* Oxford: Basil Blackwell, 1948.

———. *The Works of Jeremy Bentham.* Edited by John Bowring. Edinburgh: William Tait, 1843.

Bentley, Arthur. *The Process of Government.* Evanston, Ill.: Principia Press, 1908.

Black, James. "The Influence of Hobbes on Nahum Tate's King Lear." *Studies in English Literature* 7, no. 3 (1967): 377–85.

Blissard, William. *The Ethic of Usury and Interest: A Study in Inorganic Socialism.* New York: Charles Scribner's Sons, 1892.

Böhm-Bawerk, Eugen von. *Capital and Interest.* Translated by George D. Huncke and Hans F. Sennholz. 3 vols. South Holland, Ill.: Libertarian Press, 1959.

Botero, Giovanni. *Reason of State.* Translated by R. Peterson. London: Routledge & Kegan Paul, 1956.

Boucher, David. *Political Theories of International Relations: From Thucydides to the Present.* New York: Oxford University Press, 1998.

Bray, Michael. "Macpherson Restored? Hobbes and the Question of Social Origins." *History of Political Thought* 28, no. 1 (2007): 56–90.

Brown, Wendy. "American Nightmare: Neoliberalism, Neoconservatism, and De-Democratization." *Political Theory* 34, no. 6 (2006): 690–714.

———. *Edgework: Critical Essays on Knowledge and Politics.* Princeton: Princeton University Press, 2005.

———. *Politics Out of History.* Princeton: Princeton University Press, 2001.

Butler, Judith. *Giving an Account of Oneself.* New York: Fordham University Press, 2005.

Cavarero, Adriana. *For More than One Voice: Toward a Philosophy of Vocal Expression.* Stanford: Stanford University Press, 2005.

Cawdrey, Robert. *A Table Alphabeticall.* Gainesville: Scholars' Facsimilies & Reprints, 1966.

Caws, Peter. *Structuralism: The Art of the Intelligible.* Atlantic Highlands, N.J.: Humanities Press International, 1988.

Chambers, Simone. "The Politics of Critical Theory." In *The Cambridge Companion to Critical Theory,* edited by Fred Rush. Cambridge: Cambridge University Press, 2004.

Chaucer, Geoffrey. "Fortune: *Balades De Visage Sanz Peinture.*" In *The Riverside Chaucer,* edited by Larry D. Benson. Boston: Houghton Mifflin, 1987.

Cochran, Clarke E. "The Politics of Interest: Philosophy and the Limitations of the Science of Politics." *American Journal of Political Science* 17, no. 4 (1973): 745–66.

Coleman, Janet. "Pre-Modern Property and Self-Ownership Before and After Locke: or, When Did Common Decency Become a Private Rather Than a Public Virtue?" *European Journal of Political Theory* 4, no. 2 (2005): 125–45.

Condren, Conal. *The Language of Politics in Seventeenth-Century England.* New York: St. Martin's Press, 1994.

———. "Liberty of Office and Its Defense in Seventeenth-Century Political Argument." *History of Political Thought* 18, no. 3 (1997): 460–82.

Conestaggio, Gerolamo Franchi di. *Historie of the Uniting of the Kingdom of Portugall to the Crowne of Castill.* Translated by Edward Blount. London, 1600.

Connolly, William. *Identity\Difference.* Minneapolis: University of Minnesota Press, 1991.

———. *Political Theory and Modernity.* Ithaca: Cornell University Press, 1993.

―――. *The Terms of Political Discourse.* Princeton: Princeton University Press, 1993.
Cook, John. *Redintegratio Amoris, or a Union of Hearts.* London, 1647.
Cotgrave, Randle. *A Dictionarie of the French and English Tongues.* London: Adam Islip, 1611.
Crick, Bernard R. *The American Science of Politics: Its Origins and Conditions.* Berkeley and Los Angeles: University of California Press, 1959.
Cromwell, Oliver. *Writings and Speeches of Oliver Cromwell.* New York: Russell & Russell, 1970.
Danford, John W. *Wittgenstein and Political Philosophy.* Chicago: University of Chicago, 1998.
Daston, Lorraine. "The Moral Economy of Science." In *Constructing Knowledge in the History of Science,* edited by Arnold Thackray. Chicago: University of Chicago Press, 1995.
Deleuze, Gilles, and Felix Guattari. *A Thousand Plateaus.* Minneapolis: University of Minnesota Press, 1987.
Dempsey, Bernard W. *Interest and Usury.* Washington, D.C.: American Council on Public Affairs, 1943.
de Roover, Raymond. "The Concept of the Just Price." *Journal of Economic History* 18 (1958): 418–34.
Derrida, Jacques. *Limited, Inc.* Evanston: Northwestern University Press, 1988.
―――. "The Politics of Friendship." *Journal of Philosophy* 85, no. 11 (1988): 632–44.
de Soto, Domingo. *Tratado de la justicia y el derecho.* Madrid: Editorial Reus, 1922.
Dietz, Mary G. "Hobbes's Subject as Citizen." In *Thomas Hobbes and Political Theory,* edited by Mary G. Dietz. Lawrence: University Press of Kansas, 1990.
―――. *Turning Operations.* New York: Routledge, 2002.
Disch, Lisa. "More Truth Than Fact: Storytelling as Critical Understanding in the Writings of Hannah Arendt." *Political Theory* 21, no. 4 (1993): 665–94.
Divine, Thomas F. *Interest: An Historical and Analytical Study in Economics and Modern Ethics.* Milwaukee: Marquette University Press, 1959.
Dolan, Frederick M. "Political Action and the Unconscious: Arendt and Lacan on Decentering the Subject." *Political Theory* 23, no. 2 (1995): 330–52.
Downs, Anthony. "The Public Interest: Its Meaning in a Democracy." *Social Research* 29 (1962).
Eagleton, Terry. *Ideology, an Introduction.* New York: Verso, 1991.
Engelmann, Stephen G. *Imagining Interest in Political Thought: Origins of Economic Rationality.* Durham: Duke University Press, 2003.
Farr, James. "Conceptual Change and Constitutional Innovation." In *Conceptual Change and the Constitution,* edited by Terence Ball and J. G. A. Pocock. Lawrence: University Press of Kansas, 1988.
Fell, John. *The interest of England stated: or, A faithful and just account of the actions of all parties now pretending.* London, 1659.
Fisch, Jörg. "'Interesse' in Wörterbüchern und Lexica vom 16. bis zum frühen 20. Jahrhundert." In *Geschichtliche Grundbegriffe,* edited by Werner Conze, Otto Brunner, and Reinhart Koselleck. Stuttgart: Ernst Klett Verlag, 1982.
Fischer, David Hackett. *The Great Wave: Price Revolutions and the Rhythm of History.* New York: Oxford University Press, 1996.
Flathman, Richard E. *The Public Interest: An Essay Concerning the Normative Discourse of Politics.* New York: John Wiley & Sons, 1966.

Force, Pierre. *Self-Interest Before Adam Smith: A Genealogy of Economic Science.* Cambridge: Cambridge University Press, 2003.

Forster, Michael N. *Wittgenstein and the Arbitrariness of Grammar.* Princeton, New Jersey: Princeton University Press, 2004.

Foucault, Michel. "Discourse on Language." *The Archaeology of Knowledge.* London: Travistock Publications, 1972.

———. "Governmentality." In *The Foucault Effect: Studies in Governmentality,* edited by Graham Burchell, Colin Gordon, and Peter Miller. Chicago: University of Chicago Press, 1991.

———. "Nietzsche, Genealogy, History." In *The Foucault Reader,* edited by Paul Rabinow. New York: Pantheon Books, 1984.

———. *The Order of Things.* New York: Vintage Books, 1994.

Frank, Thomas. "The Culture Crusade of Kansas." *New York Times,* August 8, 2006. http://select.nytimes.com/2006/08/08/opinion/08frank.html.

———. *What's the Matter with Kansas? How Conservatives Won the Heart of America.* New York: Metropolitan Books, 2004.

Friedrich, Carl J., ed. *Nomos V: The Public Interest.* New York: Atherton Press, 1962.

Frost, Samantha. "Faking It: Hobbes's Thinking-Bodies and the Ethics of Dissimulation." *Political Theory* 29, no. 1 (2001): 30–57.

Gadamer, Hans-Georg. *Truth and Method.* Translated by Joel Weinsheimer and Donald G. Marshall. New York: Continuum, 1975.

———. "Vom Wort zum Begriff. Die Aufgabe der Hermeneutik als Philosophie." In *Menschliche Endlichkeit und Kompensation,* edited by Odo Marquand et al. Bamberg: Fränkischer Tag Verlag, 1995.

Gallie, W. B. "Essentially Contested Concepts." *Proceedings of the Aristotelian Society* 56 (1955): 167.

Gauthier, David. "Hobbes's Social Contract." In *Perspectives on Thomas Hobbes,* edited by G. A. J. Rogers and Alan Ryan. Oxford: Clarendon Press, 1988.

———. *Moral Dealing: Contracts, Ethics, and Reason.* Ithaca: Cornell University Press, 1990.

Gert, Bernard. "Hobbes's Psychology." In *The Cambridge Companion to Hobbes,* edited by Tom Sorrell. Cambridge: Cambridge University Press, 1996.

Geuss, Raymond. *The Idea of a Critical Theory: Habermas and the Frankfurt School.* New York: Cambridge University Press, 1981.

———. "Liberalism and Its Discontents." *Political Theory* 30, no. 3 (2002): 320–38.

Glendinning, Simon. *On Being with Others: Heidegger, Derrida, Wittgenstein.* New York: Routledge, 1998.

Gray, John H. "On the Contestability of Social and Political Concepts." *Political Theory* (1977): 331–48.

Green, Richard Firth. *A Crisis of Truth: Literature and Law in Ricardian England.* Philadelphia: University of Pennsylvania Press, 1999.

Greenblatt, Stephen. "Psychoanalysis and Renaissance Culture." In *Literary Theory/Renaissance Texts,* edited by Patricia Parker and David Quint. Baltimore: Johns Hopkins University Press, 1986.

Greenleaf, W. H. "Hobbes: The Problem of Interpretation." In *Hobbes-Forschungen,* edited by Reinhart Koselleck and Roman Schnur. Berlin: Duncker & Humblot, 1968.

Gunn, J. A. W. "'Interest Will Not Lie': A Seventeenth-Century Political Maxim." *Journal of the History of Ideas* 29, no. 4 (1968).

———. *Politics and the Public Interest in the Seventeenth Century.* Toronto: University of Toronto Press, 1969.
Gunnell, John G. *Imagining the American Polity: Political Science and the Discourse of Democracy.* University Park: Pennsylvania State University Press, 2004.
———. "Time and Interpretation: Understanding Concepts and Conceptual Change." *History of Political Thought* 19, no. 4 (1998).
Hacking, Ian. *The Social Construction of What?* Cambridge: Harvard University Press, 1999.
Hallett, Garth L. *Essentialism: A Wittgensteinian Critique.* Albany: State University of New York Press, 1991.
Hamilton, Alexander, James Madison, and John Jay. *The Federalist, with Letters of "Brutus."* Edited by Terence Ball. Cambridge Texts in the History of Political Thought. New York: Cambridge University Press, 2003.
Hampton, Jean. *Hobbes and the Social Contract Tradition.* New York: Cambridge University Press, 1986.
Hazlitt, William. "The Spirit of Controversy." In *The Collected Works of William Hazlitt: Fugitive Writings,* edited by A. R. Waller and Arnold Glover. London: J. M. Dent, 1904.
Heidegger, Martin. *What Is Called Thinking?* Translated by Fred D. Wieck and J. Glenn Gray. New York: Harper & Row, 1968.
Held, Virginia. *The Public Interest and Individual Interests.* New York: Basic Books, 1970.
Henri, duc de Rohan. *See* Rohan, Henri de
Herle, Charles. *A Fuller Answer to a Treatise Written by Dr. Ferne.* London, 1642.
Hill, Christopher. *The Century of Revolution: 1603–1714.* New York: Norton, 1980.
———. *Change and Continuity in Seventeenth-Century England.* London: Weidenfeld & Nicolson, 1974.
Hirschman, Albert O. "The Concept of Interest: From Euphemism to Tautology." In *Rival Views of Market Society and Other Recent Essays.* Cambridge: Harvard University Press, 1992.
———. *The Passions and the Interests: Political Arguments for Capitalism Before Its Triumph.* Princeton: Princeton University Press, 1977.
Hobbes, Thomas. *De Cive.* [English.] Oxford: Clarendon Press, 1983.
———. *The Elements of Law.* Cambridge: Cambridge University Press, 1928.
———. *Leviathan.* Edited by Richard Tuck. Cambridge: Cambridge University Press, 1991.
Holmes, Stephen. *Passions and Constraint.* Chicago: University of Chicago Press, 1995.
———. "The Secret History of Self-Interest." In *Beyond Self-Interest,* edited by Jane J. Mansbridge. Chicago: University of Chicago Press, 1990.
Honneth, Axel. "A Social Pathology of Reason: On the Intellectual Legacy of Critical Theory." In *The Cambridge Companion to Critical Theory,* edited by Fred Rush. New York: Cambridge University Press, 2004.
Hont, Istvan. "Commercial Society and Political Theory in the Eighteenth Century: The Problem of Authority in David Hume and Adam Smith." In *Main Trends in Cultural History,* edited by Willem Melching and Wyger Velema. Atlanta: Rodopi, 1994.
Hooker, Richard. *Of the Laws of Ecclesiastical Polity.* New York: Dutton, 1954.
Houkes, John M. *An Annotated Bibliography on the History of Usury and Interest from the Earliest Times Through the Eighteenth Century.* Lewiston, N.Y.: Edwin Mellen Press, 2004.

Hoy, David Couzens. *Critical Resistance.* Cambridge: MIT Press, 2004.
———. "Heidegger and the Hermeneutic Turn." In *The Cambridge Companion to Heidegger,* edited by Charles B. Guignon. New York: Cambridge University Press, 1993.
Johnson, Laurie M. *Thucydides, Hobbes, and the Interpretation of Realism.* DeKalb: Northern Illinois University Press, 1993.
Kahn, Victoria. *Machiavellian Rhetoric: From the Counter-Reformation to Milton.* Princeton: Princeton University Press, 1994.
Kalyvas, Andreas. "From the Act to the Decision: Hannah Arendt and the Question of Decisionism." *Political Theory* 32, no. 3 (2004): 320–46.
Kant, Immanuel. *Groundwork of the Metaphysic of Morals.* Edited by Herbert James Patton. New York: Harper & Row, 1956.
Katznelson, Ira. *Desolation and Enlightenment.* New York: Columbia University Press, 2003.
Kavka, Gregory S. *Hobbesian Moral and Political Theory.* Princeton: Princeton University Press, 1986.
Kerridge, Eric. *Usury, Interest, and the Reformation.* Burlington, Vt.: Ashgate Publishing, 2002.
Knox, T. M., ed. *Hegel's Philosophy of Right.* New York: Oxford University Press, 1967.
Koselleck, Reinhart. "Concepts of Historical Time and Social History." In *The Practice of Conceptual History: Timing History, Spacing Concepts.* Stanford: Stanford University Press, 2002.
———. "Linguistic Change and the History of Events." *Journal of Modern History* 61, no. 4 (1989): 649–66.
———. "The Temporal Structure of Conceptual Change." In *Main Trends in Cultural History,* edited by Willem Melching and Wyger Velema. Atlanta: Rodopi, 1994.
Kress, Paul F. *Social Science and the Idea of Process: The Ambiguous Legacy of Arthur F. Bentley.* Urbana: University of Illinois Press, 1970.
Laclau, Ernesto. "Identity and Hegemony: The Role of Universality in the Constitution of Political Logics." In *Contingency, Hegemony, Universality: Contemporary Dialogues on the Left,* by Judith Butler, Ernesto Laclau, and Slavoj Žižek. New York: Verso, 2000.
Laclau, Ernesto, and Chantal Mouffe. *Hegemony and Socialist Strategy.* New York: Verso, 2001.
Langholm, Odd Inge. *The Aristotelian Analysis of Usury.* New York: Columbia University Press, 1984.
———. *Merchant in the Confessional: Trade and Price in the Pre-Reformation Penitential Handbooks.* Leiden: E. J. Brill, 2003.
Laski, Harold J. *Authority in the Modern State.* New Haven: Yale University Press, 1919.
———. *Studies in the Problem of Sovereignty.* New Haven: Yale University Press, 1917.
LaVaque-Manty, Mika. "Bentley, Truman, and the Study of Groups." *Annual Review of Political Science* 9 (2006): 1–18.
———. "Dueling for Equality: Masculine Honor and the Modern Politics of Dignity." *Political Theory* 34, no. 6 (2006): 715–40.
Lewis, C. S. *Studies in Words.* Cambridge: Cambridge University Press, 1967.
Lewis, Ewart. *Medieval Political Ideas.* Vol. 1. New York: Alfred A. Knopf, 1954.
Lloyd, S. A. *Ideals as Interests in Hobbes's Leviathan.* New York: Cambridge University Press, 1992.

Locke, John. *Second Treatise of Government*. Indianapolis: Hackett, 1980.
Macaulay, Thomas. "Mill's Essay on Government: Utilitarian Logic and Politics." In *Utilitarian Logic and Politics*, edited by J. Lively and J. Rees. Oxford: Clarendon Press, 1978.
Machiavelli, Niccolò. *The Prince*. New York: Oxford University Press, 2005.
Macpherson, C. B. *The Political Theory of Possessive Individualism*. Oxford: Oxford University Press, 1962.
Mansbridge, Jane. "Self-Interest in Political Life." *Political Theory* 18, no. 1 (1990): 132–53.
Mansfield, Harvey C. "Self-Interest Rightly Understood." *Political Theory* 21, no. 1 (1995): 48–66.
Markell, Patchen. *Bound by Recognition*. Princeton: Princeton University Press, 2003.
Marx, Karl. *The German Ideology*. New York: Prometheus Books, 1998.
———. "On the Jewish Question." In *The Marx-Engels Reader*, edited by Robert C. Tucker. New York: W. W. Norton, 1978.
Mearsheimer, John J. *The Tragedy of Great Power Politics*. New York: W. W. Norton, 2001.
Meinecke, Friedrich. *Die Idee der Staatsräson in der neueren Geschichte*. Berlin: R. Oldenbourg, 1924.
Mill, John Stuart. *On Liberty and Other Essays*. New York: Oxford University Press, 1991.
———. *Utilitarianism, Liberty, and Representative Government*. Everyman's Library. New York: E. P. Dutton, 1947.
Miller, Dale T. "The Norm of Self-Interest." *American Psychologist* 54, no. 12 (1999): 1053–60.
Miller, Peter. *Defining the Common Good: Empire, Religion, and Philosophy in Eighteenth-Century Britain*. Cambridge: Cambridge University Press, 1994.
Nedham, Marchamont. *The Case of the Common-Wealth of the Kingdom Stated*. London, 1650.
———. *The Case of the Kingdom Stated, According to the Proper Interests of the Severall Parties Ingaged*. London, 1647.
———. *The Case Stated between England and the United Provinces in This Present Juncture*. London, 1652.
———. *Christiandus, or Reasons for the Reduction of France to a More Christian State in Europe*. London, 1678.
———. *Interest Will Not Lie, or a View of England's True Interest*. London, 1659.
———. *A True State of the Case of the Commonwealth*. London, 1654.
Nicholls, David. *Three Varieties of Pluralism*. New York: St. Martin's Press, 1974.
Noonan, John Thomas. *The Scholastic Analysis of Usury*. Cambridge: Harvard University Press, 1957.
Oakeshott, Michael. "Introduction." In *Leviathan*, edited by Michael Oakeshott. Oxford: Oxford University Press, 1947.
Olson, Mancur. *The Logic of Collective Action: Public Goods and the Theory of Groups*. Cambridge: Harvard University Press, 1965.
Ong, Aihwa. *Neoliberalism as Exception*. Durham: Duke University Press, 2006.
Orth, Ernst Wolfgang. "Interesse." In *Geschichtliche Grundbegriffe*, edited by Otto Brunner, Werner Conze, and Reinhart Koselleck. Stuttgart: Ernst Klett Verlag, 1982.
Parks, Robert Q. "Interests and the Politics of Choice." *Political Theory* 10, no. 4 (1982): 547–65.
Pateman, Carole. *The Sexual Contract*. Stanford: Stanford University Press, 1988.

Phillips, Dennis Charles. *Holistic Thought in Social Science.* Stanford: Stanford University Press, 1976.
Pincus, Steven. "Neither Machiavellian Moment nor Possessive Individualism: Commercial Society and the Defenders of the English Commonwealth." *American Historical Review* 103, no. 3 (1998): 705–36.
Pitkin, Hanna Fenichel. "Are Freedom and Liberty Twins?" *Political Theory* 16, no. 4 (1988): 523–52.
———. *The Concept of Representation.* Berkeley and Los Angeles: University of California Press, 1967.
———. "Slippery Bentham: Some Neglected Cracks in the Foundation of Utilitarianism." *Political Theory* 18, no. 1 (1990): 104–31.
———. *Wittgenstein and Justice.* Berkeley and Los Angeles: University of California Press, 1993.
Plamenatz, John. "Mr. Warrender's Hobbes." *Political Studies* 5, no. 3 (1957): 295–308.
Pocock, J. G. A. *The Ancient Constitution and the Feudal Law.* Cambridge: Cambridge University Press, 1957.
———. "Concepts and Discourses: A Difference in Culture? Comment on a Paper by Melvin Richter." In *The Meaning of Historical Terms and Concepts: New Studies on Begriffsgeschichte,* edited by Hartmut Lehmann and Melvin Richter. Washington, D.C.: German Historical Society, 1996.
———. *The Machiavellian Moment.* Princeton: Princeton University Press, 1975.
———. "Verbalizing a Political Act: Toward a Politics of Speech." In *Language and Politics,* edited by Michael Shapiro. New York: New York University Press, 1984.
Poovey, Mary. "Covered but Not Bound: Caroline Norton and the 1857 Matrimonial Causes Act." *Feminist Studies* 14, no. 3 (1988): 468–85.
———. *A History of the Modern Fact.* Chicago: University of Chicago Press, 1998.
Raab, Felix. *The English Face of Machiavelli.* Toronto: University of Toronto Press, 1965.
Rancière, Jacques. *Disagreement: Politics and Philosophy.* Translated by Julie Rose. Minneapolis: University of Minnesota Press, 1999.
Rawls, John. "The Idea of an Overlapping Consensus." In *Collected Papers,* edited by Samuel Freeman. Cambridge: Harvard University Press, 1999.
———. *A Theory of Justice.* Cambridge: Harvard University Press, 1971.
Richter, Melvin. "Begriffsgeschichte in Theory and Practice: Reconstructing the History of Political Concepts and Languages." In *Main Trends in Cultural History,* edited by Willem Melching and Wyger Velema. Atlanta: Rodopi, 1994.
———. *The History of Political and Social Concepts: A Critical Introduction.* New York: Oxford University Press, 1995.
Rogin, Michael. *Ronald Reagan, the Movie, and Other Episodes in Political Demonology.* Berkeley and Los Angeles: University of California Press, 1987.
Rohan, Henri de. *Of the Interest of the Princes and States of Christendom.* Translated by Henry Hunt. Paris, 1641.
Rorty, Richard. *Contingency, Irony, and Solidarity.* New York: Cambridge University Press, 1989.
Ross, Dorothy. *The Origins of American Social Science.* New York: Cambridge University Press, 1991.
Rothbard, Murray N. *Economic Thought Before Adam Smith: An Austrian Perspective on the History of Economic Thought, Volume I.* Northampton, Mass.: Edward Elgar, 1995.

Runciman, David. *Pluralism and the Personality of the State*. Cambridge: Cambridge University Press, 1997.
Rush, Fred. "Conceptual Foundations in Early Critical Theory." In *The Cambridge Companion to Critical Theory*, edited by Fred Rush. Cambridge: Cambridge University Press, 2004.
Schaar, John H., and Sheldon S. Wolin. "Essays on the Scientific Study of Politics: A Critique." *American Political Science Review* 57, no. 1 (1963): 125–50.
Schmitt, Carl. *Political Theology*. Chicago: University of Chicago Press, 2005.
Schubert, Glendon. *The Public Interest: A Critique of the Theory of a Political Concept*. Glencoe, Ill.: The Free Press, 1961.
Schumpeter, Joseph. *History of Economic Analysis*. New York: Routledge, 1992.
Searle, John R. "Social Ontology: Some Basic Principles." *Anthropological Theory* 80 (2006): 51–71.
Seigel, Jerrold E. *The Idea of the Self*. New York: Cambridge University Press, 2005.
Shapiro, Barbara J. *Probability and Certainty in Seventeenth-Century England*. Princeton: Princeton University Press, 1983.
Shklar, Judith. "The Liberalism of Fear." In *Liberalism and the Moral Life*, edited by Nancy Rosenblum. Cambridge: Harvard University Press, 1989.
Sitze, Adam. "Flight in Dark Times." *Theory & Event* 6, no. 2 (2002).
Skinner, Quentin. "The Idea of Negative Liberty." In *Philosophy in History: Essays on the Historiography of Philosophy*, edited by Richard Rorty, J. B. Schneewind, and Quentin Skinner. New York: Cambridge University Press, 1984.
———. "Language and Political Change." In *Political Innovation and Conceptual Change*, edited by Terence Ball, James Farr, and Russell L. Hanson, 6–23. New York: Cambridge University Press, 1989.
———. *Liberty Before Liberalism*. New York: Cambridge University Press, 1998.
———. "Meaning and Understanding in the History of Ideas." In *Meaning and Context: Quentin Skinner and His Critics*, edited by James Tully. Princeton: Princeton University Press, 1988.
———. *Reason and Rhetoric in the Philosophy of Hobbes*. Cambridge: Cambridge University Press, 1996.
———. *Visions of Politics*. 2 vols. New York: Cambridge University Press, 2002.
Small, Albion. *General Sociology*. Chicago: University of Chicago Press, 1905.
Smith, Adam. *An Inquiry into the Nature and Causes of the Wealth of Nations*. New York: Oxford University Press, 1993.
———. *The Theory of Moral Sentiments*. Indianapolis: Liberty Fund, 1984.
Smith, Rogers. "Identities, Interests, and the Future of Political Science." *Perspectives on Politics* 2, no. 2 (2004): 301–12.
Sorauf, Frank J. "The Conceptual Muddle." In *Nomos V: The Public Interest*, edited by Carl J. Friedrich. New York: Atherton Press, 1962.
Sorrell, Tom. *Hobbes*. New York: Routledge, 1986.
Stein, Peter. *Roman Law in European History*. Cambridge: Cambridge University Press, 1999.
Strauss, Leo. "On the Spirit of Hobbes's Political Philosophy." In *Hobbes Studies*, edited by K. C. Brown. Oxford: Basil Blackwell, 1965.
———. *Persecution and the Art of Writing*. Chicago: University of Chicago Press, 1988.
———. *The Political Philosophy of Hobbes, Its Basis and Genesis*. Oxford: Oxford, 1936.

Symonds, Joseph. *Three Treatises, Being the Substance of Sundry Discourses, Namely the Principal Interest, or the Propriety of the Saints in God, on Micah 7.7, and God's Interest in Man, Natural and Acquired, on Psalms 119.4.* London, 1653.

Taylor, A. E. "The Ethical Doctrine of Hobbes." *Philosophy* 13, no. 52 (1938): 406–24.

Taylor, Charles. "Atomism." In *Power, Possessions, and Freedom: Essays in Honour of C. B. Macpherson.* Toronto: University of Toronto Press, 1979.

———. "The Hermeneutics of Conflict." In *Meaning and Context: Quentin Skinner and His Critics,* edited by James Tully. Princeton: Princeton University Press, 1988.

———. "Overcoming Epistemology." In *After Philosophy: End or Transformation?* ed. Kenneth Baynes, James Bohman, and Thomas McCarthy. Cambridge: MIT Press, 1987.

———. "The Person." In *The Category of the Person: Anthropology, Philosophy, History,* edited by Michael Carrithers, Steven Collins, and Steven Lukes. New York: Cambridge University Press, 1985.

———. "Philosophy and Its History." In *Philosophy in History,* edited by Richard Rorty, J. B. Schneewind, and Quentin Skinner. Cambridge: Cambridge University Press, 1984.

———. *Sources of the Self: The Making of Modern Identity.* Cambridge: Harvard University Press, 1989.

———. "Theories of Meaning." In *Human Agency and Language: Philosophical Papers I.* New York: Cambridge University Press, 1985.

Ten, C. L. "Mill on Self-Regarding Actions." *Philosophy* 43, no. 163 (1968): 29–37.

Thompson, E. P. *Customs in Common.* London: The Merlin Press, 1991.

Thucydides. *The Peloponnesian War.* Translated by Thomas Hobbes. Chicago: University of Chicago Press, 1989.

Topper, Keith. *The Disorder of Political Inquiry.* Cambridge: Harvard University Press, 2005.

Trenchard, John, and Thomas Gordon. *Cato's Letters, or Essays on Liberty, Civil and Religious, and Other Important Subjects.* Vol. 1. Indianapolis: Liberty Fund, 1995.

Truman, David B. *The Governmental Process.* New York: Alfred A. Knopf, 1953.

Tully, James. *A Discourse on Property: John Locke and His Adversaries.* Cambridge: Cambridge University Press, 1980.

———. "Governing Conduct." In *Conscience and Casuistry in Early Modern Europe,* edited by E. Leites. Cambridge: Cambridge University Press, 1988.

———. "Wittgenstein and Political Philosophy: Understanding Practices of Critical Reflection." *Political Theory* 17, no. 2 (1989): 174–204.

Urbinati, Nadia. *Mill on Democracy: From Athenian Polis to Representative Government.* Chicago: University of Chicago Press, 2002.

van Houdt, Toon. "Implicit Intention and the Conceptual Shift from *Interesse* to *Interest:* An Underestimated Chapter from the History of Scholastic Economic Thought." Paper presented at "Crossroads: Writing Conceptual History Beyond the Nation State," Uppsala, Sweden, August 24–26, 2006.

———. "Just Pricing and Profit Making in Late Scholastic Economic Thought." *Supplementa Humanistica Lovaniensia* 16 (2000): 397–414.

———. "'Lack of Money': A Reappraisal of Lessius' Contribution to the Scholastic Analysis of Money-Lending and Interest-Taking." *European Journal of the History of Economic Thought* 5, no. 1 (1998): 1–35.

Vilar, Pierre. *A History of Gold and Money, 1450–1920.* New York: Verso, 1991.
Visky, Károly. *Spuren der Wirtschaftskrise der Kaiserzeit in den Römischen Rechtsquellen.* Bonn: Habelt, 1983.
Ward, James F. *Language, Form, and Inquiry: Arthur F. Bentley's Philosophy of Social Science.* Amherst: University of Massachusetts Press, 1984.
Warrender, Howard. *Political Philosophy of Hobbes.* Oxford: Oxford University Press, 1957.
Weinstein, Leo. "The Group Approach: Arthur F. Bentley." In *Essays on the Scientific Study of Politics,* edited by Herbert J. Storing. New York: Holt, Reinhart & Winston, 1962.
———. "Reply to Schaar and Wolin: V." *American Political Science Review* 57, no. 1 (1963): 157–59.
Weissman, David. *A Social Ontology.* New Haven: Yale University Press, 2000.
Wendt, Alexander. *Social Theory of International Politics.* Cambridge: Cambridge University Press, 1999.
White, Hayden. *The Content of the Form.* Baltimore: Johns Hopkins University Press, 1987.
White, Stephen K. "The Very Idea of a Critical Social Science: A Pragmatist Turn." In *The Cambridge Companion to Critical Theory,* edited by Fred Rush. Cambridge: Cambridge University Press, 2004.
Williams, J. B. "The Beginnings of English Journalism." In *The Cambridge History of English and American Literature,* edited by A. W. Ward et al., 48–61. Cambridge: Cambridge University Press, 1921.
Williams, Raymond. *Keywords: A Vocabulary of Culture and Society.* New York: Oxford University Press, 1983.
Williams, Robert R. *Hegel's Ethics of Recognition.* Berkeley and Los Angeles: University of California Press, 1997.
Winch, D. M. *Analytical Welfare Economics.* New York: Penguin, 1971.
Winthrop, John. "Christian Charitie: A Model Hereof." In *The New England Puritans,* edited by Sydney V. James. New York: Harper & Row, 1968.
Wittgenstein, Ludwig. *The Brown and Blue Books.* New York: Harper & Row, 1958.
———. *On Certainty.* New York: Harper & Row, 1969.
———. *Philosophical Investigations.* New York: Macmillan, 1958.
Wolin, Sheldon. "Fugitive Democracy." *Constellations* 1, no. 1 (1994): 11–25.
———. *Hobbes and the Epic Tradition of Political Theory.* Los Angeles: William Andrews Clark Memorial Library, University of California, 1970.
———. "Norm and Form: The Constitutionalizing of Democracy." In *Athenian Political Thought and the Reconstruction of American Democracy.* Ithaca: Cornell University Press, 1994.
———. *Politics and Vision.* Boston: Little, Brown, 1960.
———. *The Presence of the Past: Essays on the State and the Constitution.* Baltimore: Johns Hopkins University Press, 1989.
Woodhouse, A. S. P., ed. *Puritanism and Liberty, Being the Army Debates (1647–9) from the Clarke Manuscripts with Supplementary Documents.* London: J. M. Dent & Sons, 1951.
Wootton, Graham. *Interest-Groups.* Edited by Robert A. Dahl. Foundations of Modern Political Science. Englewood Cliffs, N.J.: Prentice Hall, 1970.
Xenos, Nicholas. *Scarcity and Modernity.* New York: Routledge, 1989.

Zerilli, Linda. "Wittgenstein: Between Pragmatism and Deconstruction." In *The Legacy of Wittgenstein: Pragmatism or Deconstruction*, edited by Ludwig Nagl and Chantal Mouffe. New York: Peter Lang, 2001.

Ziff, Paul. *Semantic Analysis*. Ithaca: Cornell University Press, 1960.

Zivi, Karen. "Cultivating Character: John Stuart Mill and the Subject of Rights." *American Journal of Political Science* 50, no. 1 (2006): 49–61.

Index

action
  appeals to interest as, 89
  appeals to interest as justification for, 34, 54–55, 88–89
  appeals to interest as provocation to, 21, 30, 74, 79, 89–91, 164, 201
  in Arendt, 38
  as basic unit of political analysis, 178–79, 182, 204
  equated with interest, 182
  group, 178–82, 187, 189, 200–201
  in Hobbes, 118, 127, 135–37
  identity and, 90–91, 198, 203, 207
  juridical interest and, 78
  language of interest and, 65, 105, 204
  other-regarding, 158–60
  political, 68, 70, 74, 188
  probabilistic knowledge and, 73
  self-regarding, 158–61
  verbal, 17, 19–20, 22
agency, 20–21, 65
  as constitutional claim-making, 207
  interest and, 102, 195–96
  language of interest and, 9–10, 166–67, 172, 204, 208
  as plural, 21, 208
  political, 19, 166–67, 172, 181, 188, 201
  shaped by government, 203
  social science and, 12, 188
  sovereign, 29–30, 83; as foundational concept for political thought, 208; and, 194, 196, 199, 203; language of interest and, 61, 189, 193, 196, 204; political identity and, 195; subjectivity and, 203
  uncertainty of, 74
"Agreement of the People" (Wildman), 96, 100
Arendt, Hannah, 39
  The Human Condition, 38
Aristotle, 49

Augustine, 45
autonomy
  civic humanism and, 63n15
  critical theory and, 193
  as foundational concept for political thought, 208
  government and, 143
  interest and, 6, 167, 170, 194–95
  juridical interest and, 142
  language of interest and, 103
  in liberal discourse, 140
  liberal view of, 21, 28, 69, 162, 193
  in Mill, 144, 161
  neoliberal view of, 141, 168
  as objective interest, 188–89, 193
Azpilcueta, Martinus de, 49, 52

Ball, Terence, 15n32, 47n56
Bartels, Larry, 3,4
Beccaria, Cesare Marquis of, 25
Begriffsgeschichte, 22n45, 35n18, 77. *See also* conceptual history
behavioralism, 130–31, 171–72, 185
  view of interest in, 24–25
Benhabib, Seyla, 11
Bentham, Jeremy, 5, 55–56, 146n15, 164
  Defense of Usury, 165
  Manual of Political Economy, 164
Bentley, Arthur, 188, 190, 194
  on government, 175, 179, 200–201, 203
  on groups, 170, 173, 178–82, 200–203
  importance of contestation to, 181–82
  on interests as groups, 179–80, 202
  juridical interest and, 177, 179–81, 183
  on language, 170, 174–76, 180, 182–83, 200, 204
  language of interest and, 175, 177, 179, 182, 198–200
  plural interest and, 178–83

Bentley, Arthur (*continued*)
  The Process of Government, 29, 170–74,
    176–78, 180, 183–84, 189, 199–200, 202–3
Blount, Edward, 72, 76, 103
Boccalini, Traiano, 75, 77–78, 93
Bodin, Jean, 87
body, interested, 18–19, 103–4, 176, 188, 190–92,
    195–96
Bonaventura, Federico, 75, 77–78, 93
Botero, Giovanni, 76–79, 81–82, 84–85
  Della Ragione di Stato, 75
Bush, George W., 88

Cambridge school, the, 21–22, 77
capitalism, 2, 62, 151, 165–66, 205
Case of the Kingdom Stated (Nedham), 67, 69,
    80, 90
Cato's Letters (Trenchard and Gordon), 156
Charles I, King of England, 87, 91
Charles II, King of England, 67–68
Chaucer, Geoffrey, 59n5, 60–61, 75, 82, 85, 103
  "Fortune, *Balades de Visage sanz
    Peinture*," 58
commercial society, 6, 32, 34, 62, 94, 137
commodatum, 40–42, 45n48, 48n59, 98
concepts
  conceptual change and, 16–17, 46
  conceptual history and, 13, 144
  contested quality of, 8, 194
  words and, 13–16, 22–23, 36
conceptual history, 13, 15, 21–23, 46n56
  Begriffsgeschichte, 22n45, 35n18, 77
  of interest, 5, 9, 22–26, 34, 41, 59, 171
  neoliberalism and, 153, 167, 172
  politics of, 143–44, 151, 157
  words and, 13, 36, 46, 153–54
Conestaggio, Gerolamo Franchi di, *Historie*,
    72
Connolly, William, 108n5, 195–96, 199
  The Terms of Political Discourse, 29, 171, 194
constitution, 101, 170, 201
  appeals to interest as activity of, 17–20, 38,
    93, 99, 173, 196–98
contestation, 96, 138
  agency and, 181
  appeals to interest and, 19n40, 55, 57, 87, 94,
    191, 194
  creation of groups and, 178–80, 201, 203
  democracy and, 27, 102
  equated with interest, 180
  identity and, 34, 67, 95, 155, 181, 201
  juridical interest and, 8, 61, 65, 80–81

  language of interest and, 8, 12, 14, 142, 183,
    193
contingency, 5, 81, 86, 105, 207
Cook, John, 91
Cooper, Anthony Ashley. *See* Shaftesbury, 3rd
    Earl of
critical theory, 11, 190, 193, 202, 205, 207
  of interest, 9, 12, 153, 168, 182
Cromwell, Oliver, 95, 101

damnum emergens, 44
d'Avila, Teresa, 75n50
decision, 8, 52–54, 56–57, 59, 87–88, 160–62
De Cive (Hobbes), 114, 119, 135
De Corpore Politico (Hobbes), 129n31
Defense of Usury (Bentham), 165
De iusticia et iure (Lessius), 47
de la Cruz, Juan, 75n50
democracy, 66, 101n11, 154, 165
  contestation and, 102, 105
  liberal, 32, 62, 166, 205
  self-interest and, 143, 149, 153, 156
desire, 103–4, 175–76
  duty and, 113, 128
  equated with self-preservation, 113
  in Hobbes, 115, 123–24, 129, 133, 139
  interest and, 4, 25, 86n78, 194
  sovereignty and, 133
de Soto, Domingo, 75n50
Dewey, John, 19
Digest, the (Justinian), 43
discourse
  liberal, 140, 142
  neoliberal, 25, 141, 154, 167
  political, 8, 32, 70; appeals to interest in, 55,
    167, 91, 190–91; conceptual history and,
    13; contemporary, 102; juridical interest
    and, 73; language of interest and, 6, 10, 30,
    79, 89, 102, 172; in seventeenth-century
    England, 61–66, 68, 90, 94, 164
  reason-of-state, 32, 61, 63, 76, 85, 87
Doctor Navarrus. *See* Azpilcueta, Martinus de
Durkheim, Émile, 19
Dworkin, Ronald, 4, 162

Eagleton, Terry, 193
economics, 2–3, 54, 147, 149, 166, 168
Elements of Law (Hobbes), 114, 118
Elizabeth I, Queen of England, 83
Engelmann, Stephen, 7n13, 12n25, 25, 54n79,
    62, 63n17, 72n41, 76n55, 79n63, 96n106,
    109n6

INDEX 223

false consciousness, 11, 146, 177
Farr, James, 48n62
Federalist Papers, The, 3, 180
Fell, John, 91
　The Interest of England Stated, 74
financial crisis of 2008, 2–3, 170
Flathman, Richard, 192n35
"Fortune, *Balades de Visage sanz Peinture*"
　(Chaucer), 58
Foucault, Michel, 22
Frank, Thomas, 10, 29, 169
　"The Culture Crusade of Kansas," 3
　What's the Matter with Kansas?, 1
Friedman, Milton, 146

Gadamer, Hans-Georg, 22, 23n49
Gauthier, David, 108n5, 109n6, 131–33, 138,
　143
　Moral Dealing, 113
German Ideology, The (Marx), 6
Gert, Bernard, 108n5
Geschichtliche Grundbegriffe, 35
Gordon, Thomas, *Cato's Letters*, 156
government
　in Bentley, 175, 179, 200–201, 203
　interest as activity of, 173, 193
　liberal, 3
　neoliberal, 142, 144–46, 150–51, 153, 163, 167
　See also governmentality
governmentality, 142n5, 151
Governmental Process (Truman), 171, 184–85
Grandees, the, 95–97, 100–101
Greenleaf, W. H., 108n5
Greenspan, Alan, 2–3, 10, 29, 169
group theory, 183, 184n19, 190
groups, 157, 169, 175
　action of, 178–82, 187, 189, 200–201
　in Bentley, 178–82, 200–201
　in Truman, 185–87, 189
　See also interest groups
Guiccardini, Francesco, 75
Gunn, J. A. W, 89n85, 92n92, 131n36
　Politics and the Public Interest in the Seventeenth Century, 171n4
Gunnell, John G., 15n32, 17n36

Habermas, Jürgen, 4
Hamilton, Alexander, *The Federalist Papers*, 3
Hamtpon, Jean, 108n5, 134n41
Hazlitt, William, 1
Hegel, Georg Wilhelm Friedrich, 19
　Philosophy of Right, 34–35, 41

personality and, 26, 41–45
property and, 26, 40, 42
Hegemony and Socialist Stategy (Laclau and
　Mouffe), 142n6, 205, 207
Heidegger, Martin, 16, 23n49
Helvétius, Claude, 25
Herle, Charles, 91
hermeneutics. *See* interpretation,
　hermeneutical
Hirschman, Albert O.
　history of interest and, 32–33, 35–36, 46
　on Hobbes, 131n36
　juridical interest and, 77nn60–61
　The Passions and the Interests, 31
　view of interest as rational, 6, 56, 88
historical materialism, 9
Hobbes, Thomas
　Behemoth, 123
　the body and, 135–36
　counsel and, 123–25
　De Cive, 114, 119, 135
　De Corpore Politico, 129n31
　desire and, 115, 123–24, 129, 133, 139
　Elements of Law, 114, 118
　Henri duc de Rohan and, 28, 112
　humanism of, 123
　individualism and, 121, 132
　on interest, 106–13, 121, 133, 138; as juridical,
　　112, 114, 120; as plural, 112, 123, 126, 129;
　　private, 120, 126, 132, 137; public, 119, 123,
　　126–27, 132; as related to reason, 116–20,
　　132; self–, 27, 107, 109, 128nn30–31, 131n36,
　　134n41; as related to sovereignty, 106–9,
　　112–14, 116, 121–27, 129–30, 132
　interpretations of, 127–32, 171
　language and, 110, 112, 114, 117–18, 124, 138
　Leviathan, 27, 106, 110–19, 125, 130n32
　liberalism and, 130
　multitude and, 114–26, 133
　passions and, 110, 117–18, 120, 126, 134, 136
　person and, 133–34, 136
　personality and, 28, 112–13, 120, 132
　political science and, 109, 129, 130
　propriety and, 121–22, 129, 134, 136–37
　reason and, 110–11, 123, 126, 132, 134, 136
　the self and, 133–35, 138
　self-preservation and, 132–35, 137, 139
　sovereignty and, 87, 110–11, 115, 122–25,
　　137
　speech and, 116–17
　subjectivity and, 133
holism, social, 19

Holmes, Stephen, 32–35
  account of liberalism, 146–47, 157
  conceptual history and, 29
  Passions and Constraint, 31, 142, 147
  "The Secret History of Self-Interest," 28
  on self-interest, 36n21, 143–44, 147–56, 163, 165–66
  on the rationality of interest, 56
Hooker, Richard, 28, 155–56
Hoy, David Couzens, 23n49
Human Condition, The (Arendt), 38
humanism, 59–63, 66, 68, 72–73
Hume, David, 146, 152
Hunt, Henry, 68

identity
  as contestable, 34, 67, 95, 155, 181, 201
  in critical theory, 202
  interest and, 34, 72, 91, 167, 191, 198, 202
  language of interest and, 9, 155, 172, 207
  political, 20, 69, 139, 167, 181, 195
  provocation of, 90–91, 139, 167
  sovereign agency and, 195
  of the state, 83–87, 90
  spatial, 20–21, 91
  temporal, 21, 57, 91, 198
identity politics, 21, 147
id quod interest, 39–46, 48–49, 52–54
individual, 6, 11–12, 151, 172, 202–3. *See also* person
individualism, 167, 204
  in Hobbes, 121, 132
  of interests, 6, 39
  methodological, 170
  in Mill, 158, 161
  possessive, 99, 121
  in Truman, 185–86
inflation, 27, 48, 50–55
Inquiry into the Nature and Causes of the Wealth of Nations (Smith), 3, 180
Institutes, the (Justinian), 42–44
interest
  behavioralist view of, 24, 30, 171–72
  common, 176, 189–90, 200–201
  conceptual history of, 5, 9, 22–26, 34, 41, 59, 171
  constitution of the self and, 17–20, 38, 93, 99, 173, 196–98
  contestability of, 12, 54–55, 93–95, 101, 105, 140, 157, 194–95
  democracy and, 66, 149
  as democratic, 95, 105, 116
  desire and, 4, 25, 86n78, 194
  equated with self-interest, 152, 154, 156, 166
  etymology of, 6, 31n2, 33, 38–39, 71, 75, 84
  as euphemism for usury, 6, 31, 46
  as fee on money loan, 37, 43–52
  financial, 6, 31–32, 34, 37, 39, 41, 54
  as form of knowledge, 72–80
  as foundation: of democracy, 153, 156; of liberal politics, 149; of political order, 4, 101–2, 106–7, 109, 138–39, 182
  grammar of, 38, 52, 103–4, 190, 196, 198
  of groups, 179–80, 196, 202 (*see also* interest groups)
  as having a stake or share, 16, 24, 52–54, 96–97, 100–104, 164–65
  humanistic view of, 7, 32, 41, 65, 69, 88, 148
  individualism of, 6, 11, 152
  as individual, 6, 19, 23–24, 33, 130–32, 189, 192, 195–96
  identity and, 34, 72, 91, 167, 191, 198, 202
  juridical, 7–9, 3–25, 43, 54, 57, 65, 69, 77, 91, 206; in Bentley, 170, 173, 180–81, 203; in Hobbes, 112, 114, 120; liberalism and, 28, 15; in Mill, 157–59, 161; in Nedham, 70, 74, 81; person of the state and, 85; in Rohan, 71, 78; sovereignty and, 86
  knowledge of, 3–4, 33, 78, 90, 157, 190, 192; in Bentham, 164–65; in Bentley, 187; in Connolly, 195; in Hobbes, 116, 126
  language of (*see* language, of interest)
  liberal view of, 4, 10n20, 11, 88–90, 102, 140–141
  monistic, 7n13, 24–25, 54n79, 63n17, 79–80, 205
  as motivation, 2, 89, 149–52, 161; in Bentham, 164; in Hirschman, 32, 36; in Truman, 186
  national, 5, 55, 79, 88, 190–91, 196
  neoliberal view of, 141–42, 189
  objective, 103, 176–77, 190–93, 207; as autonomy, 188–89, 193; in Arendt, 38–39; liberal approaches to, 4, 193; in Marx, 4, 193; in neoliberalism, 146; in political science, 192–93
  passion and, 52, 70–72, 152–53, 166
  as plural, 8–9, 23–25, 126, 145, 206; in Arendt, 38–39; in Bentley, 177–83; in Hobbes, 112, 123, 126, 129; in Mill, 157, 160
  plurality in, 38–40, 79–81, 114, 123, 138, 162
  political science and, 10, 24, 109, 128, 207
  political studies and, 19, 32, 199
  private, 91, 120, 126, 132, 137

property and, 91–96, 99
public, 62, 96n106, 156, 196; in Hobbes, 119, 123, 126–27, 132
as rational, 24, 32–33, 36–37, 41, 54–56, 88, 152
real, 18, 146, 188, 192, 195
as rhetoric of persuasion, 89
self-, 62, 91–92; egalitarianism of, 149, 153–56, 163–66; in Hobbes, 107, 109, 128nn30–31, 130n32, 131n36, 134n41; in Holmes, 36n21, 143–44, 147–56, 163, 165–66; in liberalism, 11, 141–43, 147, 149, 163, 165–66; as normative principle, 149, 151; as opposed to preference, 155–56, 189; as origin of interest, 16, 41, 145, 152
self-preservation and, 36, 132–34, 137
sovereign agency and, 194, 196, 199, 203
sovereignty and, 57, 72, 87, 122–23, 195, 202; in Hobbes, 106–7, 112, 116
the state and, 64, 77–79, 82–83
subjective, 103–4, 170, 176–77, 188–89; language of interest and, 174; liberal approaches to, 4; in Marx, 4, 193; in neoliberalism, 146; in political science, 192–193
subjectivity and, 133
survey research and, 187–88
usage of the term, 16–17, 156–57, 167, 180, 196–97
of voters, 1, 3, 5
interest extra rem, 44–45, 48, 52
Interest of England Stated, The (Fell), 74
interest group, 10n20, 169
in Bentley, 170, 173, 180–81, 203
in Truman, 183–84, 186
interest intra rem, 44
Interest of the Princes and States of Christendom, On The (Rohan), 27, 68, 70, 84, 112
Interest Will Not Lie, or a View of England's True Interest (Nedham), 27, 55, 67, 69, 90
interpretation, hermeneutical, 22, 23n49
Ireton, General Henry, 95–101

Jay, John, *The Federalist Papers*, 3
Johnson, Laurie, 108n5
Justinian
the *Digest*, 43
the *Institutes*, 42–44

Kalyvas, Andreas, 8n17
Kavka, Gregory, 108n5
Keywords (Williams), 31

knowledge
interest as form of, 72–80
political, 28, 88
probabilistic, 73, 76, 78n62
Kress, Paul, 173n6, 174n11, 184n19, 185n21

La Vaque-Manty, Mika, 184n19
labor, commodification of, 166
Laclau, Ernesto, *Hegemony and Socialist Strategy*, 142n6, 205, 207
language
in Hobbes, 110, 112, 114, 117–18, 124, 138
of interest, 11–12, 32, 61–69, 72, 92; action and, 103, 105, 204; agency and, 9–10, 61, 166–67, 172, 193, 204; contemporary, 104–5, 172; contestation and, 8–9, 12, 14, 146, 183, 193; critical theory and, 207; history of, 25; identity and, 9, 155, 172, 207; natural, 179–80, 182; neoliberalism and, 12n25, 141–42, 157; political discourse and, 6, 10, 30, 79, 89, 172, 102; political studies and, 10, 12, 128, 189, 192, 204, 208; politics and, 4–5, 145–46, 167, 175; subjectivity and, 105, 163, 202
natural, 174–83, 190, 194–95, 199–200; political studies and, 199, 204
scientific, 174, 180, 195
in Wittgenstein, 13–14
Laski, Harold, 173
law
canon, 40n31, 45n51, 75, 76
feudal, 40n31
natural, 128n31, 167, 195
Roman, 33–35, 39–45, 73, 75, 85
Lessius, Leonard, 48–49, 51, 53
De iusticia et iure, 47
Levellers, the, 95–101
Leviathan (Hobbes), 27, 106, 110–19, 122, 125, 130n32
liberalism, 146–47, 157, 162–63, 165–66, 193
liberty, 90, 141–42, 145
On Liberty (Mill), 158–61
Lloyd, S. A., 107n5, 122n25, 134n41
Locke, John, 24–25, 78n62, 144, 146, 163–64
Logic of Collective Action (Olson), 189
Louis XIV, King of France, 87
Loyola, Ignatius de, 75n50
lucrum cessans, 44, 46, 48, 50–53

Macaulay, Thomas, 69, 89
Machiavelli, Niccolò, 60–61, 82, 107, 149
The Prince, 73, 75

MacPherson, C. B., 97n109, 99, 121n23, 130n32
Madison, James, *The Federalist Papers*, 3, 146, 180
Madoff, Bernard, 3
Mansbridge, Jane, 191n33
Mansfield, Harvey, 32
Manual of Political Economy (Bentham), 164
Marx, Karl, 4, 7
   The German Ideology, 6
Marxism, 147, 149, 205
materialism. *See* historical materialism
Meinecke, Friedrich, 171
   Ideengeschichte, 77
Mill, James, 89
Mill, John Stuart, 144, 146, 156, 191
   Harm Principle in, 158–59, 161–62
   identity and, 157
   individualism and, 158, 161
   on interest: of community versus self-interest, 159–62; juridical, 157–59, 161; plural, 157, 160
   language of interest and, 144, 158, 159
   On Liberty, 158–61
   the self and, 144, 158–60, 162
   Utilitarianism, 159
modernity, 11, 24, 53, 102, 106, 128, 166
money, 35–36, 44, 48–54, 72, 98
   interest as fee on loan of, 37, 43–52
Montesquieu, Baron de, 146, 165
Moral Dealing (Gauthier), 113
Mouffe, Chantal, *Hegemony and Socialist Strategy*, 142n6, 205

Nedham, Marchamont, 65–66, 68, 80, 85, 96, 105
   The Case of the Kingdom Stated: According to the Proper Interests of the Severall Parties Ingaged, 67, 69, 80, 90
   Interest Will Not Lie, or a View of England's True Interest, 27, 55, 67, 69, 90
   juridical interest and, 70, 74, 81
   on plurality in interest, 80–81
   view of interest as rational, 56
neoliberalism, 24, 29, 145, 146
   conceptual center and, 153
   Connolly and, 195
   interest and, 140–41, 146, 163, 166–67
   language of interest and, 141, 157, 163
   See also government, neoliberal; discourse, neoliberal
New Model Army, 66, 95, 100
Nixon, Richard, 1
Nozick, Robert, 146

Oakeshott, Michael, 130n32
Olson, Mancur, *Logic of Collective Action*, 189
ontology, 10, 19, 173, 176, 188
Orth, Wolfgang, 41

Park, Robert, 195n42
passion, 92, 103
   in Hobbes, 110, 117–18, 120, 126, 134, 136
   interest and, 52, 70–72, 152–53, 166
   reason and, 32, 83, 164
Passions and Constraint (Holmes), 31, 142, 147
Passions and the Interests, The (Hirschman), 31
Peloponnesian War (Thucydides), 118
personality, 52–56, 60, 69, 78–79, 85, 94
   in Hegel, 35, 41–45
   in Hobbes, 28, 112–13, 120, 132
person, 18, 64, 134, 162, 188, 196, 202
   artificial, 20, 110
   in Hobbes, 133–34, 136
   in liberal theory, 140, 162
   legal, 7
   as made interested, 163, 165
   natural, 20, 82–83, 85, 151, 167, 196; in Hobbes, 126–27, 134–36; sovereign agency of, 204
   of the state, 78–87, 93, 162
Philip II, King of Spain, 83–84
Philosophy of Right (Hegel), 34–35, 41
Pincus, Steven, 62
Pitkin, Hanna, 23
pluralism, 25, 63n17, 169, 173, 187, 206
plurality, 9, 21, 131, 138–39, 153, 193
   in interests, 38–40, 79–81, 114, 123, 138, 162
   in language of interest, 39, 61
Pocock, J. G. A, 47n56
political science
   behavioralist, 130–31, 168, 171, 184
   economics and, 168
   Hobbes and, 28, 109, 129–31
   neoliberalism and, 168
   positivist, 171, 190, 198
   psychological basis of interest in, 189
   study of interest in, 10, 24, 109, 128, 207
   See also political studies
political studies
   interest and, 19, 32, 171, 195, 199
   language of interest and, 10, 12, 128, 189, 192, 204, 208
   neoliberalism and, 163
Poovey, Mary, 62
positivism, 24, 190, 198
pragmatism, 184n19

preferences, 4–5, 12, 25, 155–56, 189
Prince, The (Machiavelli), 73, 75
Process of Government, The (Bentley), 29, 170–74, 176–78, 180, 183–84, 189, 199–200, 202–3
property
    franchise and, 95, 97n109, 99–100
    interest and, 91–96, 99
    relation to propriety, 64n20
    real, 40, 42–45, 48–50, 98–99, 101
    See also propriety
propriety, 28, 80, 94
    relation to property, 64n20
    sovereignty and, 121, 123
Putney, debates at, 66, 94–101, 105

Raab, Felix, 77n60
Rainborough, William, 95, 97, 99–100
rational choice, 10n20, 12, 25, 131, 138
Rawls, John, 4, 11, 141n3, 149n22, 162
    A Theory of Justice, 11n21
Reagan, Ronald, 2
realism, 76, 190
reason, 58, 77, 92, 128, 164–65
    in Hobbes, 110–11, 123, 126, 132, 134, 136
    passion and, 32, 83, 164
reason-of-state, 68, 73, 75–76, 79–80, 87–88, 92, 112. *See also* discourse, reason-of-state
representation, 30, 66, 100, 142, 182, 191, 205
republicanism, 62, 143
Rich, Nathaniel, 95
Rohan, Henri duc de, 65–67, 69, 72–76, 96, 103, 105, 203
    contestability of the state and, 87
    Hobbes and, 28, 112
    Interest of the Princes and States of Christendom, Of the, 27, 68, 70, 85, 112
    juridical interest and, 71, 78
    on the person of the state, 78–79, 82–85, 87, 93
    plurality in interest and, 80, 81
Roman Law. *See* law, Roman
Rorty, Richard, 9n

Schaar, Jack, 184n19
Schmitt, Carl, 205
scholasticism, 7, 63
Searle, John R., 19n40
"Secret History of Self-Interest, The" (Holmes), 28
self, the, 151–53, 157
    constitution of, 18, 20

    formation of, 144, 154–55, 158–59
    in Hobbes, 133, 137–38
    knowledge of, 3, 85, 94
    in Mill, 158–60
    neoliberalism and, 155, 167
    political, 162
    See also interest, self-; self-preservation
self-preservation, 36, 132–34, 137, 141n2
Sexby, Edward, 100
Shaftesbury, 3rd Earl of (Anthony Ashley Cooper), 24–25, 67
Skinner, Quentin, 15n32, 22, 28,
    on Hobbes, 107, 111–12, 116n18, 125
    on *paradiastole*, 46, 47n56
Small, Albion, 176, 179, 199n46
Smith, Adam, 150n23
    Inquiry into the Nature and Causes of the Wealth of Nations, 3, 180
social construction, 7, 206
social science
    behavioralist, 10n20, 17n36, 138
    Hobbes and, 130
    Marxist, 10n20
    views of interest in, 102, 131, 138, 140, 181, 185
    See also political science; political studies
Sorrell, Tom, 136n45
sovereignty, 63, 66, 69, 79, 205–6
    in Hobbes, 27, 87, 110–11, 115, 122–25, 137
    identity and, 137, 206
    individual, 196
    interest and, 57, 86–87, 103, 107, 112, 202
    language and, 114
    liberal view of, 69
    propriety and, 121, 123
    subjectivity and, 133
state, the, 57, 64–66, 74–76, 81
    contestability of, 87, 93–94, 105
    contingency of, 81–82
    identity of, 83–87, 90
    interest and, 77–79, 82–83
    person of the, 78–80, 82–85, 87, 93, 162
Strauss, Leo, 11, 22, 128n31, 130n32
subjectivity, 53, 56, 63, 66, 128, 176
    appeals to interest and, 37, 56, 133
    in Hobbes, 114
    interest as means for understanding, 31
    interest-related, 26–27, 31, 35, 38 41, 52, 55
    language of interest and, 105, 163, 202
    in liberal theory, 80
    sovereign agency and, 203
Symonds, Joseph, 93–94

Taylor, A. E., 108n5, 128–29
Taylor, Charles, 22–23
Terms of Political Discourse, The (Connolly), 29, 171, 194
Theory of Justice, A (Rawls), 11n21
Thucydides, *Peloponnesian War*, 118
Trenchard, John, *Cato's Letters*, 156
Truman, David, 181, 183
　attitudes and, 186–87, 189
　behavioralism and, 188
　Governmental Process, 171, 184–85
　groups and, 185–89
　interest groups and, 184, 186
Tully, James, 12n25, 15, 24, 70n33

Urbinati, Nadia, 160n38
usury, 44–51
　conceptual history of interest and, 37
　interest as euphemism for, 6, 31, 46
utilitarianism, 62
Utilitarianism (Mill), 159

van Houdt, Toon, 48n60, 49n67

Ward, James, 173n6, 174n11, 184n19
Warrender, Howard, 108n5, 128n31, 134n41
Weber, Max, 11
Weinstein, Leo, 184n19
Wendt, Alexander, 86n78
What's the Matter with Kansas? (Frank), 1
White, Stephen, 11
Wildman, John, "Agreement of the People," 96, 100
William, Earl of Newcastle, 118
Williams, Raymond, 33
　Keywords, 31
Wittgenstein, Ludwig, 7, 13–14, 16, 175
Wolin, Sheldon, 11, 22, 28, 143, 184n19
　on Hobbes, 130–33, 138–39
　Politics and Vision, 113, 130–31, 171n4
words
　concepts and, 13–16, 22–23, 36
　conceptual history and, 13, 46, 153–54, 167
　as equivocal, 14–16
　euphemistic uses of, 46–48
　See also Wittgenstein, Ludwig

Zivi, Karen, 158n35, 160n38

www.ingramcontent.com/pod-product-compliance
Lightning Source LLC
Chambersburg PA
CBHW021402290426
44108CB00010B/351